Instructor's Manual to Accompany

THE STORY AND ITS WRITER

AN INTRODUCTION TO SHORT FICTION

William E. Sheidley

Ann Charters

University of Connecticut

A Bedford Book

St. Martin's Press · New York

PREFACE

The entries in this manual include commentaries on each story in the anthology, along with questions for discussion, writing assignments, and suggested readings. The commentaries offer brief critical analyses of the stories and suggest ways to approach them in class. Like the questions that follow, the commentaries aim to promote a lively exchange of responses and perceptions without insisting on any particular interpretation or critical methodology.

Three kinds of Topics for Writing are proposed, but not all three are proposed for each story. The topics for Critical Essays are usually phrased as sentence fragments in order to point in directions that may prove fruitful without predicating the conclusions a writer might reach. The Exercises for Reading are founded on the premise that putting words on paper can serve as a powerful aid in understanding what one reads; the Related Subjects map out nontraditional writing projects, including experiments in fiction. Instructors using the manual will readily see ways to rephrase, restructure, and reapply these assignments to suit their own purposes and the needs of their students. Some writing topics may serve equally well as discussion questions, and vice versa.

The reading lists that conclude most entries are neither exhaustive nor highly selective; they simply cite interesting and, when possible, readily available criticism that proved useful in preparing the manual or that contains information and approaches to the stories that could not be incorporated in the commentaries. Thanks are due to the authors mentioned, to whose insights and scholarship the manual is generally indebted.

At the end of the manual is a list of films made from some of the stories in The Story and Its Writer, and a list of film distributors and their addresses.

Ann Charters prepared the entries on Hawthorne, Poe, and Melville; William E. Sheidley prepared the rest.

iii

CONTENTS

Part One

The Stories

PART ONE

THE STORIES

Nathaniel Hawthorne

"Young Goodman Brown" (page 22)

Teaching "Young Goodman Brown," you should encourage students to read the introduction to The Story and Its Writer carefully, since different aspects of Hawthorne's story are analyzed throughout the discussion of the elements of short fiction. The concluding chapter, on writing about short stories, also has four student essays developing different ideas about "Young Goodman Brown."

Students often need help recognizing stories that are not intended to be read as realistic narrative. Some readers tend to take every work in the story literally; Hawthorne, however, meant "Young Goodman Brown" to be a moral allegory, not a realistic story. While most students will be able to recognize the use of symbolism, you might have to introduce them to the idea of allegory, in which the entire story is an extended metaphor representing one thing in the guise of another.

An allegory is a story that has a dual meaning -- one in the events, characters, and setting; and the other in the ideas they are intended to convey. At first, "Young Goodman Brown" holds our interest on the level of the surface narrative. But the story also has a second meaning which must be read beneath, and concurrent with, the surface narrative. This second meaning is not to be confused with the theme of the story -- all stories have themes, but not all stories are allegories. In an allegory, the characters are usually personifications of abstract qualities (faith) and the setting is representative of the relationships among the abstractions (Goodman Brown takes leave of his "Faith" at the beginning of the story).

A story is an allegory only if the characters, events, and setting are presented in a logical pattern so that they represent meanings independent of the action described in the surface story. Most writers of allegorical fiction are moralists. In a moral allegory like "Young Goodman Brown," Hawthorne is suggesting the ethical principle that

1

should govern human life. The <u>unpardonable sin</u> for Hawthorne is a
"want of love and reverence for the Human Soul," and is typified by the
person who searches into the depths of the heart with "a cold philosophical curiosity." The result is a separation of the intellect from
the heart, which is fatal in relationships among human beings, as
shown in what happens to Goodman Brown when he returns to Salem village
at the end of the story.

QUESTIONS FOR DISCUSSION

1. When is a careful reader first aware that Hawthorne intends this
   story to be read as a moral allegory?
2. One of the characters in Hawthorne's stories says, "You know that
   I can never separate the idea from the symbol in which it manifests itself." Hawthorne's flat characters such as Deacon Gookin,
   Goody Cloyse, and the minister represent symbols of social insti-
   tutions. Why did Hawthorne include them in the story?
3. How do the final three paragraphs in the story suggest an ambiguity
   in Hawthorne's attitude toward Goodman Brown?

TOPIC FOR WRITING

1. Show how a knowledge of seventeenth-century New England history
   and Puritan theology can enhance a reading of the story.

SUGGESTED READINGS

Ferguson, J. M., Jr. "Hawthorne's 'Young Goodman Brown.'" <u>Explicator</u>,
   28 (1969), Item 32.

Gallagher, Edward J. "The Concluding Paragraph of 'Young Goodman
   Brown.'" <u>Studies in Short Fiction</u>, 12 (1975), 29-30.

Robinson, E. Arthur. "The Vision of Goodman Brown: A Source and
   Interpretation." <u>American Literature</u>, 35 (1963), 218-225.

Whelan, Robert E. "Hawthorne Interprets 'Young Goodman Brown.'"
   <u>Emerson Society Quarterly</u>, 62 (1971), 3-6.

Nathaniel Hawthorne

"The Devil in Manuscript" (page 32)

"The Devil in Manuscript" is the first story about writing stories
in this anthology. In contrast to contemporary authors like Grace
Paley and John Barth, however, Hawthorne isn't suggesting the limitations of the literary form. Instead, he is giving the reader a sense
of the precarious hold of fiction by American authors in the mid-
nineteenth century literary marketplace. In a humorous way, he is also

presenting his view that literature and writers are of great importance to society; ideas found in books can catch fire and ignite an entire town, although intellectuals and artists are not generally regarded with great respect by the American public.

This story is one of the group of sketches Hawthorne published in the 1830s featuring a particularly personal type of author-character, named Oberon in "The Devil in Manuscript." As Millicent Bell described this character in her book Hawthorne's View of the Artist, the portrait is of "a solitary, introspective writer who observes the procession of the active world from some hidden point of vantage, peopling his loneliness with imaginary fancies, and seeking Fame as a bride. Yet his way of life fills him with a sense of guilt. He longs wistfully for the warmth of common affections and the love of a simple heart. As to Faust in the old chapbook stories, these are denied him by the terms of his bond. To win them he must surrender his art" (p. 136).

Stories like "The Devil in Manuscript" are among the most autobiographical in Hawthorne's work; yet, the character of Oberon is more than just Hawthorne's self-portrait as a young writer. Oberon can be taken to represent a whole category of young intellectuals who go into law or business even though their talents dispose them to the arts.

Don't forget to point out to the class that "The Devil in Manuscript" was intended as a humorous story. Hawthorne was trying to write popular-magazine fiction and thus deliberately exaggerated characters and events to amuse his readers when this story's sketch appeared in The New England Magazine in November, 1835.

QUESTIONS FOR DISCUSSION

1. Why did Hawthorne include the champagne in the story?
2. What does Oberon mean when he says a devil is concealed in his manuscript?
3. What impression does the story convey of a writer's life in Hawthorne's time?

TOPIC FOR WRITING

1. Compare and contrast the two Hawthorne stories to show the different way he treats the theme of the young idealist who renounces the community of which he is a part.

SUGGESTED READINGS

Becker, I. H. The Ironic Dimension in Hawthorne's Short Stories. New York: Carlton Press, 1971.

Bell, Millicent. Hawthorne's View of the Artist. New York, 1962.

32-45 (text pages)

Jacobson, R. J. Hawthorne's Conception of the Creative Process.
Cambridge, Mass.: Harvard University Press, 1965.

Edgar Allan Poe

"The Cask of Amontillado" (page 40)

Poe is the great master of the contrived suspense story; and "The Cask of Amontillado" is a model of narrative compression toward a single effect. Students should understand that Poe had a theory on the short story, its essential points suggested in his review of Hawthorne's tales in Part Two of the anthology.

Despite Poe's rational explanation of how a writer should compose his story, his own fiction was directed toward eliciting irrational emotions in his reader. Poe's literary style aimed at using as many extravangances of character, setting, and plot as he could invent, exploiting the reader's emotional vulnerability to disturbing images of darkness and chaos. The hectic unpredictability of the carnival season, the creepy subterranean wine cellar, and the ancient family crypt with its molding skeletons all challenge us emotionally, and make us want to read further.

In the reading, our own fears become the true subject matter of the story. As in a nightmare, Fortunato finds himself being buried alive, one of the most basic human fears. On a more conscious level, we rely on a social contract to bind us together as a human family, and Montresor's lawlessness plays on our fear that any person can take the law into his or her own hands without being checked by human conscience. Poe doesn't have to give us a great number of details about his characters; our imagination draws from the depths of the common human psyche to supply all that we need.

This story is a good example to use in stressing the importance of the student's close reading of a text. It's easy for readers to miss, in the last paragraph, the sentence, "My heart grew sick; it was the dampness of the catacombs that made it so." Yet upon this sentence rests the interpretation of Montresor's character: Can we excuse his action on grounds of insanity? Was he insane at the time he buried Fortunato alive, or did he go insane in the half century during which, he tells us, his crime has remained undetected? If the reader has not paid careful attention to that sentence in the story, he or she will have missed an essential detail in understanding it.

The book Mysterious New England, edited by A. N. Stevens (1971), suggests that Poe first heard the anecdote upon which he might have based this story when he was a private in the army in 1827. Supposedly only ten years before, a popular young lieutenant named Robert F. Massie had also been stationed at Fort Independence in Boston Harbor; when Poe was serving there, he saw a gravestone erected to the memory of Lieutenant Massie, who had been unfairly killed in a duel by a bully named Captain Green.

Feeling against Captain Green ran high for many weeks, and then suddenly he completely vanished. Years went by without a sign of him, and Green was written off the army records as a deserter.

According to the story which Poe finally gathered together, Captain Green had been so detested by his fellow officers at the fort that they decided to take a terrible revenge on him for Massie's death....

Visiting Captain Green one moonless night, they pretended to be friendly and plied him with wine until he was helplessly intoxicated. Then, carrying the captain down to one of the ancient dungeons, the officers forced his body through a tiny opening which led into the subterranean casemate... his captors began to shackle him to the floor, using the heavy iron handcuffs and footcuffs fastened into the stone. Then they all left the dungeon and proceeded to seal the captain up alive inside the windowless casemate, using bricks and mortar which they had hidden close at hand.

Captain Green shrieked in terror and begged for mercy, but his cries fell on deaf ears. The last brick was finally inserted, mortar applied and the room sealed up, the officers believed, forever. Captain Green undoubtedly died a horrible death within a few days.

QUESTIONS FOR DISCUSSION

1. How does Poe motivate the behavior of Montresor? Does the story provide any hints as to the "thousand injuries" that he has suffered? Are any hints necessary?
2. Why is the setting of the story appropriate?
3. What does Montresor's treatment of his house servants tell us about his knowledge of human psychology, and how does it prepare us for his treatment of Fortunato?
4. How does Poe increase the elements of suspense as Fortunato is gradually walled into the catacombs?

TOPICS FOR WRITING

(Remind the class that there is a student paper in Part Two of the anthology comparing and contrasting this story with "Young Goodman Brown.")

1. Montresor doesn't tell his story until a half century after the actual event. Analyze how Poe adapts the "flashback" technique to affect the reader of "The Cask of Amontillado."
2. Explicate the passages in the story in which Montresor entices Fortunato into the crypt.

40-48 (text pages)

SUGGESTED READINGS

Adler, Jacob H. "Are There Flaws in 'The Cask of Amontillado'?"
    Notes and Queries, 199 (1954), 32-34.

Carlson, E. W., ed. The Recognition of Edgar Allan Poe. Ann Arbor:
    University of Michigan Press, 1966.

Gargano, J. W. "'The Cask of Amontillado': A Masquerade of Motive
    and Identity." Studies in Short Fiction, 4 (1967), 119-126.

Edgar Allan Poe

"The Oval Portrait" (page 45)

"The Oval Portrait" is another story about writing stories, but it
is presented without the humor found in Hawthorne's "The Devil in Manuscript." Poe's intent was to dramatize his idea that art depends upon
life for its substance, often at the cost of life itself. Like Hawthorne, Poe was a Romantic writer who believed that the artist strikes
a Faustian bargain with the devil and runs the risk of developing his
genius at the cost of his general sympathy with humanity.

This little tale is also an example of the gothic fiction still
popular in American magazines during Poe's time. Both he and Hawthorne
had inherited a literary prose form when they began to write stories,
tales indebted to the gothic novel which continued to flourish in
England at the beginning of the nineteenth century. Popular writers in
this genre were Horace Walpole, Clara Reeve, William Beckford, and
Ann Radcliffe.

Gothic fiction relied on horror obtained from either natural or
supernatural causes as its primary effect. There was often an element
of medieval connotations in gothic fiction -- an atmosphere of castles,
towers, knights, and magic. The term also implied the ghostly, the
grotesque, and the horribly superhuman. Often the stories began with a
helpless traveler seeking shelter from an impending storm in the moun-
tains. He then enters a solitary castle to spend the night, and encounters a ghost who proceeds to tell him the story of an unhappy love
affair. This situation often involves a partially decomposed corpse or
a manuscript of a dead person's memoirs, which introduces a story within a story.

With its weary traveler, its gloomy castle, its light from a single candle falling on the portrait of an irresistibly lovely girl, and
so forth, Poe's short tale is indebted to the model of a gothic romance. The coincidence of the book describing the unhappy circumstances under which the portrait was painted is also standard for this
literary genre.

QUESTIONS FOR DISCUSSION

1. Do you think Poe intended you to read this tale literally or sym-
    bolically? Do the symbols in the story add up to a coherent pat-
    tern of allegory?
2. How does this story show Poe's strong interest in the theory of
    artistic creation?

TOPIC FOR WRITING

1. Rewrite the tale in the style of a David Bowie or another popular
    song lyricist; or rewrite it as a story taking place in modern
    times.

SUGGESTED READINGS

Gross, S. L. "Poe's Revision of 'The Oval Portrait.'" Modern Lan-
    guage Notes, 74 (1959), 16-20.

Thompson, G. R., "Dramatic Irony in 'The Oval Portrait': A Reconsid-
    eration of Poe's Revisions." English Language Notes, 6 (1968),
    107-114. Article revised and included in Thompson's Poe's Fic-
    tion: Romantic Irony in the Gothic Tales. Madison: University
    of Wisconsin Press, 1973.

Nikolai Gogol

"The Overcoat" (page 50)

"The Overcoat," like Gogol's work in general, has been the subject
of widely differing critical responses, some of which will surely be
replicated in class discussion. A humanitarian view that sees the
story as the vindication of a downtrodden little man coordinates fairly
well with an interpretation that stresses the story's satiric attack on
the rigid tsarist bureaucracy. Readers who note the grim joke with
which the story ends, however, find its report on the destruction of a
being too paltry even for contempt to be harrowingly cynical and heartless, while those who closely attend to the shifting narrative tone
praise Gogol for producing a masterpiece of that combination of comedy
and horror that we designate as the grotesque.

In some ways an obverse of romantic or Laforguian irony, which expresses a self-conscious revulsion from one's own emotional enthu-
siasms, the grotesque vision dissolves in grim laughter the appalled
revulsion from a world devoid of any positive value. Neither Akakii
Akakiievich Bashmachkin (whose name in Russian alludes to dung on a
shoe) nor the social and physical world with which he is at odds offers
anything admirable; and the narrator's continuously shifting under-
statements, overstatements, verbal ironies, and bathetic juxtapositions
repeatedly prevent the reader from any mistaken investment of esteem.

7

Nonetheless, the possibility that Akakii Akakiievich is our brother in ways not considered by his sentimental young colleague remains the source of the story's grip on our imagination.

Before time, which ages his coat, and the chill of the St. Petersburg winter combine to impose a need on him, Akakii Akakiievich lives in a static and self-contained world of meaningless alphabetic letters, which he finds fulfillment and delight in replicating. He is a "writer" of sorts, but a writer who -- like Gogol himself, according to Bernheimer -- hesitates to express himself in what he writes. With his fall from this undifferentiated condition into his struggle to acquire an overcoat, he is born into temporal human existence. His isolation breaks down, and so does his innocence: he makes a friend; he participates in a creative act; he experiences stirrings of sensuality; and he eventually manages to assert himself in words. He also becomes guilty of vanity, pride, lust, and deception. Having gained an identity as a man with a new coat, he now becomes vulnerable to the destruction of that identity and consequently of the self it defines, which happens in three rapid stages.

Because we see him emerge from a state approximating nonexistence, Akakii Akakiievich's brief history as a suffering human being does not appear to be much different from the radically reduced quintessence of the fate we imagine to be our own. That the retribution carried out by the shade of Akakii Akakiievich -- which suggests his vindication and the exaltation of his overcoat-identity to the stature of a myth -- can finally be nothing more than a fantasy or a joke only serves to underline the inescapable dilemma that the story propounds between the meaninglessness of remaining locked within the circle of the self and the danger of aspiring beyond it.

QUESTIONS FOR DISCUSSION

1. Characterize the narrative mode of the opening paragraphs. Can you define a consistent tone?
2. In what sense was it "impossible to bestow any other name on Akakii Akakiievich"?
3. Does Gogol share the feelings of "the poor young man" who thinks Akakii Akakiievich's complaints mean "I am your brother?"
4. Describe Akakii Akakiievich's life before his coat wore out.
5. Why does Gogol bother to make Petrovich such an unsavory character?
6. Describe Akakii Akakiievich's feelings about his new overcoat once he decides to acquire it.
7. What possible attitudes might one take toward Akakii Akakiievich's experience at the party? About his visit to the "certain important person?"
8. Near the end, the narrator speaks "of the fantastic trend taken by what is, by the bye, a perfectly true story." What is the effect of this and the narrator's other implicit acknowledgements of the fictionality of his story -- made as implausible assertions of its veracity -- on the reader?
9. Consider Nabokov's commentary on "The Overcoat" in Part Two of the

anthology (page 1147). What "gaps and black holes in the texture of Gogol's style" seem to you to "imply flaws in the texture of life itself?"

TOPICS FOR WRITING

Critical Essays

1. Satire as a diversionary tactic in "The Overcoat."
2. The "certain important person" and a very unimportant person: two sides of the same coin?
3. Akakii Akakiievich and Bartleby as versions of the artist.
4. Disappointed expectation as the goal of Gogol's style.

Related Subjects

1. Study the long sentence early in the story that begins, "Even at those hours . . ." and continues nearly to the end of the paragraph it opens. Write a similar sentence about a community with which you are familiar (e.g., college students on a campus; the residents of your neighborhood). Try to follow Gogol as closely as possible: clause for clause; phrase for phrase. How would you define the tone of what you have written? Is it the same as Gogol's tone?
2. Vladimir Nabokov concludes his commentary on the story printed in Part Two of the anthology by suggesting that "after reading Gogol one's eyes may become gogolized and one is apt to see bits of /Gogol's irrational/ world in the most unexpected places" (p. 147). Write a sketch in which, by manipulating style and diction, you cause your reader to glimpse a darker world beyond the surface appearances of things.

SUGGESTED READINGS

Bernheimer, Charles C. "Cloaking the Self: The Literary Space of Gogol's 'Overcoat.'" PMLA, 90 (1975), 53-61.

Erlich, Victor. Gogol. Yale Russian and East European Studies, No. 8, New Haven: Yale Univ. Press, 1969. Esp. pp. 143-156.

Karlinsky, Simon. The Sexual Labyrinth of Nikolai Gogol. Cambridge, Mass.: Harvard Univ. Press, 1976. Pp. 135-144.

Lindstrom, Thaïs S. Nikolay Gogol. Twayne's World Authors Series, No. 299. New York: Twayne, 1974. Especially pp. 88-96.

Ivan Turgenev

"Byezhin Prairie" (page 78)

This lyrical story may strike students, as it struck its first critics in Moscow, as disjointed and lacking a clear point. Is it, in fact, a story at all? Or is it merely a painterly sketch and compilation of peasant superstitions? Try meeting this issue head-on by exploring the plot structure. The evident climax is the death of Pavel. It has no direct causal relation to the preceding narrative events, from which it is separated by several months. Pavel does not drown, but falls from a horse. Students will see, however, that in another sense his death follows quite predictably from the night on the prairie and the superstitious tales indulged in by the boys. Although we cannot answer the question, "Why did Pavel die?" we can hardly be surprised that he did.

The next step in tracing the relationships among the story's events back from the end toward the beginning may be to determine why the boys tell ghost stories. Is it to scare themselves for fun? Or is it to achieve a kind of knowledge about the control over the unknown darkness that surrounds them by giving names and explanations to the inexplicable manifestations that emerge from it? Even death becomes less frightening if one has warning -- and one may rest at ease if one's name is not called among the doomed.

The central episode of the story epitomizes the situation "of humanity faced with the spectacle of infinity," as Frank O'Connor puts it (p. 1150), in the image of the boys gathered near the campfire and surrounded by the inscrutable night. Braver than the rest, and more admirable in the eyes of the narrator, Pavel spurns mythologizing what he cannot understand and twice ventures beyond the circle of light -- once "to face a wolf," once to fetch water. He harbors no illusions of power over the unknown, however, but voices the timeless wisdom of resignation: "No one can escape his fate."

The function of the opening section of the story may now become clear; and when it does, attention can at last focus on the true central character, the narrator, who is so unobtrusively present throughout. For when the gorgeous landscape in which he feels so comfortably at home turns with nightfall into an alien, uncanny, malevolent wilderness, and finally into an abyss into which he nearly plunges, the narrator himself becomes a "man faced with the spectacle of infinity," and he feels the anxiety that spectacle produces. His method of dealing with his situation differs little from the superstitious projections of the peasant lads: he desperately projects the scientific intellectual's myth of a straight line onto the unknown geography he traverses -- a stratagem that could as easily have led to his death as to his rescue. Somewhat embarrassed even before his dog by his helplessness, the narrator attempts to minimize the implications of his experience by means of self-ironic detachment. Although he may recognize his kinship with Pavel when the two lock eyes in the morning, the narrator can muster only a conventional response to the boy's eventual demise: "Pity! He was a splendid fellow!" The reader, however, knows

the remote and condescending attitude inherent in that remark to be
merely the narrator's self-deluding hedge against the awareness of his
own vulnerability.

QUESTIONS FOR DISCUSSION

1. Contrast the qualities of the landscape noted by the narrator
   before and after sunset. Notice instances of openness and enclo-
   sure. Can you discern a pattern?
2. What does the dog Dianka contribute to the story?
3. Note the various ways in which the story centers on the borderline
   between darkness and light, or describes a passage from one to the
   other. In what way is this preoccupation an indication of
   Turgenev's theme?
4. Define Pavel's relation to the other boys. Is he as superstitious
   as they are?
5. Trace the fluctuations of the narrator's mood throughout the
   story. How does he feel when he learns of Pavel's death? Why?
6. How does this story contribute to the social and political impact
   of A Sportsman's Sketches mentioned in the headnote (p. 77)?
7. Turgenev reports that "Byezhin Prairie" took shape in his mind in
   the following sequence: he first thought of describing peasant
   boys driving horses; second, he wrote the campfire tales; third,
   he wrote the opening in which the narrator gets lost; and finally
   he added the conclusion announcing Pavel's death. What elements
   present in each stage of development might have suggested the next
   stage to the author? Why was the story not finished until the
   last lines were written? (Note: When the story was first published in 1851 in the periodical Sovremennik, the ending was
   omitted; those who read it in that form found that it lacked a
   general thread.)

TOPICS FOR WRITING

Critical Essays

1. The landscape in "Byezhin Prairie:" backdrop or embodiment of
   theme?
2. "Byezhin Prairie" as a realistic glimpse of life and society in
   mid-nineteenth-century Russia.
3. The characterization of the narrator and his attitude toward
   Pavel as keys to the story's theme.
4. Atmospheric and symbolic settings in "Byezhin Prairie" and
   "Young Goodman Brown."

Exercise for Reading

1. As you read "Byezhin Prairie" for the first time, interrupt yourself after the narrator realizes he is lost, after he reaches the
   precipice, and after he falls asleep. Each time record in a
   paragraph or two your responses to the story to that point. After
   completing the story, do the same again, and trace the evolution

of your ideas as you proceeded.

Related Subjects

1. Retell one or more ghost stories you have heard. Describe the occasion on which you heard them. Compare both the stories and the occasion to those in "Byezhin Prairie."
2. Write a sketch or short story based on a conversation overheard. Suggest its implications for the eavesdropping narrator.

SUGGESTED READINGS

Carden, Patricia. "Finding the Way to Byezhin Meadow: Turgenev's Intimations of Mortality." Slavic Review, 36 (1977), 455-464.

Proffer, Carl, ed. From Karamzin to Bunin: An Anthology of Russian Short Stories. Bloomington and London: Indiana University Press, 1969. Pp. 17-18.

Ripp, Victor. Turgenev's Russia: From "Notes of a Hunter" to "Fathers and Sons." Ithaca and London: Cornell University Press, 1980. Pp. 49, 71-74.

Herman Melville

"Bartleby the Scrivener" (page 95)

Many students have trouble reading this story because they cannot accept what they consider the weirdness of Bartleby's character. On a first reading, the story seems to yield this interpretation. Shortly after it appeared in the November and December issues of Putnam's Monthly Magazine in 1853, for example, Richard Henry Dana, Sr., wrote to Melville's friend Evert Duyckinck saying that he admired the skill involved in creating the character of Bartleby because "the secret power of such an inefficient and harmless creature over his employer, who all the while has a misgiving of it, shows no common insight." Dana's interpretation will probably also be the way 99 percent of present-day college students will respond to the story, sharing his lack of sympathy for Bartleby.

The question is: Did Melville intend the readers of his story to feel this way? Why did he conclude his tale with the lines, "Ah, Bartleby! Ah, humanity!"?

Most sympathetic literary critics see this story as Melville's attempt to dramatize the complex question of an individual's obligation to society. Like the dead letters which Bartleby used to burn in his previous job after they were no longer needed, so his life ends when he is no longer useful to his employer. What standards should we use to judge someone's worth? How should we view those who no longer accept the world they are offered?

QUESTIONS FOR DISCUSSION

1. How did the narrator's viewpoint affect your feelings toward
   Bartleby? What details particularly influenced you one way or the
   other?
2. Did your feelings toward Bartleby change when the narrator revealed Bartleby's previous job in the Dead Letter Office?
3. How does Melville's humorous description of the two other clerks
   in the law office relieve his heavy presentation of the Wall
   Street office setting? How do these minor characters set off each
   other, the lawyer, and Bartleby?
4. Do you ever feel like saying "I prefer not to" in reply to figures
   of authority? What do you do when you feel a bit of Bartleby in
   you?

TOPICS FOR WRITING

1. Ask students to explicate the paragraph beginning, "For the first
   time in my life a feeling of overpowering, stinging melancholy
   seized me...." A close reading of this passage may bring them
   closer to realizing the complexity of Melville's portrayal of the
   lawyer's relationship to Bartleby.
2. Have students analyze the conclusion of the story. How can
   Bartleby's life be compared to a dead letter?
3. This story has an unusually prolonged and discursive exposition
   before the title character is introduced. Also, Melville doesn't
   motivate his behavior until the end of the story, after he is dead
   and the lawyer finds out about his previous job at the Dead Letter
   Office. Breaking the customary rules of starting a short story
   with a brief exposition and motivating the characters as they are
   introduced, Melville might be accused of writing a poorly structured tale. Argue for or against this accusation, remembering
   that the short-story genre was in its infancy when Melville wrote
   "Bartleby the Scrivener."
4. Part Two of the anthology has an excerpt from Melville's review
   of Hawthorne's Mosses from an Old Manse (p. 1144), discussing
   what Melville called "the power of blackness" in Hawthorne's
   tales. Can students find the same "power of blackness" in
   Melville's description of Bartleby's situation?

SUGGESTED READINGS

Dillingham, W. B. Melville's Short Fiction 1853-1856. Athens: University of Georgia, 1977.

Fogle, R. H. Melville's Shorter Tales. Norman: University of
   Oklahoma Press, 1960.

Vincent, H. P., ed. "Bartleby the Scrivener": Melville Annual for
   1965. Kent, Ohio: Kent State University Press, 1967. Includes
   Henry Murray's "Bartleby and I," pp. 3-24.

13

Gustave Flaubert

"A Simple Heart" (page 125)

Students may find Flaubert's long narrative boring and pointless, its central character too narrow and insignificant for such extended treatment, and its plot lacking the qualities of conflict, suspense, and climax customary in well-structured fiction. Rather than assuring them of the work's recognized perfection or quoting Ezra Pound's judgment that "A Simple Heart" embodies "all that anyone knows about writing," you might try placing the work in contexts that will make it more interesting and accessible.

That the tale is an autobiographically intimate recollection of the people and places of Flaubert's childhood, some of them revisited while it was being written, underlines the degree to which his objective narration controls strong personal feelings. Add that Félicité is run down by the mail coach at precisely the same spot on the road where Flaubert suffered the first onset of the epilepsy that led him to choose a life of retirement and dedicated labor at his art -- a life in many ways comparable to Félicité's own obscure and laborious existence -- and students may find themselves ready to give the story a second look.

Flaubert wrote "A Simple Heart" during the last years of his life as one of three interrelated tales, the Trois Contes, on religious themes. At this period, Flaubert had suffered the humiliation of seeing Normandy and his own home occupied by the invading Prussians; he had lost most of his money through misguided generosity to the husband of an ungrateful niece; and he watched his friends die off one by one, including the novelist George Sand, for whom he was writing "A Simple Heart" in response to her chiding him for insensitivity in his detached style of fiction. The Trois Contes, each of them in a different way, embody Flaubert's reaction to these losses. Each subjects pride and worldliness to a devastating confrontation with humility and self-abnegation.

The genre of "A Simple Heart" is the saint's life; its deceptively simple chronological structure traces the stages by which the protagonist throws off selfishness and worldly desires and, in the process, attains the spiritual purity requisite for miracles, martyrdom, and assumption into bliss. With the loss of Théodore, Félicité leaves ordinary erotic love behind her and enters upon a lifelong devotion to selfless labor. She does this not as a self-conscious and would-be heroic rejection of the world, but only because she knows of nothing else to do. The love she feels subsequently, however, is as selfless as her labor. It goes virtually unrewarded by Paul, Virginie, and Victor; but it is in a sense its own reward, for it enables Félicité to experience a vicarious life of the imagination seemingly more real than her own, as in Virginie's first communion or Victor's trip to Havana. As the world relentlessly strips her of each beloved person and finally even of the very senses by which to apprehend them, Félicité can resort to the power of her imagination, unrestrained by any conventional critical intellect. Imagination blooming into faith

14

allows her not only to find the answer to her loneliness in a parrot, but also to endow the dead, stuffed bird with spiritual life and to experience her final beatific vision of the parrot-like Holy Ghost spreading over her from heaven.

Flaubert worried that his tale would seem ironic and Félicité's confusion of the parrot Loulou with the deity absurd. On the contrary, he insisted, "it is in no way ironic, as you may suppose, but . . . very serious and very sad" (quoted by Buck, p. 105; see Suggested Readings). The question of tone should lead a class discussion straight to the fundamental issues raised by the story. Félicité's utter lack of pretension, as Culler has argued, defeats the impulse toward irony because it allows nothing for irony to deflate, while Flaubert, by avoiding commentary and committing himself to the pure and precise rendering of the facts of the case, presents the reader with the necessity, in order to give meaning to Félicité's life, of imagining a sacred order in which her vision of the parrot is not a mockery but a divine blessing and a fit reward.

QUESTIONS FOR DISCUSSION

1. One critic (Cortland) remarks that in a way Félicité's life is "entirely covered" by Flaubert's opening sentence. How is that so? In what sense does that sentence miss everything?
2. Why does Flaubert introduce his second section by defeating any excitement or special interest the reader might feel about Félicité's affair with Théodore?
3. What is the effect of Flaubert's detailed descriptions of the Norman countryside as well as the other settings and circumstances of the story?
4. Explain the purpose of Félicité's musings about the Holy Ghost in the third section.
5. Why is Virginie's first communion more meaningful to Félicité than her own reception of the sacrament?
6. Compare the reactions of Félicité and Mme Aubain to the death of Virginie. What do the differences reveal about their characters?
7. What is the effect on the reader's attitude toward Félicité of the passage that begins when she is whipped by the coachman?
8. Why does Flaubert have Mère Simon tell herself, as she sponges the sweat from the dying Félicité's temples, "that one day she would have to go the same way?"
9. Félicité means happiness, good fortune, or bliss. Is the name of Flaubert's heroine ironic?

TOPICS FOR WRITING

Critical Essays

1. The episode of Loulou's disappearance and return, and the consequences of Félicité's search for him as an epitome of the story.
2. The circumstances of Félicité's death as a key to Flaubert's theme.

125-196 (text pages)

3. The function of the brief, one-sentence paragraphs that punctuate the text at certain points.

Exercise for Reading

1. Review the story and make a list of everything Félicité loses. Is it possible to make a corresponding list of things she gains?

Related Subjects

1. Study Flaubert's description of Mme Aubain's house in the first section and write a similar description of a house you know.
2. Write an obituary for Félicité such as might have been published in the Pont-l'Évêque newspaper. Are you satisfied with the result?

SUGGESTED READINGS

Buck, Stratton. Gustave Flaubert. Twayne's World Authors Series No. 3. New York: Twayne, 1966. Especially pp. 103-108.

Cortland, Peter. A Reader's Guide to Flaubert. New York: Helios Books, 1968. Pp. 127-146.

Cross, Richard K. Flaubert and Joyce: The Rite of Fiction. Princeton, N.J.: Princeton Univ. Press, 1971. Pp. 17-25.

Culler, Jonathan. Flaubert: The Uses of Uncertainty. Ithaca, N.Y.: Cornell Univ. Press, 1974. Especially pp. 11-19, 208-211.

Leo Tolstoy

"The Death of Ivan Ilych" (page 152)

No one who comes to "The Death of Ivan Ilych" from a direction other than that of War and Peace and Anna Karenina is likely to share the opinion of some Tolstoy scholars that it is parable-thin in its evocation of life, providing only a transparent surface of detail through which Tolstoy's allegorical intentions are exposed to view. The story is studded with brilliantly realistic representations of experiences that the reader encounters with a twinge of sometimes embarrassed recognition -- Peter Ivanovich's struggle with the pouffe, for example. But it is nonetheless a product of the period following Tolstoy's religious crisis and a story written by one whose explicit theory of art rested on a utilitarian moral didacticism.

The story's effectiveness depends on Tolstoy's avoiding, until the last possible moment, preaching the sermon that, as the headnote suggests, he eventually means to preach. The opening section places us in the shoes of Peter Ivanovich, causing us to sympathize with the desire to look away from death, at the same time that it subjects that desire to a devastating satiric attack. Then, by returning to a long, chronological survey of Ivan Ilych's life, Tolstoy forces us to do exactly the opposite of what Peter Ivanovich does: to confront death and its meaning in an extended and excruciatingly matter-of-fact account. What we see is not a life, but a death -- or a life viewed as death. For Ivan Ilych's life, as he eventually comes to realize, is a slow but accelerating process of dying. The narration, however, decelerates, so that the reader may expect it to be nearly over around section VI, whereas in fact there are six more (albeit shorter) sections to come, containing a series of painful revelations that burst through the screen of unawareness that Ivan Ilych has built up to hide himself from reality.

Tolstoy tortures the reader just as Ivan Ilych is tortured, so that the precept finally advanced by the story arrives as the answer to the reader's fervent need. Ivan Ilych is not a particularly bad man; and -- bad or good -- all men, as Gerasim remarks, come to the same spot. Tolstoy makes this recognition virtually intolerable by his vivid rendering of Ivan Ilych's suffering. Then he offers a way out by proposing that one simple motion of the soul toward charity can release the sufferer from his mortal anguish. Tolstoy prepares us for this revelation by stressing the relief Ivan Ilych finds in the kindness of Gerasim, whose health, strength, and repose are bound up with his simple acceptance of sickness and death as necessary parts of life. Some critics have claimed that Tolstoy's art fails to encompass the illumination Ivan Ilych receives at the end, which rests on doctrines extrinsic to the text; but, at least it can be said that he avoids sentimental piety by providing for an ironic interpretation when he caps Ivan Ilych's triumphant assertion, "Death is finished. . . . It is no more!" with the paradoxical conclusion, "He drew in a breath, stopped in the midst of a sigh, stretched out, and died."

The preoccupations and activities of Ivan Ilych and his peers during Ivan Ilych's lifetime in the society portrayed by Tolstoy contrast sharply with those of the unselfish peasant Gerasim. They are directed to no constructive end, serving only to gratify the ego with a sense of power and to hide the fear of death under a surface awareness of pleasure and propriety. Ivan Ilych is never more content than when manipulating the inert objects which are so plentiful in the story -- as when decorating his new house -- and he does his best to relate to people as he relates to things, insulating himself from true human contact. After he has received his death blow from the quite inert knob of a window frame, however, Ivan Ilych experiences a similar dehumanizing treatment from the doctors, his wife, and his friends, none of whom can bear to face the implications of his evident mortality. As his sickness steadily reduces him to a state of infantile dependency, Ivan Ilych comes to recognize first his own powerlessness and then the error in his strategy of living. Finally, as the coffin-womb he has built for himself falls away and he is reborn into the light of spiritual understanding, he sees the fundamental truth he has worked so hard to deny: the feelings of others are as real as his own. At this moment, moved by pity for his wife and son, he at last finds something worthwhile to do; and, in doing it, he attains the sense of ease and "rightness" that has previously eluded him. That the single positive act of Ivan Ilych's life is to die may be seen as either a grim irony

17

or an exciting revelation, depending on the perspective from which the reader views it. But, either way, the conclusion of the story embodies the kernel of Tolstoy's social theme. As Wasiolek puts it, "Death for Tolstoy now, as the supremely shared experience, is the model of all solidarity, and only the profound consciousness of its significance can bring one to the communion of true brotherhood" (p. 179; see Suggested Readings).

QUESTIONS FOR DISCUSSION

1. How does the authorial voice qualify our view of Ivan Ilych's survivors' reactions to his death in section I?
2. Evaluate Peter Ivanovich's view of Ivan Ilych's son when he meets him near the end of section I.
3. Comment on the implications of Ivan Ilych's hanging a medallion bearing the motto respice finem (consider the end) on his watch chain.
4. What is wrong with Ivan Ilych's marriage? With his work? With his ambitions?
5. By examining the authorial comments in sections III and IV, define the attitude toward Ivan Ilych that Tolstoy asks the reader to share. Does this attitude change?
6. Consider the opening sentence of section VI. Is this section a low point in the story? If so, what kind of rise ensues?
7. Why does Ivan Ilych find relief in having his legs supported by Gerasim?
8. What is the effect of the shift to the present tense about one-third of the way through section VIII?
9. In section IX, Ivan Ilych complains to God in language similar to that of Job. Compare and contrast their plights.
10. What is the meaning of Ivan Ilych's reversion to childhood shortly before his death?
11. How might Ivan Ilych's dream of the black sack be interpreted?

TOPICS FOR WRITING

Critical Essays

1. The opening section as a story in itself, but one fully understood only after reading sections II–XII.
2. Bridge as an epitome of the life that Ivan Ilych and his friends try to live.
3. Tolstoy's use of symbolic, descriptive details.
4. "The Death of Ivan Ilych" and "A Simple Heart" compared and contrasted, stressing their endings.

Exercise for Reading

1. Stop after reading section I and write a paragraph or two on the theme and tone of the story as you understand it so far. After reading the rest of the story, write a paragraph evaluating your

original response. This exercise could serve as preparation for
the first topic under Critical Essays above.

Related Subjects

1. Using "The Death of Ivan Ilych" as the basis of your knowledge of
    society, write a manifesto calling for revolution or reform.
2. Write a sermon, using the demise of Ivan Ilych Golovin as your
    occasion.

SUGGESTED READINGS

Christian, R. F. Tolstoy: A Critical Introduction. Cambridge:
    Cambridge Univ. Press, 1969. Pp. 236-238.

Greenwood, E. B. Tolstoy: The Comprehensive Vision. New York: St.
    Martin's Press, 1975. Pp. 118-123.

Simmons, Ernest J. Introduction to Tolstoy's Writings. Chicago:
    Univ. of Chicago Press, 1968. Especially pp. 148-150.

Wasiolek, Edward. Tolstoy's Major Fiction. Chicago: Univ. of Chicago
    Press, 1978. Especially pp. 165-179.

Mark Twain

"A Story without an End" (page 198)

It will be hard to discuss this story without propounding possible
endings. Debating the merit of various alternatives should lead the
class repeatedly back to the set of circumstances specified by Twain
and restated in the concluding paragraph. The story depends on a
highly artificial combination of character traits and coincidences for
its humor; and the violation of any of these devices in an ending that
might unveil Mr. Brown, or might find him self-possessed enough to explain his predicament to the ladies, would violate the story's delicate
tonal balance. Twain has written neither a farce nor a romance, but
has delighted in his ability to construct a solutionless conundrum.
This tour de force is neither a comic nor a witty tale, to use his
terms as quoted in the headnote, but rather a humorous story that calls
the reader's attention directly to its dependence on the skillful manner in which it is told. Its true subject has nothing to do with love,
charity, manners, or life in backwoods Missouri. It is instead a story
about writing stories -- not a surprising conclusion at all when one
recalls the opening and closing sections.

Among various things that the story reveals about the art of fiction, one that warrants particular scrutiny is its demonstration of how
to make a reader laugh. Both Brown's naked pursuit of his buggy and
the ladies' tedious recapitulation of their day's perambulations to a
trouserless young man, who responds as if he were fully clothed,

19

exemplify Bergsonian incongruity, in which behavior is made laughable by being mechanically continued into circumstances where it is drastically inappropriate. Twain intensifies the impact of his comic irony through understatement as well, withholding any remark about Brown's reaction to his situation until the reader has had ample opportunity to imagine it for himself, and then confining himself to the briefest of comments.

QUESTIONS FOR DISCUSSION

1. Examine the details noted in the first four paragraphs of the inset story. Are any of them unnecessary?
2. Why does Twain say that Brown sought to secure his horse's compassion?
3. Why does Twain risk an explanation as implausible as "the train jumped off a bridge" for the loss of the story's ending?
4. Discuss the effect of the frame on our apprehension of the story. Do we ever forget that the story is in a frame?

TOPICS FOR WRITING

Critical Essays

1. Diction as the key to Twain's tone.
2. Lying versus fictionalizing: what Brown could learn from the artist.

Exercise for Reading

1. Try reading the inset story aloud to someone and the whole story to someone else. How do the listeners' reactions differ?

Related Subject

1. Choose a possible ending from those suggested in class discussion; rewrite the inset story as much as necessary to make it fit. Try changing the point of view: have Brown tell it in the first person, or see everything through Mary's eyes.

Ambrose Bierce

"An Occurrence at
Owl Creek Bridge" (page 206)

What is the reason for the enduring interest of this contrived and improbable tale? Surprise endings frequently draw groans similar to those that greet bad puns, but Bierce's final twist is more likely to elicit shock and recoil. Perhaps the story's success results more from its realization of an intimate and familiar fear than from its sharp, vivid style or its tense pacing of the narrative. The idea of

continued life is all that the human mind, unable to imagine mere
"darkness and silence," can propose in view of impending death. By
narrating a fantasy of escape so persuasively that we succumb to it,
and then by revealing it with the snap of a neck to have been only a
fantasy, Bierce forces us to recognize once again the reality of our
mortal situation.

If, out of the desire to evade that recognition, the reader seeks
to repudiate the story as a piece of literary chicanery, he or she will
not succeed. A clear-headed review of section III reveals that the exciting tale of escape could not have been real. Even before Farquhar
enters the nightmare forest with its strange constellations and peculiar, untravelled roadway, he has experienced a preternatural height-
ening of sensory awareness that happens only when one sees with the
eyes of the mind; and, he has undergone sensations better explained by
reference to a slow-motion expansion of a hanging than to his imagined
plunge into Owl Creek. The images of his dream emerge from Farquhar's
instinctual desire to live, and Bierce renders them with such clarity
that the reader can cherish them as well. The same intensity of sensory awareness marks Bierce's conjecture about what it must be like
when the noose jerks tight. We feel the constriction, see the flash
of nervous discharge, and hear the cracking vertebrae.

Our close participation in the imaginary and real sensations of
dying countervails the doomed man's symbolic isolation, which is the
burden of section I. While the executioners enact the formal rituals
that establish distance from the victim, who is being expelled from the
human community (even the sentinels are turning their backs on him),
Bierce leads the reader into an empathic communion with him. The
agency of this imaginative projection is the coolly exact observational
style, which carries us across the plank -- Farquhar's first thought to
which we are privy is his approval of this device -- and into the
psyche of the condemned.

Before launching into Farquhar's dying fantasy, however, Bierce
goes back, in section II, to narrate the events leading up to the execution. Besides establishing for Farquhar an identity with which we
can sympathize, this passage presents him as active rather than acted
upon, and so generates a momentum that continues into the story of his
escape. The section ends with one of several stark, one-line revelations that conclude passages of uncertainty, illusion, or false conjecture in the story: "He was a Federal scout;" "What he heard was the
ticking of his watch;" "Peyton Farquhar was dead. . . ." This device
of style expresses Bierce's major theme: whatever we dream of, life is
entrapment by death, and time is running out.

QUESTIONS FOR DISCUSSION

1. In what ways does section I suggest the idea of a psychological
   time much slower than actual time?
2. Why is it appropriate that the execution should take place on a
   bridge over a river?
3. What is the function of Farquhar's conjectures about escape at the

21

end of section I?
4. In what ways does Bierce try to gain the reader's sympathy for Farquhar? Why does he need to do this?
5. Which events in section III might be read as dislocations of sensations experienced by a man in the process of being hanged?
6. Contrast the descriptive style of a passage from section III with that of a passage from section I.
7. What would be the result if Farquhar's imagined reunion with his wife took place after the snapping of his neck?

TOPICS FOR WRITING

Critical Essays

1. Bierce's handling of time and chronology in "An Occurrence at Owl Creek Bridge."
2. The fiction of effect as a fiction of despair in Gogol, Poe, and Bierce.

Related Subject

1. Compare the near-death experience widely discussed in the popular press of late with the experience of dying as envisioned by Flaubert, Tolstoy, and Bierce.

SUGGESTED READINGS

Wiggins, Robert A. Ambrose Bierce. Univ. of Minnesota Pamphlets on American Writers, No. 37. Minneapolis: Univ. of Minnesota Press, 1964. Especially pp. 24-25.

Woodruff, Stuart C. The Short Stories of Ambrose Bierce: A Study in Polarity. Pittsburgh: Univ. of Pittsburgh Press, 1964. Pp. 153-163.

Henry James

"The Real Thing" (page 215)

According to the narrator, the real thing, which might be fine for representation by the mechanical means of photography, is constraining to his artistic imagination. Mr. and Mrs. Monarch become colossal figures crowding his canvas and blocking his creativity. By contrast, Miss Churm and Oronte, because they have to pretend to be the subject being painted, enter into "the deceptive atmosphere of art" and help its "alchemy" to take place. No master artist himself, the narrator is unable to transform the Monarchs into anything but themselves, and his effort to do so results in monstrous misrepresentations. Because he needs to produce pot boilers, he does not try to paint a portrait of the Monarchs -- although to be a painter of portraits is his stated ambition. But, he sees them so clearly -- and what he sees involves so little plasticity -- that he cannot draw illustrations of fiction with them before him.

He can paint their portrait in the words of the story, however, and as he does so they come to life for both the artist and reader. Although the narrator first regards them as types and appraises them like animals, they have gained dignity and individuality and have become objects of compassion by the latter stages of the story. If the narrator persists in blaming the defects of his art on the defects of his models, he seems willing at least to accept his limitations and to place a higher value on his human contact with the Monarchs.

The rigidity of the Monarchs may symbolize both the intractability of the real world upon which the artist struggles to work and the literal-minded insensitivity of the audience with which he seeks to communicate; but, their chief interest as characters lies in how that rigidity at last dissolves. Hampered by their twenty years of inane leisure on the country-house circuit, the Monarchs are less "a compendium of everything /most objectionable/ in the social system" of England, as Jack Hawley would have it, as they are the victims of that social system. Trained as real gentlefolk, they reveal that insofar as that real thing is seen as mere surface manners and physical appearance, it may appear an empty shell, devoid of sensitivity and imagination. Clinging desperately to the facade of their social status even when the money to support it no longer exists, the Monarchs find themselves unemployable at any job beneath their station. But their integrity and tenacity, epitomized in the solidity of their marriage, give them strength. The story's conclusion suggests that their experience in the studio, which is indeed for them as for the narrator "a place to learn to see," has taught them how to relinquish the self-defeating proprieties of their rank and to accept a new role as servants, a role which they can perform effectively and which will enable them to survive. The alchemy of the studio has not "sublimated," but lowered them in social rank; still, in freeing them from having to continue to be "the real thing," it may have released them to explore the myriad possibilities of being themselves.

The sympathy that the story generates for the Monarchs, and that leaves fond memory for them in the mind of the reader and of the narrator, arises from the narrative method defined in the headnote. Whatever James planned in his notebook (see Part Two, p. 1153), attention to the "nuances of perception" is as crucial to "The Real Thing" as it is to The Ambassadors; and it stimulates an alertness in the reader that enables him to enter sympathetically into the Monarchs' plight. Consider the opening section. Most of the information so painfully gleaned in those pages is recapitulated in summary form in the second section. The narrator's claim to have gathered so much from that first interview challenges the reader to be similarly perceptive, just as the opening paragraph, with its deliberate mystifications and plentiful clues about the narrator's profession, requires the reader to become actively engaged in deciphering the text. If he does so, the reader will be rewarded by feeling the full power of the last line of that section as it poignantly anticipates the end of the tale.

215-234 (text pages)

QUESTIONS FOR DISCUSSION

1. Why do the Monarchs have such difficulty announcing their business when they first come to the narrator's studio? Contrast their approach with that of Oronte.
2. Why is the narrator afraid the Monarchs might prove artistic? Do they?
3. Consider your reactions to the Monarchs on one hand and to Miss Churm and Oronte on the other. Which pair deserves the greater respect?
4. Why is the narrator happiest drawing Major Monarch's trousers and Mrs. Monarch's back or profil perdu?
5. What is Jack Hawley's role in the story? Why does the narrator need his opinion? Why does he hesitate to take his advice?
6. Why does the narrator think it ideal to have the Monarchs as his servants rather than as his models?
7. How serious are the narrator's artistic ambitions? Do you agree with his theory of art? Does his inability to deal with the real thing suggest that he is not the real thing as an artist? As a man?

TOPICS FOR WRITING

Critical Essay

1. The steps James took beyond the plan for "The Real Thing" that he was evolving in his notebook entry printed in Part Two (p. 1153) in order to arrive at the finished story.

Exercise for Reading

1. Examine the four sections of the story individually, noting what is accomplished in each with regard to four processes that take place in the story: the unrolling of the plot; the growth of the Monarchs; the growth of the narrator; and the exploration of the theme.

SUGGESTED READINGS

Labor, Earle. "'The Real Thing': Three Levels of Meaning." In Tompkins, cited below, pp. 29-32. Originally published in College English, 23 (1962), 376-378.

Tompkins, Jane P. "Introduction" to Twentieth Century Interpretations of "The Turn of the Screw" and Other Tales, ed. Tompkins. Englewood Cliffs, N.J.: Prentice-Hall, 1970. Pp. 1-10, especially pp. 6-7.

Toor, David. "Narrative Irony in Henry James's 'The Real Thing.'" In Tompkins, cited above, pp. 33-39. Originally published in The University Review, 24 (1967), 95-99.

Winner, Viola Hopkins. <u>Henry James and the Visual Arts</u>. Charlottes-
ville: Univ. of Virginia Press, 1970. Pp. 108-111.

Sarah Orne Jewett

"A White Heron" (page 236)

Jewett portrays Sylvia, whose very name associates her with the
woodland, as torn between the natural world in which she is so fully at
home and the first stirrings of the "great power" of love in her
"woman's heart." Her project of pleasing the young hunter and winning
the treasure of his gratitude, in the form of ten dollars, leads her
out of her shyness and into the heroic adventure of climbing the great
pine tree. As a result of her efforts, Sylvia grows within herself.
The reader worries that she may be tempted into betraying the white
heron and thus into surrendering something essential to her own integrity, but Sylvia, in her vision from the top of the tree and her face-
to-face meeting with the heron, has gained the perspective necessary
to hold firm.

Jewett's rich evocation of the landscape and the emotional intensity with which she narrates the climactic action contribute to the
story's deeper resonances. If Sylvia recalls the woodland goddess
Diana -- and similarly guards her chastity -- she also resembles those
heroes and heroines of myth and folklore who must go to some symbolic
world-navel or towering height in quest of wisdom, or who must suffer
an initiation that involves mastering their fear of the (sometimes
phallic) <u>other</u> and reintegrating their identities in order to cope with
it. Sylvia rejects the destructive gun and mounts the pine tree, "a
great mainmast to the voyaging earth," electing the fecund life of a
natural world she is still discovering over the destructive promises of
the "ornithologist," whose grounds are populated with dead, stuffed
birds. While the narrator ends fretting over Sylvia's having consigned herself to loneliness and love-longing, nothing in the story
suggests that she would be better off having sold herself for ten dollars and a whistle.

Students may find it easier to approach the story through its
autobiographical dimensions. According to Pool, who builds on F. O.
Matthieson's early study, Jewett remained childlike and single through
her life, treasuring the love of her father, who used to take her on
long rambles through the countryside when she was a girl. "As Sylvia
elects to keep her private and meaningful secret, so is she choosing
for Miss Jewett too. . . . She chooses, psychologically, to remain a
child, with Sylvia" (Pool, p. 225; see Suggested Readings). But if
she chooses to remain a child, it is a child in terms she met in
reading Wordsworth, whom she admired: as one privy to the indwelling
spirit of the natural world.   ∤

The imagery that surrounds Sylvia is uniformly associated with
<u>mother</u> nature until she ventures up the tree and meets the heron. Her
adventure enables her to reject assertively the young man and the

advancing modern world of science and machinery with which he is associated. This is a step forward from her original strategies of withdrawal and concealment. The antinomy, however, is not resolved. The
only perfect marriage in the story is between the nesting herons; and
Jewett offers no key to a satisfactory union between the world of
nature and the civilization that threatens to despoil it.

QUESTIONS FOR DISCUSSION

1. Sarah Orne Jewett is known as a local colorist. To what extent
   is the locale of this story its subject? To what extent does the
   story transcend its specific Maine setting?
2. Discuss the presentation of the cow Sylvia is driving as the story
   opens. What does her "loud moo by way of explanation" actually
   explain?
3. Comment on the men, apart from the hunter, mentioned in the story.
   Is the absence of men from Sylvia's world a significant factor in
   the story?
4. As a child in town, Sylvia had the reputation of being "afraid of
   folks." Is she? Does she have reason?
5. Explain Sylvia's reaction when she hears the hunter's whistle.
   Why does Jewett briefly switch to the present tense here? Does
   she do so elsewhere?
6. Comment on the omniscient-narrative point of view used in this
   story. How is it controlled? What does the narrative voice contribute to the story?
7. Describe the character and appurtenances of the young hunter, and
   contrast them with those of Sylvia. How important are his evident
   gentleness and good intentions?
8. How does Jewett charge the pine tree and Sylvia's climb to the top
   of it with special meaning? What does she see up there that she
   has never seen before?
9. What do Sylvia and the heron have in common?
10. Analyze the last paragraph. What has Sylvia lost? What has she
    preserved? What has she gained?

TOPICS FOR WRITING

Critical Essays

1. Elements of folk and fairy tale in "A White Heron."
2. Sylvia's nighttime excursion as a journey into the self.
3. Maternal and sexual imagery in "A White Heron."
4. "A White Heron" as a rejection of modern-industrial society.

SUGGESTED READINGS

Brenzo, Richard. "Free Heron or Dead Sparrow: Sylvia's Choice in
    Sarah Orne Jewett's 'A White Heron'." Colby Library Quarterly,
    14 (1978), 36–41.

Hovet, Theodore R. "America's 'Lonely Country Child': The Theme of Separation in Sarah Orne Jewett's 'A White Heron'." Colby Library Quarterly, 14 (1978), 166-171.

_____. "'Once Upon a Time': Sarah Orne Jewett's 'A White Heron' as a Fairy Tale." Studies in Short Fiction, 15 (1978), 63-68.

Pool, Eugene Hillhouse. "The Child in Sarah Orne Jewett." In Appreciation of Sarah Orne Jewett. Ed., Richard Cary. Waterville, Maine: Colby College Press, 1973. Pp. 223-228, esp. p. 225. Originally published in Colby Library Quarterly, 7 (1967), 503-509.

Guy de Maupassant

"The String" (page 245)

Without its masterful use of the kind of sharp observation Maupassant learned from Flaubert (see headnote in text), "The String" would be a lifeless tale of flat characters in a contrived set of circumstances with a preformulated theme. Maupassant's pictures of the peasants on their way to market or of Maître Hauchecorne groping for the string and then, caught in the act, pretending to be absorbed in something important are painted with such clarity and freshness that we believe what he shows us must be true. Because his vision is convincing, Maupassant's message strikes with the force of revelation.

Maupassant was fascinated with delusions and their effect on behavior. In "The Necklace," for example, a couple destroy their lives trying to accumulate enough money to replace borrowed jewels they believed to be diamonds and had lost, only to learn too late that they were paste. In "The String," Maitre Hauchecorne is destroyed by a false presumption of his guilt by those around him. He cannot clear himself of suspicion, and people's reaction to what they take to be his hypocrisy drives him into a terminal depression.

Students will readily acknowledge that Maitre Hauchecorne has been unjustly treated, but the story will make little sense aesthetically until they recognize that the main cause of his trouble lies not in an unfortunate coincidence but rather in his character and that of the society Maupassant portrays. Maître Hauchecorne does not find the wallet, but he would lie about it if he did, just as he dissembles when he becomes aware that Maître Malandin's eyes are upon him as he picks up the string. Maître Hauchecorne is called from the cozy dinner at the inn to answer his accuser, and thereafter his severance from the community that nourishes and sustains him becomes ever more complete. Ironically, it is by maintaining his innocence at such lengths that he cuts himself off from his fellows, who would be quite happy to admire him for his cleverness if he would acknowledge his deceit.

The reader may wish to register dismay at the society based on cunning, trickery, and suspicion that Maupassant depicts, but those qualities are nonetheless the basis of human interaction in the world of the story. Maître Hauchecorne and Maître Malandin "had once had a quarrel _together_" (my emphasis), and they were "both good haters." By insisting on his innocence, Maître Hauchecorne lies to a deeper extent than to that which he is accused. Further, he represents himself as morally superior to those around him, which Maître Hauchecorne well knows to be untrue, so that he finds himself in the doubly ironic position of being fully aware of his own responsibility for the "unjust" ostracism that is inflicted upon him.

QUESTIONS FOR DISCUSSION

1. Why is Maître Hauchecorne embarrassed to be seen stooping for the string? Should he be?
2. Describe what this sentence contributes to the story: "The peasants looked at cows, went away, came back, perplexed, always in fear of being cheated, not daring to decide, watching the vendor's eye, ever trying to find the trick in the man and the flaw in the beast."
3. Describe the atmosphere at Jourdain's. Why does Maupassant have Maître Hauchecorne called to the Mayor's office from here?
4. Why do Maître Hauchecorne's old friends seem to admire him for doing what he denies?
5. To what extent and in what ways does Maupassant seek to engage our sympathy for Maître Hauchecorne? Does Maître Hauchecorne deserve his ironic fate? What does Maupassant seem to think of the characters and society he portrays?
6. Does this story exploit an improbable coincidence to tell a grim joke, or does it offer a valid insight into human nature?

TOPICS FOR WRITING

Critical Essays

1. The thin line between cynicism and sentimentality: Maupassant's tone in "The String."
2. The impossible situations of Mark Twain's Mr. Brown and Maupassant's Maître Hauchecorne.
3. Local color and universality of theme in Jewett and Maupassant.
4. The tragedy of Maître Hauchecorne.

Related Subject

1. Study the descriptive passage that opens the story, noticing how Maupassant makes us see things in a new way. Then write a similar descriptive sketch of your own, trying to discover something heretofore unnoticed about what you describe.

SUGGESTED READING

Downs, John A. "Maupassant's 'La Ficelle' and Bazan's 'Billet de Mille'." Studies in Philology, 57 (1960), 663-671.

Guy de Maupassant

"Miss Harriet" (page 250)

Try approaching this story by exploring the relationship of the prelude to the tale. Not only does it introduce most of the motives that will be developed in the body of the story; it also provides, through its artful rendering of the landscape, the bridge through which the story gains access to a relevant past. Further, by showing that Léon's recollections reveal something unexpected to the people that hear them, Maupassant implies that his own story may have a similar meaning for the reader. There is a comfortable sensuality in the description of the countryside that crystallizes in the simile of the young girl slipping off her nightgown and that is reflected in the desire of "the little Baroness de Sérennes," whose sexual behavior has already been called subtly into question, for a love story "that will make us all laugh." Léon, out of the depth of his experience, tells quite a different kind of tale.

It starts, however, in a deceptive manner. The easy, careless daubing of the young painter involves loving the landscape like a young girl and loving young girls as if they were part of the landscape. In Miss Harriet, however, he meets one who loves the landscape -- nature -- with a heightened intensity. The religious quality of her attitude exalts it, but we come quickly to understand her feelings to be the result of passion, the thwarted longing for what she cannot have.

Miss Harriet is first fascinated with Léon's painting because it allows him to possess nature, complete with a suffusion of divine glory, in a concrete way that she cannot. But just as Léon's art remains continuous with his sexuality (which Maupassant makes clear particularly in the first several paragraphs of Léon's narration and in the contents of some of his paintings), so Miss Harriet's pantheistic transports cannot be dissociated from her repressed erotic desires. When all her sublimated emotions come into focus in her love of the young artist and burst into consciousness, she is literally shattered. Léon, though he acknowledges feeling "as surprised as if I had witnessed a miracle, and as troubled as if I had committed a crime," finds the English spinster's love as queer and pathetic as her religious enthusiasm, and much more difficult to share than her admiration for the Norman landscape.

Having known no man but her father, Miss Harriet has transferred her affection to a fatherly deity and projected his image on the universe. No human lover could replace this dream so vastly enlarged by passion, certainly not young Léon, who immediately betrays Miss

Harriet's love by snatching a few trivial kisses with Céleste. That the collapse of her vision should drive Miss Harriet to suicide is not surprising. Maupassant's masterstroke, however, is to recognize that in her despair she would not be capable of the romantic exaltation of a leap from the cliffs at sunset to be at last united with her vision, but that she would merge with the landscape in the only manner her disillusionment has left open, burying herself deep in the unilluminated earth to decompose by plunging down the well. Miss Harriet's final act may seem a grotesque parody of Léon's sensuous, naked plunge into the deep hole of a stream, but it is nonetheless a version of that union with the other that both love and art of the romantic variety seek.

In an interesting discussion of "Miss Harriet," from which an excerpt is included in Part Two of the anthology, Sean O'Faolain expresses his simultaneous admiration and distaste for what he terms the relentless realism and elementalism of Maupassant, whose vision he finds to be cynical and unredeemed. But "Miss Harriet," however elemental the passion it studies and however brutal its denouement, develops its attack on the evil of the world with extreme subtlety. That Miss Harriet's death arises from a longing similar to that which motivates Léon in both his sexual and artistic daubing criticizes his careless attitude and provides him with an important insight. He first expresses what he has learned when he kisses the corpse, a gesture that recognizes a deep truth about the intertwining of love and death that he has hitherto ignored; and he continues to express it by telling his tale for the edification of the sophisticated party in the drag. The connection between love and death is one of the abiding mysteries of literature. The reward for confronting it in this story is a heightened sense of natural beauty and the gentle wisdom that makes Léon's such a pleasant voice of admonition.

QUESTIONS FOR DISCUSSION

1. How can we tell the social class of the people in the prelude? What can we infer about their sexual behavior?
2. Comment on the appropriateness of Maupassant's description of the landscape at sunrise, in the prelude, to what follows. What about his magnificent description of the hare?
3. Consider the tone implied by Léon Chenal's introduction of his story. Is that tone carried through the narrative? What other attitudes might one take toward the experience? What do we think of Léon in view of the attitude he expresses?
4. Examine Léon's several descriptions of Miss Harriet, beginning with his first view of her as "a pickled herring adorned with curling papers" and continuing through to his description of the "glassy corpse" on which he bestows a kiss. Does his view of her change to embody the changing meaning she has for him?
5. Why do the people of the village call Miss Harriet "the demoniac?"
6. Discuss Miss Harriet's purchase and release of the fish. What is her motive? Why does her action upset the fisherman so?
7. Miss Harriet and Léon Chenal are characterized in part as national

stereotypes. Why? Does the story have a point to make about the French and English cultures?

8. How good are Léon's paintings as described in the story? What changes might be expected in his work as a result of the experience he narrates?

9. Léon sees "a species of madness . . . an exasperated desire, impatient and impotent, for the unrealised and unrealisable" lurking in Miss Harriet's eyes. What, exactly, does she want? Why is such a desire insane?

10. Why does Miss Harriet jump down the well instead of jumping off a cliff?

11. What is the effect on the reader of the detailed rendering of the extrication of Miss Harriet's body from the well? Of the experience itself on Léon?

12. Examine the last paragraph of the story. What attitude does it suggest? What other attitudes might one take toward this story?

TOPICS FOR WRITING

Critical Essays

1. "Miss Harriet" as a theory of fiction. Or, "Ut pictura poesis:" "Miss Harriet" and "The Real Thing."
2. Eros and agape: Maupassant's critique of two kinds of love.
3. Description and theme in "Miss Harriet."

Exercise for Reading

1. After reading the story in its entirety, return to the prelude and annotate it carefully, listing passages in the main story that are anticipated in some way by the details of the opening.

Related Subject

1. Imagine "Miss Harriet" as a film. Write a scenario for all or part of it, concentrating on how you would handle the visual elements of the story.

SUGGESTED READINGS

Dugan, John Raymond. _Illusion and Reality: A Study of Descriptive Techniques in the Works of Guy de Maupassant_. The Hague: Mouton, 1973.

O'Faolain, Sean. _The Short Story_. New York: Devin-Adair, 1951. Pp. 134-43. (Excerpt appears in Part Two of the anthology, pp. 1156-1157.)

Kate Chopin

"Regret" (page 267)

"Regret," especially considered in conjunction with Jewett's
"A White Heron" or Maupassant's "Miss Harriet," can open the door to
an interesting discussion on a highly topical question: Must a woman
who rejects the traditional female roles of marriage and motherhood
thereby consign herself to isolation and loneliness? Chopin's quiet
sympathy for Mamzelle Aurélie, whose peculiarities characterize her
without making her in the least grotesque, differs from both the
impassioned concern of Jewett and the chilly irony of Maupassant.
The result is a treatment of the woman's dilemma that is perhaps
more insightful and balanced. Chopin faces squarely all that her
heroine has lost and the regret she feels as a result of becoming
aware of it, but she never implies that Mamzelle Aurelie was a fool
to have lived as she has.

A consideration of the substantive issues raised by the story
should not, however, divert attention from matters of style and
structure. Chopin's comment on Maupassant (included in Part Two, p.
1127) describes the virtues of her own work even better than it does
those of her master. Like Maupassant's, her "direct and simple"
observations are precisely directed toward her artistic purpose.
With a few deft observations about her figure, clothing, and activities, Chopin establishes Mamzelle Aurélie's masculine, even military
bearing, and then proceeds to trace the rapid stages by which looking
after the children awakens not only her maternal feelings but also
her power to relate to others as individuals. At the start, Mamzelle
Aurélie deals in categories -- chickens, negroes, children -- and
pursues her "line of duty" toward them. But when she finds it
impossible to put the children to bed the way she would shoo the
chickens to the henhouse, she begins to listen -- to the children and
to Aunt Ruby -- and she begins to learn new ways. Her adaptation to
the children (efficiently set forth in the paragraph beginning "Ti
Nomme's sticky fingers . . .") and their adaptation to their temporary home (reflected in their whereabouts at the moment of Odile's
return) are narrated without a trace of emotional excess. Simply,
"Mamzelle Aurélie had grown quite used to these things." Even after
the children are taken away, when she feels her loneliness for the
first time, Mamzelle Aurélie's identity does not dissolve; she cries,
but "like a man." (Would Maupassant have had her commit suicide with
her fowling piece?)

Chopin's artistry marks her handling of other elements of this
remarkably compact story as well. That Odile departs in a rush to
the bedside of her sick mother, and that she returns, joyous that her
mother is not dying, to delighted screams of welcome from her own
daughter cannot be without meaning for Mamzelle Aurélie, the only
character in the tale who is no one's mother or child. Although she
leads an active life managing her farm, in her relations with other
people Mamzelle Aurélie remains as Chopin symbolically portrays her,
standing on her gallery (porch), "looking and listening."

QUESTIONS FOR DISCUSSION

1. What does Chopin's choice of words in the first descriptive phrase that she offers about Mamzelle Aurélie -- "a good strong figure" -- imply about her attitude toward her heroine?
2. How does Chopin arouse and control the reader's anticipation of the epiphany or revelation toward which the story builds?
3. Discuss Odile and Aunt Ruby as foils for Mamzelle Aurélie. In what ways is she superior to them?
4. How does Chopin avoid saccharine sentiment in portraying the four children, while still making it credible to the reader that Mamzelle Aurélie should come to love them?
5. Note Chopin's use of sense imagery other than the visual. What do such images contribute to the story's impact on the reader?
6. How important is Chopin's use of Cajun dialect and local color? What would the story lack without them?

TOPICS FOR WRITING

Critical Essays

1. Mamzelle Aurélie and Miss Harriet.
2. The stages of Mamzelle Aurélie's awakening.

Related Subject

1. Write a review and evaluation of "Regret" from a feminist point of view.

SUGGESTED READING

Seyersted, Per. Kate Chopin: A Critical Biography. Baton Rouge: Louisiana State University Press, 1969. Pp. 125-130.

Joseph Conrad

"An Outpost of Progress" (page 272)

The bald and multiplying ironies of this story begin and end with the narrator's sarcasm in the title and in his view of the trading company as "The Great Civilizing Company (since we know that civilization follows trade)." Although the savagery of "the land of darkness and sorrow," with its brutality, ignorance, superstition, and human sacrifice, is singularly repellent and merits the narrator's haughty disdain, the principles of European civilization are equally dehumanizing. The society that produced Kayerts and Carlier "had taken care of those two men, forbidding them all independent thoughts, all initiative, all departure from routine; and forbidding it under pain of death. They could only live on condition of being machines."

At the beginning of the story, the pair seem childlike inno-
cents. The narrator has little sympathy for their stupid optimism
and self-congratulatory comradeship, but they seem nonetheless,
within their limits, entirely benign. Even Makola/Henry Price,
despite the narrator's comment that he worships "the Evil Spirit that
rules the lands under the equator," appears harmless. But Makola and
his two masters stand at the point where the savagery of Africa and
the soullessness of imperialist Europe collide to breed horrors.
Makola sells men into slavery for a haul of ivory for the company,
with a deeper insight into its true motives and values than Kayerts
and Carlier, whose innocence and propensity for illusionary plati-
tudes blinds them for a time to the truth about the enterprise they
are a part of. Conrad compares them to "blind men in a large room,
aware only of what came in contact with them (and that only
imperfectly), but unable to see the general aspect of things." They
are blind to themselves as well. They continue to feel superior to
the natives and "that beast Makola" even as they buy into his slave
deal and then, under the strain of isolation and poor nutrition,
gradually abandon orderly and civilized relations and face each
other at last in a brutal struggle to the death over a sugar cube.
Their squabble is childish in motive and absurd in action, which not
only expresses their nature as Conrad has portrayed them but also
predicates Kayerts's recoil and suicide. Carlier has his eye blown
out by Kayerts's revolver, but Kayerts's mind itself becomes
unhinged when his conviction of innocence gives way to the recognition that he has, out of fear, murdered his unarmed comrade, who
may very well have been coming (as Kayerts himself was coming) to
surrender and sue for peace.

Near the beginning of the story, the narrator remarks that "the
contact with pure unmitigated savagery, with primitive nature and
primitive man, brings sudden and profound trouble to the heart." In
their blindness, Kayerts and Carlier do not see the darkness that
surrounds them -- until, like the rank grass that invades their
courtyard, it becomes part of themselves. Was it part of them all
along? Surely the ease with which they fall in line with Makola's
schemes and lies suggests as much, and the grotesque picture of the
corpse of Kayerts sticking its tongue out at the Managing Director
implies that Conrad spies the root of the evil in the acquisitive-
ness that has brought Europeans into the jungle to begin with.

The headnote quotes Conrad's playful remark that the tale is
"the lightest part of the loot I carried off from Central Africa."
Its theme is heavy enough, however -- too heavy, perhaps, for him
to handle without the distancing of a sarcastic and cynical narrative voice. In "Heart of Darkness" Conrad returned to the same
material, and by reflecting it through the brooding mind of the
narrator Marlow he found a way to confront its sobering implications
with full seriousness.

QUESTIONS FOR DISCUSSION

1. Why does the story present a long description of Makola/Henry
   Price almost immediately? Explain why he is a central figure
   in the story.
2. Who is the protagonist? What are the terms of his conflict?
   When does he receive an illumination? What does he learn?
3. Discuss the relationship between Kayerts and Carlier. What is
   their friendship based on? What do their differences in background and character contribute to the story?
4. Why are Kayerts and Carlier so lazy?
5. Consider Conrad's use of phrases like "pioneers of trade and
   progress." Why are they ironic? At one point, Carlier says,
   "In a hundred years, there will be perhaps a town here. Quays,
   and warehouses, and barracks, and -- and -- billiard rooms.
   Civilization, my boy, and virtue -- and all." Analyze and
   comment on this declaration.
6. What is Gobila's function in the story? What does he reveal
   about the two cultures that collide in the action Conrad
   narrates?
7. Discuss the armed band of traders, and the ten station men who
   become their slaves, as fruits of the Europeanization of Africa.
   Compare them with Henry Price.
8. After the slave deal, Kayerts and Carlier feel "that something
   from within them was gone, something that had worked for their
   safety, and had kept the wilderness from interfering with
   their hearts." Explain.
9. Throughout most of the story, the narrator uses heavy verbal
   irony to maintain a distance between the reader and the characters. In the final fight, however, that distance collapses and
   we find ourselves locked closely into the consciousness of
   Kayerts. How does Conrad accomplish this effect? What purpose
   does it serve?
10. As Kayerts contemplates the corpse of Carlier, he loses his
    grip on his own identity and almost comes to think that he him-
    self is the dead man. Why? In what sense might he be
    substantially correct?
11. Comment on the ending of the story. Why does Kayerts hang
    himself on the arrival of the steamer? What dimension of
    meaning would be lost if the story ended without the steamer
    returning?

TOPICS FOR WRITING

Critical Essays

1. Innocence and primitivism in "An Outpost of Progress."
2. Why there are no "noble savages" in Conrad's tale.
3. Conrad's attack on colonialism.

272-356 (text pages)

Exercise for Reading

1. Mark all passages in which an omniscient narrator speaks
   directly in general terms or implies a value judgment through
   obvious irony. Does a consistent attitude and set of ideas
   emerge? How do they compare with the implied theme embodied in
   the narrative as a whole?

Related Subject

1. R. A. Gekoski has suggested that Kayerts's "wrong-headed
   lucidity" as he attempts to rationalize the death of Carlier
   resembles the cogitations of Raskolnikov in Dostoevsky's Crime
   and Punishment and the darkest thoughts of Conrad himself as
   expressed in his letters to his friends. The grotesque suicide
   of Kayerts, then, may represent Conrad's effort to distance
   himself from ideas that seem to him a moral abyss. Using
   Kayerts's thoughts as a starting point, write a philosophical
   analysis of the moral vision they imply. What arguments (based
   on the story or otherwise) might be used to sustain Kayerts?
   What kinds of arguments might be used against his position?

SUGGESTED READINGS

Gekoski, R. A. Conrad: The Moral World of the Novelist. New York:
   Barnes & Noble, 1978. Pp. 43-47, 150.

Watt, Ian. Conrad in the Nineteenth Century. Berkeley: University
   of California Press, 1979. Pp. 49, 75, 159, 175-176.

Joseph Conrad

"Heart of Darkness" (page 290)

At the center of the concentric layers out of which Conrad
constructs this story lies a case of atavism and the collapse of
civilized morality similar to that detailed in "An Outpost of
Progress." Like Kayerts, Kurtz casts aside all restraint and
becomes as wild as his surroundings; or rather, the darkness around
him calls out the darkness within his innermost being. But while
Kayerts is a contemptible fellow in the eyes of the narrator of "An
Outpost of Progress," Kurtz is a man of heroic abilities and
exemplary ideals. Out of weakness, Kayerts crumbles; Kurtz explodes,
unable to control his own strength.

Conrad does not replace the ironic distance from which we regard
Kayerts with an intimate inside view of Kurtz. To do so would
destroy the aura of mystery and special significance that marks the
story's theme as a profound revelation, the "culminating point of
[Marlow's] experience," gained at "the farthest point of navigation."
Instead, he positions Kurtz in the midst of an impenetrable jungle,

at "the very heart of darkness," as far from home and as remote from
familiar frames of reference as possible. Then he causes the reader
to approach him through a series of identifications that make the
revelation of his debasement a statement not just about Kurtz, but
about us all.

Conrad creates this effect mainly through his use of Marlow as
narrator, and no discussion of the story can avoid exploring his
function. He is on the one hand a kind of prophet -- his pose
resembles that of an idol or Buddha -- whose wisdom arises from his
having looked beyond the veil that screens the truth from common
view ("the inner truth is hidden -- luckily, luckily"), and on the
other hand an adventurer like the heroes of epic poems, descending
into Hades and emerging shaken with his dark illumination. But
Marlow's vision is neither of heaven nor of hell. His journey up
the Congo River is in fact a descent into the inner reaches of the
human soul. Forced by a combination of circumstances and precon-
ceptions into a special association with Kurtz, Marlow recognizes in
that "shadow" the intrinsic darkness of human nature, in which he
shares. When he plunges into the jungle to redeem Kurtz, who has
crawled away on all fours to rejoin the "unspeakable rites" of his
worshipers, Marlow embraces what Kurtz has become no less than what
he once was or might have been, acknowledging his own kinship with
the deepest depravity. Kurtz dies crying, "The horror! the horror!"
-- apparently having regained from his rescuer enough of his moral
bearings to recoil from his own behavior. Marlow, who judges the
truth "too dark -- too dark altogether," preserves the innocence of
Kurtz's "intended," leaving her "great and saving illusion" intact.

Conrad may be suggesting that only by a conscious lie or by
willful blindness can we avoid sinking into the savagery that surrounds us, that dwells under externally maintained restraint within
us, and that animates our civilization in various guises, such as
"the flabby, pretending, weak-eyed devil of a rapacious and pitiless
folly." The conquest of the earth, which is what the civilized
society portrayed in the story is engaged in, "is not a pretty thing
when you look into it too much," Marlow says. "What redeems it is
the idea only . . . an unselfish belief in the idea -- something you
can set up, and bow down before, and offer sacrifice to . . . ."
But such idolatry of our own idea is not far from its horrible perversion into the worship of himself that the would-be civilizer
Kurtz sets up. It leads to a civilization aptly portrayed in Kurtz's
symbolic painting of a blindfolded woman carrying a torch through
darkness. If Conrad offers a glimmer of light in the dark world he
envisions, it is in the sympathetic understanding that enables
Marlow to befriend Kurtz and to lie for Kurtz and his intended, even
at the cost of having to taste the "flavour of mortality" he finds
in lies, which he detests like the death it suggests to him.

QUESTIONS FOR DISCUSSION

1. What does Conrad gain by having his story told by Marlow to a
    group of important Londoners on a yacht in the Thames estuary?
    What is implied by the association of the Thames with the
    Congo? by Marlow's assertion, "And this also . . . has been one
    of the dark places of the earth"?
2. Marlow enters on his adventure through a city he associates
    with "a white sepulchre"; he passes old women knitting who
    remind him of the Fates; the company office is "as still as a
    house in a city of the dead." Locate other indications that
    Marlow's journey is like a trip into the underworld. What do
    they suggest about the story's meaning?
3. In what ways is the French warship "shelling the bush" an apt
    image of the European conquest of Africa? What does this
    historical theme contribute to our understanding of Marlow and
    Kurtz?
4. Discuss the Company's chief accountant. Why is it appropriate
    that Marlow first hears of Kurtz from him?
5. Marlow calls the men waiting for a post in the interior
    "pilgrims." Explain the irony in his use of the term.
6. Marlow is associated with Kurtz as a member of "the gang of
    virtue." Explain the resonance of that phrase.
7. Describe the journey up the Congo as Marlow reports it in the
    pages that follow his remark, "Going up that river was like
    travelling back to the earliest beginnings of the world . . . ."
    In what ways does Conrad make it a symbolic journey as well as
    an actual one?
8. Discuss Marlow's attitudes toward the natives. What do they
    mean to him?
9. As the boat draws near Kurtz's station, people cry out "with
    unrestrained grief" from the jungle. Why?
10. After the attack of the natives is repulsed and the narrative
    seems at the point of reaching the climax toward which so much
    suspense has been built -- the meeting with Kurtz -- Conrad
    throws it away by having Marlow stop to light his pipe and speak
    offhandedly and abstractly about what he learned. Why? Does
    this passage actually destroy the suspense? Is the story
    rendered anticlimactic? Or is the climax changed? What is the
    true climax of the story?
11. Why do you think the heads on stakes are facing Kurtz's house?
12. Discuss the Russian and his attitude toward Kurtz. Why does
    Conrad trouble to add this European to Kurtz's train of
    cultists?
13. Marlow is astonished that the Manager calls Kurtz's methods
    "unsound." Why? What does this passage reveal about each of
    them?
14. Explain what happens to Marlow when he goes into the bush after
    Kurtz. Explain what happens to Kurtz. Why does Marlow call
    Kurtz "that shadow"?
15. Marlow claims to have "struggled with a soul"; he tells Kurtz
    that if he does not come back he will be "utterly lost." Is
    Marlow a savior for Kurtz? Is Kurtz saved?

16. Why does Marlow lie to Kurtz's "intended"?
17. Contrast the last paragraph of the story with the opening.
18. Comment on the title of Kurtz's pamphlet, "On the Suppression of Savage Customs," and on the significance of its scrawled postscript, "Exterminate all the brutes."

TOPICS FOR WRITING

Critical Essays

1. Conrad's use of foreshadowing.
2. Traditional symbolism and literary allusion as a way of universalizing the theme of "Heart of Darkness."
3. The function of the frame.

Exercise for Reading

1. Marlow frequently concludes a segment of his narrative with a generalization that sums it up and takes on a quality of special significance, such as, "I felt as though, instead of going to the centre of a continent, I were about to set off for the centre of the earth"; or, "It was like a weary pilgrimage among hints for nightmares." Locate as many such passages as you can. What do they reveal about the mind of the narrator?

Related Subject

1. Conrad frequently uses an impressionist technique that Ian Watt has called "delayed decoding." When the steamboat is attacked, for example, Marlow first sees "little sticks" flying about, and only later recognizes them as arrows. Find other instances in the story, and then write a narrative of your own using a similar method.

SUGGESTED READINGS

Berthoud, Jacques. Joseph Conrad: The Major Phase. New York: Cambridge University Press, 1978. Pp. 41–63.

Conrad, Joseph. Heart of Darkness: An Authoritative Text, Backgrounds and Sources, Criticism. Edited by Robert Kimbrough. Revised edition. New York: Norton, 1971.

Gekoski, R. A. Conrad: The Moral World of the Novelist. New York: Barnes & Noble, 1978. Pp. 72–90.

Anton Chekhov

"A Trifle from Real Life" (page 358)

This story provides an opportunity to show how a mastery of technique can transform a banal and even sentimental theme into a

profound and chilling insight into human nature. From his title up
to the last paragraph, Chekhov withholds all trace of conventional
moral opprobrium. The narrator adopts an urbane tone such as
Belayeff himself might use in detailing his affair with Olga Ivanovna
to his cronies at the racetrack, and although he implies an ironic
attitude by calling Belayeff "my hero," he remains scrupulously
objective in recounting Belayeff's reception of the secrets Aliosha
confides in him. But Belayeff's callous and self-centered response
comes as no surprise to the attentive reader, who remembers that the
man has never paid any attention to the child before and that he
enters into the fateful conversation because "Aliosha's pale face and
fixed, dark eyes unexpectedly reminded Belayeff of Olga as she had
appeared in the first pages of their romance." Meanwhile, Chekhov
has portrayed Aliosha in such a way that the reader feels his
attractiveness, shares his delight in the secret meetings with his
father, and sympathizes with his hopes and concerns. Then, when the
full extent of Belayeff's and Olga's selfish disregard for Aliosha's
feelings becomes clear, it strikes the reader with some of the same
force with which it falls on the innocent boy. He has in fact been
deceived not only by Belayeff, whom he has regarded as kind, but also
by his parents, both of whom pretend to be more concerned about him
than they are.

QUESTIONS FOR DISCUSSION

1. The narrator twice refers to Belayeff's affair as the "pages" of
    a "romance." Considering this, what is the implication of the
    phrase "from real life" in the title?
2. Why does Chekhov call his story a trifle? Is it?
3. Why does Belayeff talk to Aliosha, whom he has never noticed at
    all before?
4. Comment on the simile that compares the acrobatic Aliosha to a
    martyr.
5. Examine the character of Aliosha's papa. To what extent do you
    approve of his behavior? of his promises?
6. Belayeff's last words in the story are "Leave me alone! . . .
    This is more important than words of honour. This hypocrisy,
    these lies, are intolerable!" What do these exclamations reveal
    about his character?
7. Evaluate Olga Ivanovna's decision to go in search of Pelagia to
    confirm Belayeff's report of what Aliosha has told him.
8. Does the last sentence make a positive contribution to the
    story? Would you propose a different ending?

TOPICS FOR WRITING

Critical Essays

1. Chekhov's use of the technique he expounds in the excerpts from
    his letters (included in Part Two, p. 1129), in his character-
    ization of Aliosha and in the story at large.
2. Aliosha's story -- truth or fantasy? How we can tell?

Related Subjects

1. Adapt the story as a one-act play. Compare the reactions of
    readers to the original story and to your adaptation.
2. Experiment with revisions to Chekhov's last paragraph. What
    happens to the story when this paragraph is changed?

Anton Chekhov

"The Lady with the Dog" (page 363)

Anna Sergeyevna comes to Yalta because she wants "to live, to
live!" Gurov begins his affair with her because he is bored and
enjoys the freedom and ease of a casual liaison. At the outset both
are undistinguished, almost clichés -- a philandering bank employee
escaping from a wife he cannot measure up to, a lady with a dog and
a "flunkey" for a husband. By the end of the story, however, after
having been captured and tormented by a love that refuses to be
filed away in memory, the two gain dignity and stature by recognizing
that life is neither exciting nor easy; and by taking up the burden
of the life they have discovered in their mutual compassion, they
validate their love.

Chekhov develops the nature of this true love, so ennobling and
so tragic, by testing it against a series of stereotypes that it
transcends and by showing a series of stock expectations that it
violates. Anna Sergeyevna reacts differently from any of the several
types of women Gurov has previously made love to, and Gurov finds
himself unable to handle his own feelings in the way he is accustomed
to. Anna Sergeyevna proves neither a slice of watermelon nor a
pleasant focus of nostalgia. Most important, as the conclusion
implies, she will not remain the secret core of his life, bought at
the price of falsehood and suspicion of others.

In observing the evolution of the lovers, the reader is led
through a series of potential misconceptions. We may want to despise
Gurov as a careless breaker of hearts, but it is clear that he has
one of his own when he sees Anna Sergeyevna as a Magdalene. Later,
when Gurov is tormented by his longings for Anna Sergeyevna, we are
tempted to laugh the superior realist's laugh at a romantic fool:
Surely when Gurov arrives at S-----, disillusionment will await him.

And in a sense it does. Just as there was dust in the streets
at Yalta, the best room in the hotal at S----- is coated with dust;
reality is an ugly fence; and even the theater (where The Geisha is
playing) is full of reminders of how unromantic life really is. But
Anna Sergeyevna has not, as Gurov supposes at one point, taken
another lover, nor has she been able to forget Gurov.

The antiromantic tone is but another oversimplification, and
the story comes to rest, somewhat like Milton's Paradise Lost, at a
moment of beginning. The lovers' disillusionment about the nature
of the struggle they face creates in them a deep compassion for one

another, which finds its echo in readers' final attitude toward them
as fellow human beings whose lives are like our own and who deserve
a full measure of our sympathy. Or perhaps they draw our pity;
surely their fate, which Chekhov so skillfully depicts as probable
and true, inspires tragic fear. Gurov and Anna Sergeyevna have met
the god of love, and Chekhov awes us by making him seem real.

QUESTIONS FOR DISCUSSION

1. Why does Gurov call women "the inferior race"?
2. At the end of section I, Gurov thinks that there is "something
    pathetic" about Anna Sergeyevna. Is there? What?
3. Why is Anna Sergeyevna so distracted as she watches the steamer
    putting in?
4. How does Anna Sergeyevna differ from other women Gurov has known,
    as they are described in the paragraph that ends, "the lace on
    their lingerie seemed to him to resemble scales"? Compare this
    passage with the paragraph in section IV that begins, "His hair
    was already beginning to turn gray."
5. In view of what follows, is it appropriate that Gurov should see
    Anna Sergeyevna as a Magdalene?
6. What is the function of the paragraph that begins, "At Oreanda
    they sat on a bench not far from the church"?
7. What "complete change" does Gurov undergo during his affair with
    Anna Sergeyevna at Yalta? Is it permanent?
8. Explain Gurov's remark at the end of section II: "High time!"
9. Why is Gurov enraged at his companion's remark about the
    sturgeon?
10. Discuss the possible meanings of the objects Gurov encounters in
    S-----: the broken figurine, the long gray fence, the cheap
    blanket, and so on.
11. Seeing Anna Sergeyevna enter the theater, Gurov "understood
    clearly that in the whole world there was no human being so near,
    so precious, so important to him . . . ." What is Chekhov's
    tone in this statement?
12. Explain Anna Sergeyevna's reaction to Gurov's arrival. Why does
    she volunteer to come to Moscow?
13. Discuss the implications of Gurov's "two lives" as Chekhov
    explains them in section IV. Do you agree with the generali-
    zations about the desire for privacy with which the paragraph
    ends? Relate these ideas to the story's ending.
14. What will life be like for Gurov and Anna Sergeyevna? Anna has
    previously said, "I have never been happy; I am unhappy now, and
    I never, never shall be happy, never!" Is she right?

TOPICS FOR WRITING

Critical Essays

1. Chekohv's characterization of the wronged spouse in "The Lady
    with the Dog."
2. Gurov and Belayeff (in "A Trifle from Real Life") -- a compari-
    son of two Chekhovian adulterers.

3. The meaning of the three geographical locales in "The Lady with the Dog."

Exercise for Reading

1. On your first reading of the story, stop at the end of each section and write down your judgment of Gurov and Anna Sergeyevna and your prediction of what will happen next. When you have finished reading, compare what you wrote with what turned out to be the case and with your final estimate of the protagonists. To the extent that your initial impressions were borne out, what points in the text helped to guide you? To the extent that you were surprised, explain what led you astray. What might Chekhov have wanted to accomplish by making such misconceptions possible?

SUGGESTED READINGS

Kramer, Karl D. The Chameleon and the Dream: The Image of Reality in Chekhov's Stories. The Hague: Mouton, 1970. P. 171.

Rayfield, Donald. Chekhov: The Evolution of His Art. New York: Barnes & Noble, 1975. Pp. 197-200.

Smith, Virginia Llewellyn. "The Lady with the Dog." In Anton Chekhov's Short Stories: Texts of the Stories, Backgrounds, Criticism. Edited by Ralph E. Matlaw. New York: Norton, 1979. Excerpted from Smith, Anton Chekhov and the Lady with the Dog (New York: Oxford University Press, 1973), pp. 96-97, 212-218.

See also the selection from Vladimir Nabokov's Lectures on Russian Literature in Part Two, p. 1158.

Edith Wharton

"Roman Fever" (page 378)

As the headnote points out, nearly every detail of the seemingly meandering narration that leads up to the final sequence of three dramatic revelations has a function in preparing for the climax. Wharton knits better than Grace Ansley, and her story does not fully unravel until the last words are spoken. When the secret is finally out, the reader experiences a flash of ironic insight that Wharton has been preparing from the beginning through her masterful delineation of the characters and their situation.

Face to face with "the great accumulated wreckage of passion and splendour" that spreads before them, and deserted in their advancing age by the pair of daughters who are now their sole concerns, the two widows may evoke the reader's condescending pity. They seem as small and pale as the images of one another each sees, in Wharton's metaphor, "through the wrong end of her little telescope." But as the two characters become differentiated, Alida Slade takes on depth and coloration. As the story of her flashy but parasitic life and of the jealousy and guilty resentment she has harbored toward her friend gradually emerges, the reader can no longer pity her but can hardly admire her either. Her revelation that it was she, not Delphin Slade, who wrote the letter inviting Grace to a tryst in the Colosseum may be unexpected, but it follows perfectly from her character as Wharton has established it. The blow it strikes to Mrs. Ansley is severe, and it seems the more cruel to the reader, who has no reason as yet to revise the original estimate of her as merely pitiable. Mres. Ansley staggers, but to the reader's surprise and gratification she gradually recovers herself. Impelled by the shock for once to assert herself, she caps Mrs. Slade's revelation with an even more dramatic one of her own.

Grace Ansley's reticence, and the quietness of her life in contrast to Alida Slade's, express neither emotional pallor nor weakness of character. She had the spunk to take what she wanted from Delphin Slade twenty-five years before, and she has been content with her memory ever since, not needing, as Alida Slade would have needed (and indeed has needed), to get reassurance by parading her conquest in public. Thus it is Mrs. Ansley who manifests greater independence and vitality. Mrs. Slade, by contrast, has been conventional and dependent. Widowhood is such an uncomfortable lot for her because she can no longer shine with the reflected brilliance of her husband. Barbara may be unlike Horace Ansley because Delphin Slade was really her father, but her differences from Jenny derive from the fact that Grace Ansley, not Alida Slade, is her mother.

Wharton has constructed her plot with a precision O. Henry would have admired, but she has based it less on contrivances of circumstance than on an understanding of her characters. By placing them in a setting that spans millenia -- from ancient Rome to the airplane -- she implies the universality of the passions, triumphs, and defeats that maek up the lives of even these New York society ladies, whose wealth and status do not protect them from the human condition after all.

QUESTIONS FOR DISCUSSION

1. What do Barbara and Jenny think of their mothers? How accurate is their estimate?
2. Why does Grace Ansley place an "undefinable stress" on "me" and "I" in replying to Alida Slade's questions about her reaction to their view of the Roman ruins?
3. Why does Alida Slade consider Grace and Horace Ansley "two nullities"?
4. Compare and contrast the two ladies' responses to widowhood and advancing age. Who takes it harder? Why?
5. Alida Slade remembers "that Mrs. Horace Ansley, twenty-five years ago, had been exquisitely lovely. . . ." Explain the importance of this fact to Mrs. Slade, to Mrs. Ansley, and to the structure of the plot.
6. What is "Roman Fever" -- literally and figuratively?
7. Why has Alida Slade "always gone on hating" Grace Ansley?

8. What reaction does Alida Slade seem to have expected from Grace
   Ansley in response to her confession that she forged the letter?
   Why?
9. Alida Slade remarks, "Well, girls are ferocious sometimes."
   What about ladies?
10. Near the end of the story, why does Grace Ansley pity Alida
    Slade? Why does Mrs. Slade at first reject that pity?
11. Comment on the meaning of the way the ladies walk off stage.

TOPICS FOR WRITING

Critical Essays

1. The importance of setting in "Roman Fever."
2. Edith Wharton's manipulation of point of view.
3. "Roman Fever" and Wharton's principles of the short story as
   stated in the excerpt from her book, The Writing of Fiction
   (included in Part Two, p. 1131).

Exercise for Reading

1. On your first reading of the story, mark passages whose significance is not entirely clear -- such as Grace Ansley's
   peculiar intonations when acknowledging her memory of a former
   visit to Rome. After reading the story to the end, return to
   the marked passages and write explanations of them.

Related Subjects

1. Which of the two ladies is more guilty of reprehensible behavior?
   Consider arguments on both sides, or organize a debate.
2. Write a story of your own about a secret that comes out or a
   misunderstanding that is resolved. Try to make both the
   perpetuation of the error or deception and the emergence of the
   truth dependent on character rather than circumstance.

Rudyard Kipling

"The Wish House" (page 390)

Kipling confronted two parallel problems in constructing "The
Wish House": He had to find a way to convince the reader that the
selfless love felt by Mrs. Ashcroft is real, serious, and sincere,
and he had to persuade the reader to accept the superstition through
which she expresses it. The elements of setting, characterization,
event, and structure that make up the story constitute his masterful
solution to these artistic problems.

Kipling's most important decision was to follow the precedent
of many tales of the strange or supernatural, putting his story into
a frame and having it told by a fictional narrator. As J. M. S.
Tompkins has pointed out, Kipling can thus fit "the substance of a

novel into the words of a short story." Mrs. Ashcroft speaks of a
past whose remoteness is repeatedly called to our attention by references of how much things have changed: Lorries roll by, radio
antennae spring up, and horse manure no longer fills the streets of
London, but Mrs. Ashcroft and her companion remember a preindustrial
world of "hoppin'" and "hayin'" almost old enough to be "once upon
a time." Furthermore, as Mrs. Fettley remarks, Mrs. Ashcroft,
mortally ill with cancer, is "further off lyin' now than in all [her]
life" and has nothing to gain by deluding her friend or the reader
with her incredible tale.

What she may gain by deluding herself is another question, however, and Kipling, like Hawthorne and other writers who work on the
fringes of the supernatural, is careful to provide the alternate
possibility of a naturalistic explanation. The story is much better
as a tale of the power of love than as a case history of a neurosis,
however, and the substance of the poems that Kipling printed with
it when he originally published it confirms his intention.

Whether or not Gracie Ashcroft actually cures 'Arry Mockler by
taking his ills upon herself in the form of the ulcer on her ankle,
her desire to sacrifice herself for him, her joy at his recovery,
and the love on which these choices are based, are unquestionably
real and pure. Kipling ensures that the reader will understand her
devotion to 'Arry as sincere by the skill with which he introduces
it. The incident of her quarrel with the pitchfork-wielding Polly
Batten establishes Gracie's attractiveness, which makes her loyalty
to 'Arry a voluntary act and not just her lot for lack of an alternative. That Jim Batten felt her appeal is confirmed by the clear
implication that she bore his child, and the history of her marriage
indicates that, like Mrs. Fettley, she sets little store in fidelity
for its own sake.

Mrs. Ashcroft would like to believe that she once "set a heap
by" her husband, but the recollection of her feelings for him is
obliterated by her qualitatively stronger attachment to 'Arry. In
fact, her marriage, her affairs, and Mrs. Fettley's intrigue with
the railroadman all serve as foils to set off a quite different kind
of love. When she meets 'Arry Mockler, Gracie recognizes "that I'd
found me master, which I 'adn't ever before," and she claims to have
"never been like that before." But the overmothered and much
younger 'Arry is no prize in objective terms, and Gracie makes no
sentimental claims when asked, "What did ye get out of it?" "The
usuals," she replies.

The idea of a love not defined in terms of getting enters the
story with Sophy Ellis, who wants to suffer for those she loves
simply to do them good. This form of self-sacrificing charity might
seem remote from the sexual love with which the story has been
concerned until then, but Kipling is careful to connect the two
emotions through Gracie's remark, "you know how liddle maids first
feel it sometimes -- she come to be crazy fond o' me, pawin' an'
cuddlin' all whiles." Indeed, it might be said that Mrs. Ashcroft
learns her new kind of love from Sophy. Her willingness to suffer
pain out of her desire for 'Arry has already been neatly established

when she pours scalding water on her arm, but after she learns Sophy's secret she conceives the very different idea of taking on 'Arry's sickness and pain as a compensation for the bitter truth that "I couldn't ever get 'Arry -- 'ow could I?" When she finds that the charm has worked, however, she rejoices, "I've got ye now, my man. . . . You'll take your good from me 'thout knowin' it till my life's end." The reader, guided by Mrs. Fettley's companionable concern, has no choice but to wonder at the power of a love that has brought Mrs. Ashcroft a sense of purpose and value through years of lonely pain.

Kipling, however, refrains from insisting that Mrs. Ashcroft is not a fool, just as he does not insist that the reader accept the superstition on which the story is based. Gracie's harrowing and unforgettable question -- "It do count, don't it -- de pain?" must finally remain unanswered in the story, although there is no doubt that Kipling's heart would hold with Mrs. Fettley's reassurance -- "Twill be -- 'twill be, Gra." Gracie Ashcroft's passion raises her to tragic stature. To borrow Tompkins's terms, once again her "masterful sacrifice of herself for her unknowing and departed lover is a self-fulfillment and a self-purgation."

QUESTIONS FOR DISCUSSION

1. Describe the position of Mrs. Ashcroft and Mrs. Fettley in the world that surrounds them. What effect does their isolation from the hustle and bustle of the modern world have on the story?
2. What is the possible implication of Mrs. Ashcroft's grandson's resemblance to Jim Batten?
3. What can we imagine that the conversations Kipling skips over by leaving white spaces have been about? Why does he omit them? Why does he introduce them into the story to begin with?
4. What does Gracie's remark about her husband -- "for you know Liz, what a rover 'e was" -- suggest about the two women and their relationship?
5. When asked "What did ye get out of it?" of her affair with 'Arry, Gracie replies, "The usuals." What are the usuals, as she reports them here and in the paragraphs that follow? Why, then, does her love for him become the dominant reality of her life?
6. What is the artistic purpose of Gracie's scalding herself on the arm?
7. Describe Sophy Ellis. Why is she an appropriate person to introduce Gracie to the Token?
8. When Gracie offers to nurse 'Arry in London, he replies, "I won't take it, . . . for I can give ye naught." What change in her has taken place that makes this response inappropriate?
9. Discuss Kipling's narration of Gracie's visit to the Wish House. What makes it effective? Does it seem real or fantastic?
10. When do we become aware that the charm has worked?
11. What does Gracie mean when she says, "I've got ye now, my man"? Comment on the significance of her choice of words.
12. What does Gracie want her pains to be "counted" for?
13. Comment on the way the nurse's arrival affects the reader's estimate of Gracie Ashcroft.

TOPICS FOR WRITING

Critical Essays

1. Gracie Ashcroft -- tragic heroine or fool?
2. Sophy Ellis as a symbol of love.
3. Old wives' tales: Wharton's "Roman Fever" and Kipling's "The Wish House."
4. Kipling's Mrs. Ashcroft and Flaubert's Félicité as versions of transcendent love.
5. The importance of dialect in "The Wish House."

Exercise for Reading

1. After you have completed the story, review its contents and organize them into two outlines -- one for the chapters of a novel told in chronological order by a third-person narrator, and one for the five acts of a classical tragedy. Which outline corresponds more closely to Kipling's story? Which version do you think would advance Kipling's theme more effectively?

Related Subject

1. Write the interior monologue of Liz Fettley as she rides home from this, her last visit to Gracie Ashcroft.

SUGGESTED READINGS

Dobree, Bonamy. Rudyard Kipling: Realist and Fabulist. New York: Oxford University Press, 1967. Pp. 53-55.

Tompkins, J. M. S. The Art of Rudyard Kipling. Revised edition. London: Methuen, 1965. Pp. 4-8, 154, 171-173, 207-208, 219-220, 231, 234, 244-245.

Wilson, Angus. The Strange Ride of Rudyard Kipling: His Life and Works. New York: Viking, 1977. Pp. 286-288.

Stephen Crane

"The Open Boat" (page 405)

Crane's story fictionalizes an actual experience. A correspondent himself, Crane happened to be aboard the Commodore when it went down, and he included in his newspaper report of the event this passage (as quoted by E. R. Hagemann):

> The history of life in an open boat for thirty hours
> would no doubt be instructive for the young, but none is
> to be told here now. For my part I would prefer to tell
> the story at once, because from it would shine the
> splendid manhood of Captain Edward Murphy and of
> William Higgins, the oiler, but let it suffice at this
> time to say that when we were swamped in the surf and
> making the best of our way toward the shore the captain
> gave orders amid the wildness of the breakers as clearly
> as if he had been on the quarter deck of a battleship.

It is good that Crane did not write "at once" but let his experience
take shape as a work of art which, instead of celebrating the
"splendid manhood" of two or four individuals, recognizes a profound
truth about human life in general -- about the puniness of man in
face of an indifferent nature and about the consequent value of the
solidarity and compassion that arise from an awareness of our common
fate. Crane's meditation on his experience "after the fact" enables
him to become not simply a reporter but, as he puts it in the last
line of the story, an _interpreter_ of the message spoken to man by
the world he confronts.

Crane portrays the exertions of the four men in the boat without
glamorizing them. His extended and intimate account of their hard
work and weariness wrings out any false emotion from the reader's
view of the situation. By varying the narrative point of view from
a coolly detached objective observer to a plural account of all four
men's shared feelings and perceptions to the correspondent's rueful,
self-mocking cogitations, Crane defeats our impulse to choose a hero
for adulation, while at the same time driving home the point that the
condition of the men in the dinghy -- their longing, their fear, and
their powerlessness in the face of nature and destiny -- reflects
our own. By the end, what has been revealed is so horrible that
there can be no triumph in survival. The good fortune of a rescue
brings only a reprieve, not an escape from what awaits us. Billie
the oiler drowns, but there is no reason it should have been he, or
only he. His death could be anybody's death.

Crane's narration builds suspense through rhythmic repetition,
foreshadowing, and irony. We hear the surf periodically: Our hopes
for rescue are repeatedly raised and dashed; night follows day,
wave follows wave, and the endless struggle goes on. The correspondent's complaint against the cruelty of fate recurs in diminuendo,
with less whimsy and self-consciousness each time.

These recurrences mark the men's changes in attitude -- from
the egocentric viewpoint they start with, imagining that the whole
world is watching them and working for their survival, to the
perception of the utter indifference of nature with which the story
ends. Some stages in this progression include their false sense of
security when they light up the cigars; their isolation from the
people on shore, epitomized by their inability to interpret the
signal of the man waving his coat (whose apparent advice to try
another stretch of beach they nonetheless inadvertently follow);

their experience of aloneness at night; their confrontation with the
hostility of nature in the shark; and finally, their recognition that
death might be a welcome release from toil and suffering. They
respond by drawing together in a communion that sustains them,
sharing their labor and their body heat, huddled together in their
tiny, helpless dinghy. Even their strong bond of comradeship, however, cannot withstand the onslaught of the waves. When the boat is
swamped, it is every man for himself: each individual must face
death alone. Because of the fellowship that has grown up among them,
however, when Billie dies, each of the others feels the oiler's
death as his own. The reader, whom Crane's narrative has caused to
share thirty hours at sea in an open boat, may recognize the implication in what is spoken by "the sound of the great sea's voice to
the men on shore."

QUESTIONS FOR DISCUSSION

1. Contrast the imagery and the tone of the first paragraph with
   those of the second. Why does Crane continually seek to
   magnify nature and to belittle the men who are struggling with
   it? Find other instances of Crane's reductive irony, and
   discuss their effects.
2. How does Crane convey the men's concentration on keeping the
   boat afloat?
3. Explain Crane's use of the word probably in the first paragraph
   of section II.
4. Why does the seagull seem "somehow gruesome and ominous" to the
   men in the boat? Compare and contrast the seagull with the
   shark that appears later.
5. Comment on the imagery Crane uses to describe changing seats in
   the dinghy (stealing eggs, Sevres).
6. What is it that the correspondent "knew even at the time was
   the best experience of his life?" Why is it the best?
7. What is the purpose of Crane's litotes (understatement) in the
   line from section III, "neither the oiler nor the correspondent
   was fond of rowing at this time"?"
8. What is the effect on the reader of the men's lighting up
   cigars?
9. Discuss the meaning of the correspondent's question, "Was I
   brought here merely to have my nose dragged away as I was about
   to nibble the sacred cheese of life?"
10. What do you think the man waving a coat means? Why is it
    impossible for him to communicate with the men in the boat?
11. "A night on the sea in an open boat is a long night," says
    Crane. How does he make the reader feel the truth of that
    assertion?
12. At one point the correspondent thinks that he is "the one man
    afloat on all the oceans." Explain that sensation. Why does
    the wind he hears sound "sadder than the end"? Why does he
    later wish he had known the captain was awake when the shark
    came by?

13. Why does the correspondent have a different attitude toward the poem about the dying soldier in Algiers from the one he had as a boy?
14. Examine the third paragraph of section VII. How important are the thoughts of the correspondent to our understanding of the story? What would the story lose if they were omitted? What would the effect of this passage be if Crane had narrated the story in the first person? If he had made these comments in the voice of an omniscient third-person narrator?
15. Define the correspondent's physical, mental, and emotional condition during his final moments on the boat and during his swim to the beach.
16. Define and explain the tone of Crane's description of the man who pulls the castaways from the sea.
17. Why does Crane make fun of the women who bring coffee to the survivors?

TOPICS FOR WRITING

Critical Essays

1. Crane's handling of point of view in "The Open Boat."
2. The importance of repetition in Crane's narrative.
3. Imagery as a key to tone in "The Open Boat."

Exercise for Reading

1. After reading the story once rapidly, read it again with a pencil in hand, marking every simile and metaphor. Then sort them into categories. What realms of experience does Crane bring into view through these devices that are not actually part of the simple boat-sea-sky-beach world in which the story is set? Why?

Related Subject

1. Write an eyewitness account of some experience you have under- gone that would be suitable for newspaper publication. Then note the changes you would make to turn it into a fictional narrative with broader or more profound implications -- or write that story.

SUGGESTED READINGS

Adams, Richard P. "Naturalistic Fiction: 'The Open Boat.'" In Stephen Crane's Career: Perspectives and Evaluations. Edited by Thomas A. Gullason. New York: New York University Press, 1972. Pp. 421-429. Originally published in Tulane Studies in English, 4 (1954), 137-146.

405-433 (text pages)

Cady, Edwin H. Stephen Crane. Twayne's United States Authors Series, No. 23. Revised edition. Boston: G. K. Hall, 1980. Pp. 150-154.

Hagemann, E. R. "'Sadder than the End': Another Look at 'The Open Boat.'" In Stephen Crane in Transition: Centenary Essays. Edited by Joseph Katz. DeKalb: Northern Illinois University Press, 1972. Pp. 66-85.

Kissane, Leedice. "Interpretation through Language: A Study of the Metaphors in Stephen Crane's 'The Open Boat.'" In Gullason, ed., Stephen Crane's Career. Pp. 410-416. Originally published in Rendezvous (Idaho State University), 1 (Spring 1966), 18-22.

Stephen Crane

"The Bride Comes to Yellow Sky" (page 424)

Students will readily notice that Crane works with a gallery of stereotypes made familiar in popular Westerns from the dime novel through contemporary cinema and TV. They may object to these clichés and, perhaps even more vehemently, to the story's anticlimactic ending. Against the background of such a response, it should not be difficult to move toward an understanding of Crane's true intent.

With superb technical control, Crane toys with the reader as Scratchy Wilson toys with the town, setting up one false expectation after another while steadily building toward the thematic statement that comes into focus in the image that concludes the story. In section I he explicitly offers for our delight the Embarrassed Hick Newlyweds. Along with the porters and dining-car waiters, we smile in condescension. The information that this bridegroom Jack is in fact Jack Potter, town marshall and mainstay of law and order in Yellow Sky, only serves to heighten the comedy of his hasty retreat from the alarmed station agent, who may in fact be running after the couple for other reasons than to laugh at them. Sections II and III give us the Old West: laconic Texans, silent Mexicans, a garrulous greenhorn, a drunken cowboy on a rampage, and an impending gunfight. The tension mounts. But in section IV, instead of fireworks, we get talk, and a semblance of good manners. The marshall keeps order without a gun, and Scratchy Wilson, expressing his own and perhaps the reader's disappointment with his "I s'pose it's all off now," walks off into the sands of history.

Crane hints at the structure of his tale when he observes the two lines of the railroad and the Rio Grande converging across the schematic landscape to meet at Yellow Sky. But what might represent the suspense of two converging lines of action colliding in an explosive climax turns out in fact to suggest something a good deal more subtle and meaningful -- the quiet extinction of the rough-and-tumble society of the American frontier by the westward advance of modern civilization. When Scratchy Wilson walks away, it is as "a simple child of the earlier plains," overwhelmed by his "glimpse of another world" in the person of Jack Potter, married and unarmed. Potter, too, has been offered a glimpse of another world, and he has been uncomfortable in face of it. In the Pullman car his brick red hands, so fit for drawing a six-gun or shoeing a horse, seem awkward and out of place. But when he tips the porter he is learning a new task, and the image of the Pullman, symbol of his "new estate," revisits his mind as he stands jaw-to-jaw with Scratchy in the street.

Both of these western heroes, in fact, have already succumbed to the influence of the society of the East. Scratchy's most picturesque piece of equipment, his maroon flannel shirt, has been made on the East Side of New York, and Jack Potter has betrayed Yellow Sky and ridden the railroad that fascinates him eastward to San Antonio to get married. In the marvelous image that opens the story, all of Texas is rushing eastward. Whatever was real in the myth of the Old West is doomed when the railroad brings sophistication, settled customs, and a bride to Yellow Sky -- doomed to funnel down Scratchy's footprints into the past.

Crane does not let it go without regret. The east sends to Yellow Sky not only the elegance of the railroad with its intimidating employees, but also the craven and inept drummer. Scratchy Wilson, on the other hand -- though Crane diminishes him with mock heroic diction and the placid regard of the serene adobes -- turns out to be truly noble at heart, bound to his "ancient antagonist" with a respect that places shooting him, now that he is married, completely out of the question.

QUESTIONS FOR DISCUSSION

1. Why are the newlyweds ill at ease in the Pullman? How does the treatment they receive from the porters and waiters affect the reader's estimate of them?
2. Discuss the possible implications of Jack Potter's pride in the railroad.
3. Why and how does Crane prevent the reader from romanticizing the love between Jack and his bride? How does he show it to be true?
4. Why does Jack feel he has betrayed his town by getting married?
5. What does Jack think the station agent wants? Is he right?
6. Describe the scene in the Weary Gentleman saloon. What is the function of the drummer?
7. How does section II affect the reader's estimate of Jack Potter?
8. Discuss Scratchy Wilson's clothing. What does it suggest about the relationship between the east and the west?
9. How scary is Scratchy Wilson? What techniques does Crane use to belittle him? Why should he want to?
10. Discuss the function of the dog.

424-450 (text pages)

11. The paragraph in section IV that begins "There was a silence
    . . ." may be termed the high point of the story's suspense.
    Comment on the language Crane uses to describe the bride's view
    of the situation.
12. Why does Jack Potter suddenly remember the Pullman car?
13. Explain Scratchy Wilson's reaction to the news of Jack's
    marriage.
14. Discuss the combined implications of the images with which the
    story begins and ends. To what extent do they summarize the
    story that they bracket?

TOPICS FOR WRITING

Critical Essays

1. Crane's use of mock-heroic irony in "The Open Boat" and "The
   Bride Comes to Yellow Sky."
2. The Old West grows up -- Crane's theme of childhood in "The
   Bride Comes to Yellow Sky."
3. "The Bride Comes to Yellow Sky": parody, celebration, or
   lament?

SUGGESTED READINGS

Bernard, Kenneth. "'The Bride Comes to Yellow Sky': History as
    Elegy." In Stephen Crane's Career: Perspectives and Evalua-
    tions. Edited by Thomas A. Gullason. New York: New York
    University Press, 1972. Pp. 435-439. Originally published in
    The English Record, 17 (April 1967), 17-20.

Solomon, Eric. Stephen Crane: From Parody to Realism. Cambridge,
    Mass.: Harvard University Press, 1966. Pp. 251-256.

Tibbetts, A. M. "'The Bride Comes to Yellow Sky' as Comedy." In
    Gullason, ed. Stephen Crane's Career. Pp. 430-434. Originally
    published in English Journal, 54 (April 1965), 314-316.

Willa Cather

"Paul's Case" (page 435)

Students may feel repelled by this story and reject its ending
as heavy-handed. The structure of the plot, which pits a sensitive
adolescent against an ugly and confining bourgeois society, invites
us to admire Paul's rebellion and to glamorize his suicide, but
Cather takes great pains to make Paul as unattractive in his way as
the family, school, and neighborhood he hates. Quite apart from his
supercilious mannerisms, which his teachers feel some inclination to
forgive, Paul's quest for brightness and beauty in the world of art
and imagination is subjected to Cather's devastating criticism, so

54

readers who were ready to make a stock tragic response to his demise may find it difficult to care.

Try meeting this objection directly by examining the implications of the story's concluding passage. The vision presented here comes close to formulaic naturalism. Paul is not only caught in a universal machine, he is himself a machine. The imagination that has sustained him against the ugliness of his surroundings is dismissed as "a picture making mechanism," now crushed. The world against which Paul rebels is plain, gray, narrow, and monotonous. Its combination of saints (Calvin, Washington) and customary homilies precludes all that is in itself beautiful, pleasant, and fulfilling in the present moment. Paul's reaction, however, is merely the obverse. His habitual lies reflect his general resort to the artificial. He may be "artistic," but not in the sense of being creative, and his romantic fantasies involve no more satisfactory relations with others than does his ordinary life. Paul's world is so intolerable to his sensitivity that he is driven to escape from it, even at the cost of sitting in the cellar with the rats watching him from the corners. His escape inevitably becomes a form of self-destruction, as manifested in his criminal act -- which to him feels like confronting "the thing in the corner" -- and finally in his suicide. Paul passes through the "portal of Romance" for good, into a dream from which "there would be no awakening."

If it could be termed a choice, it would clearly be a bad choice, but Cather presents it rather as a symptom of Paul's "case," a disease of life from which he suffers, has suffered perhaps since his mother died when he was an infant, and for which, at first glance, there seems to be no cure. No wonder readers may be inclined to dismiss the story as unduly negative because unduly narrow. But Cather, at the same time that she meticulously documents the inexorable progress of Paul's illness, defines by implication a condition of health whose possible existence gives meaning to Paul's demise. As Philip L. Gerber explains: "Although [Cather] extolled the imaginative, her definition of imagination is all-important; for rather than meaning an ability 'to weave pretty stories out of nothing,' imagination conveyed to her 'a response to what is going on -- a sensitiveness to which outside things appeal' and was an amalgam of sympathy and observation."

Paul's refuge is the product of the first, false kind of imagination, but the reality and the power of an imagination of the second sort is evident throughout the story, in the masterful evocations of Cordelia Street, of the school and its all-too-human teachers, and not least of Paul himself. When Paul's case finally becomes extreme enough to break through the insensitivity of bourgeois Pittsburgh, the world of the street that bears the name of King Lear's faithful daughter at last begins to live up to its name, sympathizing with Paul's plight and offering to embrace him with its love. To Paul, however, whose own unregenerate imagination is still confined to making pretty pictures rather than sympathetic observations, the advances of Cordelia Street seem like tepid waters of boredom in which he is called upon to submerge himself. The potential for growth and change that is reflected in his father's abandoning his usual frugality to pay back the money Paul has stolen, and in his coming down from the top of the stairs into Paul's world to reach out to him, escape Paul's notice -- but not that of the reader.

QUESTIONS FOR DISCUSSION

1. Describe Paul's personality as Cather sets it forth in the opening paragraph of the story. Is this someone we like and admire?

2. Why do Paul's teachers have so much difficulty dealing with him? What does the knowledge that Cather was a teacher in Pittsburgh at the time she wrote this story suggest about her perspective on Paul's case?

3. What techniques does Cather use to establish the reader's sympathy for Paul? What limits that sympathy?

4. Contrast the three worlds -- school, Carnegie Hall, and Cordelia Street -- in which Paul moves. Why does Cather introduce them in that order?

5. What is the effect of Cather's capitalizing the word Romance?

6. Discuss the three decorations that hang above Paul's bed. What aspects of American culture do they refer to? What do they leave out?

7. Explore the allusion embodied in the name Cordelia Street. Why does Paul feel he is drowning there?

8. Discuss Paul's fear of rats. Why does he feel that he has "thrown down the gauntlet to the thing in the corner" when he steals the money and leaves for New York?

9. Explicate the paragraph that begins, "Perhaps it was because, in Paul's world, the natural always wore the guise of ugliness. . . ." To what extent does this paragraph offer a key to the story's structure and theme?

10. Describe the effect of the leap forward in time that occurs in the white space before we find Paul on the train to New York. Why does Cather withhold for so long her account of what has taken place?

11. What is admirable about Paul's entry into and sojourn in New York? What is missing from his new life?

12. Why does Paul wink at himself in the mirror after reading the newspaper account of his deeds?

13. On the morning of his suicide, Paul recognizes that "money was everything." Why does he think so? Does the story bear him out?

14. What is the effect of Paul's burying his carnation in the snow? Of his last thoughts?

15. Compare Cather's account of Paul's death with accounts of dying in other stories, such as Flaubert's "A Simple Heart," Tolstoy's "The Death of Ivan Ilych," and Bierce's "An Occurrence at Owl Creek Bridge."

TOPICS FOR WRITING

Critical Essays

1. "Paul's Case" as an attack on American society.
2. Cather's commentary on Katherine Mansfield (printed in Part
    Two, p. 1172) as a basis for criticism of "Paul's Case."

Exercise for Reading

1. Cather's story is punctuated by several recurrent images and
    turns of phrase. Locate as many such repetitions as you can
    and take note of their contexts. What does this network of
    internal connections reveal?

SUGGESTED READINGS

Daiches, David. Willa Cather: A Critical Introduction. Ithaca,
    N. Y.: Cornell University Press, 1951. Pp. 144-147.

Gerber, Philip L. Willa Cather. Twayne's United States Authors
    Series, No. 258. Boston: G. K. Hall, 1975. Pp. 72-73, 101,
    141, 163.

Gertrude Stein

"As a Wife Has a Cow" (page 452)

This example of the hundreds of pieces of writing Stein produced in her Modernist onslaught against conventional literary
expectation was published in 1926 with illustrations by the Cubist
Juan Gris. It can best be apprehended by drawing an analogy to the
schools of post-Impressionist painting by which she was influenced.
As Michael J. Hoffman puts it, Stein attempted "a use of language
in which words cease to be purveyors of conventional meaning and
become plastic counters to be manipulated purely in obedience to the
artist's expressive will, just as painters manipulate nonsemantic
line and color." Abstracting from her prose fiction the familiar
elements of plot, character, and setting, Stein has arrived in this
work at the point of retaining nothing but words.

Using the words as sounds, Stein deploys them in patterns of
repetitions and transformations reminiscent of a musical composition
made up of a theme and variations. Like music, "As a Wife Has a
Cow" seems to have little or no paraphrasable meaning, but it nonetheless remains coherent, complete, and satisfying to hear.

While words are sounds, however, they are also intrinsically
semantic. In order to neutralize as much as possible their potential
for meaning something, Stein causes them to refer to themselves as
words. She renders them polysemous -- having more than one

57

syntactically possible referent. At the same time, she indulges in
the pleasures of rhyme, cadence, and repetition characteristic of
"autotelic" language (as Carolyn Copeland calls it) -- language
spoken as an end in itself, as in nonsense chants and infant babble.

But Stein's story is not infant babble. It is a meticulous
record of what she calls in the excerpt from one of her lectures
(printed in Part Two, p. 1133) "the thing moving excitedly inside
in me" as she is writing. One way to make at least partial sense of
the story, then, is to hear the words on the page as a record of the
consciousness of the writer resolving to compose the story, becoming
entangled with the words she conceives, and fighting herself free
from the unintended implications they keep arousing. When the end
is finally reached, a change from the provisional intention for the
story has taken place: What was "nearly all of it to be as a wife
has a cow, a love story" has reached its definitive, immutable form
as "My wife has a cow." The statement is equivalent to the story
insofar as it embodies the previous statements made about the words
that comprise it (and the words that make up the statements, and
so on). It is a love story, perhaps, because "the thing moving
excitedly" has embraced its words with "my."

According to Virgil Thomson, Stein liked to refer to this "love
story" as her Tristan and Isolde. Thomson describes another work as
similar to this one because "it counts on repetition, subtle and
exhaustive, for much of its power, just as Romantic music does. It
also avoids picture-words -- the nouns of image and the verbs of
motion. It is full of prepositions and pronouns, of adverbs and
auxiliaries, of all the kinds of words that express connection." If
the Cubist analysis and simultaneous musical development of verbal
connection arrives, at the concluding line seems to assert, at the
final possession by the mind of the words being explored, then "As a
Wife Has a Cow: A Love Story" may indeed be said to deserve its
apparently gratuitous subtitle.

QUESTIONS FOR DISCUSSION

1. Try to construe Stein's syntax by adding punctuation and by
    italicizing some words to show that they are meant as words,
    not as semantic units referring to something: for example,
    "In came in there [;] came in there, come out of there [!]
    In came in[,] come out of there [!] Come out there in [i.e.,
    . . . come out . . . there. In. . . ,' above] came in
    there. . . ." What is the effect of this procedure on your
    attention as a reader?
2. Compare the words and phrases to musical notes and chords.
    Can you hear rhythmic patterns, recurrent themes, counter-
    points, and codas?
3. Compare the paragraphs that begin "When he can. . . ," "Not
    and now. . . ," "And in that. . . ," and "Have it as
    having. . . ." What do they have in common structurally?
    Contrast their development with that of the paragraph that

begins "And to in six and another." Does the last sentence of
that paragraph explain its first sentence? How would you
punctuate that first sentence?
4. Who might Stein be referring to by <u>they</u> near the end?
5. Can the last paragraph be understood as a resolution reached by
the writer in response to a consideration of <u>expectation</u> and
<u>preparation</u> in the previous paragraphs?

TOPICS FOR WRITING

<u>Critical Essays</u>

1. "As a Wife Has a Cow" and the "actual present." (See the headnote on page 451.)
2. Stein's effort to avoid meaning.
3. Visual and diachronic structures in "As a Wife Has a Cow":
Stein's verbal imitation of modern painting and traditional
music.

<u>Exercise for Reading</u>

1. Read the story aloud, following the cadences set up by the
words. Try stressing different words to make the sentences as
coherent as possible. Repeat this process several times. Then
write about the ideas and sensations the story evokes as you
read it.

<u>Related Subject</u>

1. Starting with any phrase that catches your ear, write a paragraph imitating Stein. What characteristics of the words you
use command most of your attention? Does what you have written
read like entire nonsense? Does it tell a comprehensible
story? If either is the case, your imitation will have failed.

SUGGESTED READINGS

Copeland, Carolyn Faunce. <u>Language & Time & Gertrude Stein</u>. Iowa
City: University Press of Iowa, 1975. Especially pp. 74–122.
(Contains no direct commentary on "As a Wife Has a Cow.")

Hoffman, Michael J. <u>Gertrude Stein</u>. Twayne's United States Authors
Series, No. 268. Boston: G. K. Hall, 1976. (Contains no
direct commentary on "As a Wife Has a Cow.")

Kawin, Bruce F. <u>Telling It Again and Again: Repetition in Literature and Film</u>. Ithaca, N. Y.: Cornell University Press, 1972.
Pp. 131, 144–146.

Stein, Gertrude. A Book Concluding with As a Wife Has a Cow: A Love
    Story. West Glover, Vt.: Something Else Press, 1973. (Reprint
    of the 1926 edition, with facsimiles of the original litho-
    graphs.)

Jack London

"To Build a Fire" (page 456)

While the protagonist of "To Build a Fire" lacks sufficient
imagination to concern himself with "significances, " or to "meditate
. . . upon man's place in the universe," London's story leads us
directly to these issues. Its setting and structure strip man's
confrontation with death in an alien and indifferent or even hostile
universe down to a starkly simple example, while its slow and
detailed pace brings home the reality of that confrontation with all
the force of actual experience.

The nameless traveler across the blank Arctic landscape is as
well equipped as any man for coping with his situation. He is
resourceful, cautious, tenacious, and able to tolerate a great deal
of discomfort. More experience in the Yukon would not have improved
his ability to cope: It would simply have supplied him with such
wisdom as is propounded by the old-timer: Don't try it, or don't
try it alone. But avoidance can only be temporary. Man must face
death, and face it alone. London places his character on "the unprotected tip of the planet," exposed to the frigid emptiness of the
universe, and the story details how it overcomes him.

London defines the man's condition by contrasting it with that
of the dog, which is at home in the hostile environment. Fitted by
nature with adequate defenses against the cold and guided by unfailing
instinct in deciding what to do, the dog provides an unsentimental
perspective on the man's struggles. Although the man's judgment is
a poor substitute for canine instinct and although his improvised
technology, despite its provision of fire, proves disastrously less
reliable than husky fur, the man's consciousness of his situation,
his errors, and his eventual dignity in accepting his death earn him
a heroic stature impossible for the dog, which London portrays as a
dog, not as a person deserving credit for his decisions and hence his
survival. At the end, the husky has more in common with "the stars
that leaped and danced and shone brightly in the cold sky" than with
the human spirit that has passed from the frozen corpse, leaving
behind its mark in the dignity of the posture that the corpse retains.

Readers may disagree over whether the story -- which, as Earle
Labor has shown, corresponds remarkably with Greek tragedy as
defined by Aristotle -- conveys a tragic sense of order or the black
pessimism characteristic of the mature London. Surely all readers
will, however, acknowledge the powerful effect that the story
creates, thanks to London's artful use of foreshadowing, repetition,
and close observation of authentic detail. As numbness and frost

invade· and gradually seize the body of the man, the metaphysical chill accompanying the recognition of mortality creeps irresistibly into the reader's mind. Each detail of the story contributes to this single impression -- the atmosphere; the cold, ironic voice of the narrator; and most poignantly, perhaps, the contrasting moments of warmth by the fire at lunch, the remembered comfort of which is strangely echoed in the repose of the dying man's last thoughts.

QUESTIONS FOR DISCUSSION

1. Describe the atmosphere established in the first two paragraphs.
2. What techniques does London use to impress the reader with the man's solitude? Why does he refrain for so long from mentioning the dog?
3. How cold is it? How does London make clear what such cold is like? Why is it important for him to do so?
4. London tells us that the man lacks imagination. What good would imagination have done him?
5. Why is the dog reluctant to follow the man? Why does it follow him anyway? Trace the dog's attitudes throughout the story.
6. The man keeps close track of time and distances. Why is that important to him? What significance might it have for the reader?
7. What is the reason for London's careful introduction of the hazards of the hidden spots of water in such detail before the man actually slips into one? What would be the difference if he withheld these explanations until afterwards?
8. What does the man do at half past twelve when he arrives at the forks? What does his behavior reveal about his character? In what way are those traits important to the subsequent action?
9. The words of an old-timer from Sulphur Creek enter the man's memory at intervals in the story. Trace the changes in his response to them. What does the old-timer have in common with the dog?
10. Several times London associates the cold with outer space. Consider the possible implications of this connection.
11. Why does London wait until after lunch to have the man fall into the water?
12. What mistake does the man make in building his second fire? Why does he commit that error?
13. While his second fire is getting started, the man indulges in some distinctly prideful thoughts. Is pride his downfall? Explain.
14. How do we feel about the man as he struggles to build his third fire?
15. What is wrong with the man's plan to kill the dog, warm his hands in the dog's body, and then start another fire?
16. At one point the man crawls after the dog on all fours, like an animal; at another he feels that he is flying like the god Mercury. What do you think London means to imply by these comparisons?

17. Although the man readily accepts the likelihood that he will
    lose parts of his body to the frost, he refuses to acknowledge
    that he is going to die until nearly the end. Contrast his
    behavior before and after he makes that recognition.
18. By the end, does the man still lack imagination?
19. Explain the effect of the last paragraph's being narrated from
    the dog's point of view.

TOPICS FOR WRITING

Critical Essays

1. Instinct vs. judgment in "To Build a Fire."
2. London's use of foreshadowing and repetition.
3. London's treatment of the partial source of the story, Jeremiah
   Lynch's Three Years in the Klondike (London, 1904). (Quoted in
   Franklin Walker, Jack London and the Klondike, pp. 256-257; see
   Suggested Readings, below.)

Exercise for Reading

1. After reading the story, make a list of the elements that
   compose it, such as man, dog, cold, old-timer, fire, water, etc.
   Read it again, classifying each passage into the appropriate
   category or categories. Invent new categories as needed, but
   keep your list as short as possible. Draw a diagram showing
   how the elements are related. Does your diagram reveal or
   confirm anything about the meaning of the story?

Related Subject

1. Write a story or vignette involving a human being and an
   animal. Imitate London by telling part of it from the animal's
   point of view but without anthropomorphizing the animal in any
   way.

SUGGESTED READINGS

Labor, Earle. Jack London. Twayne's United States Authors Series,
    No. 230, New York: Twayne, 1974. Pp. 63-70.

McClintock, James I. White Logic: Jack London's Short Stories.
    Grand Rapids, Mich.: Wolf House Books, 1975. Pp. 116-119.

Walker, Franklin. Jack London and the Klondike: The Genesis of an
    American Writer. San Marino, Calif.: The Huntington Library,
    1966. Pp. 254-260.

Sherwood Anderson

"Hands" (page 470)

Anderson's story might be called a portrait. Like a formal painted portrait, it depicts Wing Biddlebaum not only as he exists at a given moment but also in conjunction with certain props in the background that reveal who he is by recalling his past and defining his circumstances. The focal image of the portrait is Wing's hands, around which the other elements of the picture are organized and to which they lend meaning. Further, the story depends for a portion of its effect upon a series of painterly tableaux, from the sunset landscape with berry pickers with which it begins to the silhouette of Wing as a holy hermit, saying over and over the rosary of his lonely years of penance for a sin he did not commit.

In keeping with this achronological narration (which William L. Phillips has shown may in part result from Anderson's thinking his way through the story as he wrote it), neither Wing nor George Willard experiences any clear revelation or makes any climactic decision. Wing never understands why he was driven out of Pennsylvania, and George is afraid to ask the questions that might lead them both to a liberating understanding of Wing's experience.

The reader, however, is not permitted to remain in the dark. With the clear understanding of how the crudity and narrow-minded suspicion of his neighbors has perverted Wing's selfless, "diffused" love for his students into a source of fear and shame comes a poignant sorrow for what is being wasted. Wing's hands may be the pride of Winesburg for their agility at picking strawberries, but the nurturing love that they betoken is feared by everyone, including George, including even Wing himself, whose loneliness is as great as his capacity to love -- from which, by a cruel irony, it arises.

QUESTIONS FOR DISCUSSION

1. Define Wing Biddlebaum's relationship to his community as it is implied in the first paragraph. To what extent is the impression created here borne out?
2. Why does Wing hope George Willard will come to visit? Does George ever arrive?
3. Wing's name, which refers to his hands, was given to him by "some obscure poet of the town," and telling the full story of those hands "is a job for a poet." What connotations of _wings_ are appropriate? Why is _Wing_ a better name for Biddlebaum than, say, _Claw_, or _Hook_, or _Picker_?
4. Could Wing himself have been a poet? Why does he tell his dreams only to George?
5. Why did the people of the town in Pennsylvania nearly lynch Adolph Meyers? Why was he unable to defend himself?

6. Are the people in Ohio any different from those in Pennsylvania?
    Explain. What about George Willard? Evaluate his decision not
    to ask Wing about his hands.
7. What other hands do we see in the story? Compare them with
    Wing's.
8. Explain the implications of our last view of Wing. What is the
    pun in the last line?

TOPICS FOR WRITING

Critical Essays

1. The crucifixion of Wing Biddlebaum.
2. Anderson's Wing and Flaubert's Félicité.
3. Anderson's comments on "Form, Not Plot, in the Short Story"
    (included in Part Two, p. 1135) as a key to his art in "Hands."

Exercise for Reading

1. After reading the story once, jot down your response, including
    your feelings about Wing, George, the townspeople, and the
    narrator. Also write, in one or two sentences, a summation of
    the story's theme as you understand it. Then reread the para-
    graphs of the story in the order they would have followed had
    Anderson told the story in chronological order. Would your
    responses differ? Would the story have an identical theme?
    Explain.

Related Subject

1. Anderson claimed to have written this story at a sitting and to
    have published it without rearrangements or major additions or
    deletions of material. Imitating Anderson's process, write a
    vignette about a person unknown to you whom you see in a photo-
    graph. Start with the scene in the photo and end with the same,
    interpolating previous incidents and background information
    as they occur to you.

SUGGESTED READINGS

Burbank, Rex. Sherwood Anderson. Twayne's United States Authors
    Series, No. 65. New York: Twayne, 1964. Pp. 64-66.

Phillips, William L. "How Sherwood Anderson Wrote Winesburg, Ohio."
    In The Achievement of Sherwood Anderson. Edited by Ray Lewis
    White. Chapel Hill: University of North Carolina Press, 1966.
    Pp. 62-84, especially pp. 74-78. Originally published in
    American Literature, 23 (1951), 7-30.

Sherwood Anderson

"Death in the Woods" (page 474)

If "Hands" is a portrait, "Death in the Woods" is a madonna, a
religious image of the earth mother, the principle of connectedness
by which life is fostered and sustained. Anderson's depiction of
the woman whose job it is to feed animal life, "in cows, in chickens,
in pigs, in horses, in dogs, in men," congeals in the visionary
revelation of her death scene. To the men and boys who stand around
her, the moonlit glimpse of her naked breast -- effectively foreshadowed in the incident in which, as a girl, she had her dress
ripped open by the German farmer she was bound to -- conveys a
sense of wonder: They look upon a marble statue of a beautiful
young woman in the snow. Near her, or perhaps around her, lies the
oval track left by the dogs, at once a prayer ring and a symbol of
the interdependence and endless continuity of the life she has
served.

It is appropriate that the basis of Mrs. Grime's scant economy
is eggs, whose various connotations are obvious enough. As the
nurse of living things, Mrs. Grimes establishes bonds and fosters
community. The world with which she must deal, however, corrodes
those bonds. When we first see her she is struggling alone:
"People drive right down a road and never see a woman like that."
The men she feeds are rapacious and cruel -- to her and, as in the
fight between Jake and the German farmer, to each other. The town
treats them all with cold suspicion. Even the butcher who loads
her grain bag out of pity would deny the food to Mrs. Grimes's
husband or son: "He'd see him starve first." Not Mrs. Grimes, who
tacitly reaffirms her theme: "Starve, eh? Well things had to be
fed. . . . Horses, cows, pigs, dogs, men." When she dies the
forces for harmony and union that she embodies achieve a momentary
victory, as the townspeople fall into a ragged communal procession
to witness her death -- a ceremony as instinctive as the ring-
running of the dogs, if somewhat less orderly and beautiful.

Anderson's story progresses from an apprehension of drab
poverty and ugliness to a discovery of wonder and beauty. The
agency that distills religious and aesthetic emotion out of the
profane world of the story is the inquiring imagination of the
narrator, who muses over his recollections, reconstructs his story
from fragments, and in doing so explains the process of synthesis
that takes place as he writes. In its progress from the ordinary to
the mystical, from ugliness and privation to a soul-nourishing
beauty, the story records a triumph of the creative imagination,
which penetrates the surfaces of things to find within them their
inherent mythic truth.

What makes that triumph possible is the narrator's subtly
expressed identification with Mrs. Grimes. The fascination that
causes him to cling to his recollections and finally to work them
through may arise, as William J. Scheick argues, from the shock of
his initiation into an awareness "of the relation between feeding,

sex, and death" that blocks his sexual development; or it may arise from a sense of the hitherto unexpressed mythic implications of the scene in the woods. In either case, the narrator recognizes that the death of Mrs. Grimes has meaning for him -- as one who has worked for a German farmer, who has himself watched dogs run in a ring, and who has kept silent; as one who is fed by women; and as one who must die. The story's circular structure, like the ring of dogs and the ring of men around the corpse, transforms compulsion into worship, just as Anderson's art transforms the report of a frightening death into a celebration of life and of the power of the sympathetic imagination to render its beauty.

QUESTIONS FOR DISCUSSION

1. Discuss the style of the opening paragraph. What qualities of the old woman's life are reflected in the syntax and rhythms of the prose?

2. How does Anderson modulate from generalization through recollection to specific narration? What change in narrative mode takes place in section II with the paragraph that begins, "One day in Winter. . ."? Does the story ever return to its original mode? Where?

3. "Her name was Grimes" -- appropriately?

4. What does the narrator mean when he calls the Grimes men "a tough lot"? Are they alone in this in the story?

5. Describe the woman's life with the German farmer. How important to the story is the farmer's having torn "her dress open clear down the front"?

6. How big a part does love play in the relations between people in this story? What other factors are prominent -- exploitation? mistrust? violence?

7. Does the butcher's generosity seem a welcome change? How does the butcher compare with Mrs. Grimes as a nurturer of life?

8. How does Anderson prepare us to accept it as probable that Mrs. Grimes would sit down under a tree and freeze to death?

9. Describe the behavior of the dogs. How does Anderson explain it? How does the narrator know it took place?

10. Comment on the tonal effect of the passage, "It had been a big haul for the old woman. It was a big haul for the dogs now."

11. What does the corpse look like in the moonlight? Why does Anderson give a concise description of the corpse near the beginning of section IV rather than saving the whole revelation until the men and boys arrive on the scene at the end of that section?

12. Comment on the implications of this line: "Either mother or our older sister would have to warm our supper."

13. Explain the possible meanings of the word everything in the first sentence of section V.

14. Discuss the narrator's remarks about why he has told the story. What is "the real story I am now trying to tell"? To what extent is it a story about the narrator himself? About stories and storytelling?

TOPICS FOR WRITING

Critical Essays

1. Circles: -- image and structure in "Death in the Woods."
2. The narrator's struggle "To tell the simple story over again."
3. The role of the community in "Death in the Woods" and "Hands."
4. Mrs. Grimes and the mythic roles of woman.

Exercise for Reading

1. On a second reading, make notes about the narrator. Rearrange his activities, experiences, and concerns into chronological order. What is the narrator's story? What is his conflict? What does he achieve? What does he learn?

Related Subject

1. Read several myths from Ovid's Metamorphoses. Rewrite the story of Mrs. Grimes as an Ovidian myth. What changes of tone are necessary? What important themes have you had to abandon? What have you had to invent?

SUGGESTED READINGS

Burbank, Rex. Sherwood Anderson. Twayne's United States Authors Series, No. 65. New York: Twayne, 1964. Pp. 125-129.

Joselyn, Sister Mary. "Some Artistic Dimensions of Sherwood Anderson's 'Death in the Woods.'" Studies in Short Fiction, 4 (1967), 252-259.

Scheick, William J. "Compulsion toward Repetition: Sherwood Anderson's 'Death in the Woods.'" Studies in Short Fiction, 11 (1974), 141-146.

A. E. Coppard

"The Higgler" (page 486)

A higgler is an itinerant trader in poultry and dairy products; he is also one who higgles, a stickler for petty advantages in bargaining. Coppard's story revolves around the sharp-trading suspiciousness associated with the higgler's profession. Applying his business savvy to the offer of a bride, Harvey Whitlow ironically passes up the best deal that ever comes his way. Coppard follows the principles he sets forth in his remarks on the short story genre (printed in Part Two, p. 1138) by structuring his narrative to build, in a manner characteristic of the oral tale, toward the surprising revelation of a disastrous misunderstanding.

The narrative voice that tells the story likewise takes on the intonations we might expect from a neighbor or friend of Harvey, gossiping about his fate, but it does so only from time to time. "The Higgler" is no mere tale, but a carefully crafted evocation of the life it portrays, and one, despite Coppard's disclaimer, with novelistic overtones and suggestions of larger social and moral themes. Harvey Whitlow's name hints at his limitations. Having decided Mary is above him, he can conceive of relations with her only in terms of romantic fantasy, or eventually -- perhaps inspired by Grandmother Fundy -- of adultery. Mary's repeated explanation, "I was fond of you -- then," is ambiguous, however, and Harvey's speculations about what his life will be like as a working bailiff may be just as deluded as his previous suspicions about Mrs. Sadgrove's offer of a bride. For may not Mary mean by <u>then</u> an epoch before she learned, through his "war story" about the execution of a pig, of Harvey's callous nature? Harvey accompanies his grotesque tale with some decidedly lowbrow remarks about the French language, which she speaks well, and when he is finished she turns away and walks off to the house.

The attentive reader, by contrast, experiences no surprise. The tale of the pig expresses Harvey's personality as already established in his remark to the handsome gander that he never kills anything before Saturday and in his casual destruction of the field mouse, so vividly described by Coppard as Harvey's fellow worker in the orchard. What <u>should</u> trouble the reader is the association in Harvey's mind of small rodents with Mary (who has "hair like a squirrel, lovely") and of the gander with Mrs. Sadgrove. The first time she sees him, Mrs. Sadgrove looks at Harvey "as uncomprehendingly as a mouse might look at a gravestone," and it is fitting that Harvey, who declares his willingness to "buy any mottal thing," should be assigned the nightmare task of preparing her grotesquely stiffening corpse for burial.

QUESTIONS FOR DISCUSSION

1. What is Harvey Witlow's problem at the outset? In what terms does he phrase it? Do his concerns extend beyond the economic?
2. Describe Prattle Corner. Does Harvey see it clearly?
3. Mrs. Sadgrove claims to drive a hard bargain. Why does Coppard introduce her in these terms?
4. Discuss Harvey's thoughts about the gander and his way of dealing with it. Is there a similar conflict in his response to Mary?
5. How would you characterize the voice that speaks the first paragraph of section II? Is it the same as the voice that speaks the next paragraph? What is the effect of this modulation?
6. What is the unspoken emotional import of the scene in which Harvey handles the swarm of bees? Is he always so brave?
7. Why does Harvey wonder if something is the matter with Mary? What is the reason for her silence? Why can Harvey not divine it?

8. Why does Harvey crush the field mouse?
9. If you were Mary, what would you think of Harvey's story about shooting the pig?
10. Comment on the implications of this line: "The distracted higgler hummed and haa-ed in his bewilderment as if he had just been offered the purchase of a dubious duck."
11. Explain what happens in section IV. Why does Coppard end the section as he does?
12. What does Coppard emphasize about Harvey's wedding to Sophy in section V? Why?
13. Discuss the imagery of light and darkness in section VI, beginning with the sunset. Why does Coppard provide such a backdrop for his final scene?
14. How accurately do you think Harvey understands what Mary means when she reveals, "I was fond of you -- then"?

TOPICS FOR WRITING

Critical Essays

1. Harvey Witlow and the peasants in Maupassant's "The String."
2. How Coppard makes the higgler a sympathetic character.
3. Coppard's landscapes, animals, and weather (see Exercise for Reading, below).
4. The importance of names in "The Higgler."
5. Love, money, and death: "The Higgler" as a postwar story.

Exercise for Reading

1. Coppard is noted for his elaborate descriptions of the landscape and weather conditions. Locate such passages throughout the story. What purposes do they serve beyond local color? What about his interiors? His minor characters?

Related Subjects

1. Study Coppard's description of the gander in section I. Then write a similar description of about the same length and structure that characterizes an animal you can observe.
2. Invent the plot for a story that depends on a misunderstanding of one person's desires by another. Then list the attributes of both characters that would be necessary to make the misunderstanding plausible and not entirely dependent on happenstance.

James Joyce

"An Encounter" (page 508)

What does the "queer old josser" do down at the end of the field? Students will want to know, but they may (out of innocence or embarrassment) hesitate to ask. Rather than assuring them that letters by Joyce imply that he did indeed intend masturbation, or rather than adding to their discomfort by returning the question with "What do you think?", use the interest aroused by the passage to start a discussion of the story's narrative method and the theme it embodies. Our uncertainty about the man's action results from the uncertainty of the narrator, who does not look and who even as he reports the event makes no indelicate conjecture. The reader sees the man as the boy sees him, and whatever diagnosis we may arrive at to explain his behavior, he retains for us some of the aura of mystery and danger that he holds for the narrator.

In their encounter with the old man, the boys at last meet the real adventure they have been seeking. Joyce prepares us for this revelation of reality in careful stages. Spurred by Wild West fantasies to a hunger for "wild sensations" and a desire to escape the bleak routine of school, the narrator and Mahony set out from home looking for excitement. (Leo Dillon does not even take the first step.) The anticipated idyll, however, leads only to the discovery of industry, poverty, and commerce. Mahony's attempt to "play the Indian" on a "crowd of ragged girls" evokes not the imagined freedom of the American West but the suffocations of the rigid Irish social and religious divisions. At last the romantic dream dwindles to the vague hope that the Norwegian seamen will have green eyes. They do not, and the boys resign their quest in gloom: "The sun went in behind some clouds and left us to our jaded thoughts and the crumbs of our provisions."

Their own resources spent, our heroes are in need of a super-natural aid, which dodders into the story in the person of an old man with startling green eyes. His unsettling talk initiates them into mysteries quite different from what they expected to find. Romance, whether of adventure or of love, becomes as repellent in his mouth as his yellow, gapped teeth, and although the boys are naturally unable to respond to the longing for human contact that he so strangely tries to voice, the experience of listening to him leaves the narrator "penitent" for his previous uncharitable attitude toward Mahony and perhaps, by extension, for his similar condescension toward National School boys and other real things he does not yet understand. The adventure-personalities assumed by the boys fit uncomfortably, and the narrator, pretending bravery as he calls to "Murphy," is "ashamed of my paltry stratagem" but glad enough to be reunited with his friend.

"An Encounter" is packed with Joyce's usual stylistic and symbolic riches; each passage rewards careful scrutiny. Extending the implications suggested above to relate the story to the general theme of Dubliners, the old man in his green-black suit, with his "bottle-green" eyes, can be seen as an embodiment of the reality of the Ireland that Joyce himself had to escape. Obsessed with private fantasies, at war with himself, and trapped in his isolation, the man sums up much of what the boys have seen in their excursion through Dublin. His interest in romantic fiction and his sadism are not foreign to the boys themselves: He represents what they may become if they cannot break free. Beyond the end of their truncated excursion, however, lies the Pigeon House, yet to be explored -- even Father Butler does not go there. Joyce leaves it to the reader to imagine what kind of flight may be made from there.

QUESTIONS FOR DISCUSSION

1. What kind of reading do the boys find in their Wild West magazines? How faithful are the stories and the games based on them to the reality of the Old West?
2. What does Joe Dillon's vocation imply about him? About the priesthood he enters?
3. Examine the title The Halfpenny Marvel, relating it to the larger context of the story.
4. "National School boys" are mentioned twice in the story. What opinion of them is held by those who mention them? Is it justified?
5. The narrator remarks, "real adventures . . . must be sought abroad." Is he right?
6. What is the narrator's mood as he waits for his friends? On what is it based?
7. Contrast the personality of Mahony with that of the narrator. How important are their differences to the story's theme?
8. Summarize the boys' "adventures" before they meet the old man.
9. Why do you think the narrator hopes the Norwegian sailors will have green eyes? Norwegians may be associated with the Vikings, who raided Ireland in the Dark Ages. Are the Norwegians doing something similar?
10. Comment on the appearance of the old man as he approaches the boys, passes them, and then returns. What effect does Joyce gain by so methodically tracing his steps?
11. Develop a theory to explain the old man's sexual talk, his withdrawal, and his return in a sadistic mood. What can we imagine the boys mean to him? What effect does his monologue have on him? On the boys?
12. Discuss the old man's short-lived "liberalism" and its meaning for the narrator. Why does the narrator propose that he and Mahony adopt the pseudonyms Murphy and Smith?
13. Account for Mahony's behavior when the cat reappears.
14. In the Wild West games, the narrator has been one of "the reluctant Indians who were afraid to seem studious or lacking in robustness." Does that description account for his response to his "real adventure"? Why is he afraid the man will seize him by the ankles? Is he in any real danger? If not, what is he afraid of?

71

508-545 (text pages)

TOPICS FOR WRITING

Critical Essays

1. The quest structure of "An Encounter."
2. Adult males and adolescent boys: "An Encounter" as an initiation.
3. The three parts of "An Encounter" and their respective functions.
4. "An Encounter" as a self-discovery.

Exercise for Reading

1. Joyce's story is highly economical. Select a passage of a paragraph or two for detailed explication. Relate its words, phrases, images, ideas, and actions to other parts of the story. Define what it accomplishes in advancing Joyce's plot, symbolism, and theme.

Related Subjects

1. Recall a fantasy game that you played as a child. What suggested it to you? What gratifications or experimentations do you now see that it involved?
2. Write a personal narrative about an "adventure" you set out on that ended with a surprise or a disillusionment.

SUGGESTED READINGS

Beck, Warren. Joyce's "Dubliners": Substance, Vision, and Art. Durham, N. C.: Duke University Press, 1969. Pp. 79-95.

San Juan, Epifanio, Jr. James Joyce and the Craft of Fiction: An Interpretation of "Dubliners." Rutherford, Madison, and Teaneck, N.J.: Fairleigh Dickinson University Press, 1972. Pp. 45-53.

Senn, Fritz. "An Encounter." In James Joyce's "Dubliners": Critical Essays. Edited by Clive Hart. New York: Viking, 1969. Pp. 26-38, 171.

James Joyce

"The Dead" (page 514)

"The Dead" is an apprehension of mortality. Joyce's carefully detailed scrutiny of the party, with all its apparent vivacity, serves only to reveal the triviality, transience, and emptiness of what passes in Dublin for life. The story involves a series of supersessions. Miss Ivors's friendliness is superseded by rigid politics, and she departs. Her kind of fervor is superseded by the

72

"hospitality" of the dinner table that Gabriel feels so good about and that he celebrates in his speech. That conviviality, however, is exposed as mostly hypocritical, as each person reveals a selfish preoccupation -- including Gabriel, who uses his oration to reassure himself after his self-esteem has been wounded by Miss Ivors. The long evening, however, generates in the heart of Gabriel a strong surge of love for Gretta that supersedes his selfishness. It is edged with jealousy and self-contempt, Gabriel's habitual weaknesses; nonetheless, the reader feels for a while that out of the waste of the soiree at least this rejuvenation has been salvaged. But Gabriel is longing for something just as dead as Michael Furey, and Gretta's devastating disclosure of a dead lover's power over her mind brings the "thought-tormented" Gabriel to his final recognition of the predominance of death. Like the monks of Mount Melleray, all people in Ireland, dead or alive -- from the aged Aunt Julia on down -- seem to be sleeping in their coffins.

While Gabriel's vision is triggered by the revelation of a dead man's sway over the emotions of his wife and of his consequent power to thwart Gabriel's desire, it is supported by the pervasive imagery of snow, chill, and death that comes to fulfillment in the last paragraph. The snow has been falling intermittently throughout the story. Gabriel is blanketed with it when he arrives on the scene, and images of cold and dampness pervade the narration. Last year "Gretta caught a dreadful cold"; Bartell D'Arcy has one this year. The girl in the song he sings holds her death-cold infant in a soaking rain. Not only are the physical descriptions of some characters so vivid that one almost sees the skulls beneath the flesh; even the warm, lively, cheerful elements of the story contribute to the final impression of morbidity. The Misses Morkan are giving what may be their final dance. The alcoholic antics of Mr. Browne and Freddy Malin consist only of ersatz good humor. And Gabriel himself, on whom everyone depends, can barely sustain his nerve and perform his function as master of the revels, keeper of order, and sustainer of life.

In the moribund and sterile world presided over by his three spinster aunts, Gabriel is called upon to play a role not unlike that of a year-god at this Christmas season. (The party probably takes place on Epiphany, January 6.) From the outset he is willing, but in three sequential encounters he fails. Each failure strikes a blow at his naiveté, his self-confidence, and his sense of superiority. His first two defeats are followed by accomplishments (handling Freddy, his performance at dinner), but their effect on him is cumulative. Gabriel's cheerful banter with the pale, pale Lily does not suit her, as one who has been hurt in love, and his Christmas gift of a coin can do little to ease her "great bitterness." Afterwards, his pretensions to take care of people are subjected to merciless ridicule in the "galoshes" passage. With Miss Ivors Gabriel is more circumspect than with Lily, but that does not prevent him from being whipsawed between her political hostility and her personal affection. This confusing interaction not only causes Miss Ivors to abandon the company and Gabriel in his speech to reject the entire younger generation of Ireland, it also sets the

stage for his ultimate failure with Gretta. Gretta's favorable response to Miss Ivors's plan for a trip to Galway now seems to Gabriel a
betrayal, and the association of this trip with Gretta's love for
the long-dead Michael compounds the feelings of alienation and self-
contempt that Miss Ivors's disapproval fosters in him.

Gabriel's failures and self-doubts should not diminish him
unduly in the reader's eyes: Joyce portrays him as aesthetically
sensitive, charitable, and loving. The "generous tears" he sheds
out of sympathy for Gretta's sorrow may not redeem anyone in a
world devoted to death, but they are the distillation of a compassion
quite opposite to the self-serving hypocrisy that has passed for
friendly conversation at the Misses Morkan's ball. By the end of
the story Gabriel no longer feels superior to his compatriots. He
recognizes that when Aunt Julia dies his speechifying will be use-
less. He turns his mind away from the past and toward a future in
which, as he feels his old identity fade and dissolve, at least the
theoretical possibility of growth and change exists. The ambiguity
of Gabriel's much-debated "journey westward" reflects the uncertainty
of any future, but Gabriel's readiness to embrace it represents a
major step forward from his rejection of Miss Ivors's proposition in
favor of a recycling of the European Continent.

QUESTIONS FOR DISCUSSION

1. Contrast the mood of the first paragraph with that of the
   second. Why does Joyce move from anticipation to rigidity?
2. Why are the Misses Morkan so eager for Gabriel to arrive?
3. What is the basis of Gabriel's error with Lily?
4. Explain Gabriel's hesitation to quote Browning.
5. What does Gabriel's interest in galoshes reveal about him?
6. Comment on the other men present at the dance besides Gabriel.
   Why does Joyce limit his cast so narrowly?
7. Discuss the reception of Mary Jane's "Academy piece."
8. What does Miss Ivors want from Gabriel? Why is he so upset by
   his conversation with her? Why does she leave early? Figuratively, what does she take with her when she goes?
9. Explain Gabriel's longing to be out in the snow. Is Gabriel
   "thought-tormented"?
10. Explain the irony of Julia's singing "Arrayed for the Bridal"
    to Mary Jane's accompaniment. What is the effect of the
    subsequent conversation, in this regard?
11. Comment on the relevance of the dinner-table conversation to the
    themes of the story.
12. Why is Gabriel so cheerful when carving and when proposing his
    toast? Is he justified? Why does he imagine people standing in
    the snow before he begins to speak?
13. What is the effect of Joyce's ending the tribute to the Misses
    Morkan with a glimpse of Freddy conducting the singers with his
    fork?

14. Comment on Gabriel's anecdote about "the never-to-be-forgotten Johnny." Can it be read as a summation in a minor key of the party now ending? Of the life of the Morkan family? Of their society?

15. Discuss the scene in which Gabriel watches Gretta listening to D'Arcy. What is Gabriel responding to? What is Gretta responding to? What do they have in common? Trace their moods as they proceed to the hotel.

16. Why is Gabriel so humiliated when he learns that Michael Furey is dead? What other effects does this revelation have on him? Explain what he realizes in the last section of the story.

17. Discuss the final paragraph. What does its poetic beauty contribute to the story? What is our final attitude toward Gabriel?

TOPICS FOR WRITING

Critical Essays

1. Gabriel Conroy and women.
2. Why "The Dead" is a Christmas story.
3. Gabriel Conroy's death wish.
4. Gabriel Conroy -- failed redeemer.
5. Habit and hypocrisy in "The Dead."

Exercise for Reading

1. After your first reading of the story, scan it again, marking the following: all references to cold, dampness, and snow; all references to death, illness, or people dead at the time of the story; all references to warmth, light, fire, and the like; all references to youth, young people, children, and the like. Catalogue your findings and write a paragraph on the importance of these elements in the story.

Related Subject

1. For a specific occasion, plan and compose an after-dinner speech with several headings like Gabriel's. Then analyze your speech, explaining what you were trying to accomplish for your audience -- and for yourself. Compare your intentions with Gabriel's.

SUGGESTED READINGS

Beck, Warren. Joyce's "Dubliners": Substance, Vision, and Art. Durham, N. C.: Duke University Press, 1969. Pp. 303-360.

Bernstock, Bernard. "The Dead." In James Joyce's "Dubliners": Critical Essays. Edited by Clive Hart. New York: Viking, 1969. Pp. 153-169, 177-179.

514-552 (text pages)

Loomis, C. C., Jr. "Structure and Sympathy in 'The Dead.'" In
Twentieth Century Interpretations of "Dubliners." Edited by
Peter K. Garrett. Englewood Cliffs, N. J.: Prentice-Hall,
1968. Pp. 110-114. Originally published in PMLA, 75 (1960),
149-151.

San Juan, Epifanio, Jr. James Joyce and the Craft of Fiction: An
Interpretation of "Dubliners." Rutherford, Madison, and Tea-
neck, N. J.: Fairleigh Dickinson University Press, 1972.
Pp. 209-223.

Virginia Woolf

"Moments of Being" (page 547)

The narrative present of Woolf's story lasts only a few
seconds, but it covers an event of dramatic importance for both
characters. Students may be confused by the stream-of-consciousness
technique, which allows Woolf to transform such a trivial occasion
into a moment of transcendence and which is also intrinsic to the
story's theme. Try approaching "Moments of Being," then, by sorting
out its contents into present and past time. Julia's comment about
Slater's pins, the reverberation of the last chord of the fugue,
Fanny's groping for the pin while Julia retrieves and grasps the
carnation, Julia's remark about last Friday, Fanny's finding the
pin, their kiss, Julia's reiterated criticism of Slater's pins, and
the reinstallation of the flower take place in the present. Other
events belong to the past: Fanny recalls a conversation with Miss
Kingston about her memories of Julius and Julia Craye, an exchange
about the use of men with Julia after a previous lesson, a remark
of Julia's about Kensington, and another about men being ogres.
Still other events -- and these are the ones that contribute most to
our sense of Julia's plight -- depend entirely on Fanny's conjecture,
as she reconstructs Julia's life in her imagination. By the time
Fanny, still groping for the pin, has seen Julia holding the flower
and has envisioned her loss of a suitor, she has developed an understanding of Julia that sees her as passionately drawn to the beauty
of a world outside herself and at the same time, of her own volition,
sealed off from possessing it. Julia's surprisingly ordinary remark
about the pins has spurred Fanny to identify with her, to look at
her from the inside, and to accept her peculiarities. When she
turns to confront Julia's ecstatic gaze of admiration (skillfully
foreshadowed by Woolf two pages earlier), she finds that her
conjectures have brought her into contact with Julia's innermost
being. Because of what she has so sensitively construed about her
teacher, Fanny finds herself able, by being embraced, to grant
Julia the possession of beauty that has always been denied her.
When they kiss, the two women participate in a moment of union with
a reality beyond the self, a kind of marriage that Woolf celebrates
in the splendid ambiguity of the conclusion.

QUESTIONS FOR DISCUSSION

1. Why does Julia's remark about pins give Fanny food for thought?
2. Explain how Miss Kingston fits into the story. Why does Woolf not mention her again after the second page?
3. How is Julius Craye's profession appropriate?
4. Why does Woolf twice repeat the statement that none of the Crayes ever married?
5. What prevents Julia Craye from possessing and enjoying the carnation entirely and altogether? What enables her at last to possess what she seeks at the end of the story?
6. How important is independence to Julia Craye? How important are safety and health?
7. Does Fanny Wilmot deserve the love she receives from Julia? If so, on what basis does she deserve it?

TOPICS FOR WRITING

Critical Essays

1. Woolf's style as an embodiment of theme in "Moments of Being."
2. "A dead white star": Woolf's Julia Craye.

Exercise for Reading

1. Reorganize the story into chronological order, noticing what information about the past depends on report, what on Fanny Wilmot's speculation. Why does Woolf pack the whole story into such a brief moment? What would be lost if it were narrated in chronological order?

Related Subject

1. Write a two- or three-page stream-of-consciousness narration and compare it to Woolf's story. What techniques does Woolf use to gain focus, coherence, and point?

SUGGESTED READING

Fleishman, Avrom. "Forms of the Woolfian Short Story." In Virginia Woolf: Revaluation and Continuity. Edited by Ralph Freedman. Berkeley: University of California Press, 1980. Pp. 44-70, especially pp. 60-62.

Franz Kafka

"The Metamorphosis" (page 554)

This story admits the broadest range of explications -- bio-
graphical, psychoanalytic, religious, philosophical. Here is one
way it might be read: As the sole supporter of his family after the
collapse of his father's business, Gregor Samsa has selflessly
devoted himself to serving others. Bringing home "good round coin
which he could lay on the table for his amazed and happy family" has
given him great satisfaction, and his only ambition has been to send
his sister, "who loved music, unlike himself," to study at the
Conservatorium. After his metamorphosis, Gregor can no longer
justify his existence by serving others. Instead, he must come to
terms with himself <u>as</u> himself, an alien being whose own nature and
needs are perhaps only by a degree more strange to Gregor than those
of the human Gregor Samsa would have been, if somehow he had
confronted them rather than deferring to the version of himself
projected by the supposed needs of his family.

Kafka simultaneously traces Gregor's painful growth to self-
willed individuality and the family's liberation from dependence
upon him, for the relationship of dependence and exploitation has
been crippling to both parties. Gregor learns what food he likes,
stakes his sticky claim to the sexually suggestive picture of the
woman with the fur muff (which may represent an objectification of
his libido), and, no longer "considerate," at last <u>comes</u> <u>out</u>,
intruding his obscene existence upon the world out of a purely
self-assertive desire to enjoy his sister's music and to be united
with its beauty. With this act Gregor has become fully himself;
his death soon after simply releases him from the misery of his
existence.

It is also a final release of the family from dependence and
from the shame and incompetence that it entails. As an insect,
Gregor becomes quite obviously the embarrassment to the family that
they have allowed him to be when he was human. Step by step they
discover their ability to support themselves -- taking jobs, coping
with what is now merely the troublesome burden of Gregor, and
learning finally the necessity of escaping from the prison that his
solicitousness has placed them in. Gregor's battle with his father
strangely transmutes the Oedipal conflict. It is triggered by
Gregor's becoming a being for whom there is no longer room in the
family, just as if he were a youth growing to sexual maturity, but
the result is that the father, who has previously been reduced to a
state of supine inertia by Gregor's diligent exertions, returns to
claim his full manhood as husband and paterfamilias.

Emerging from their apartment, "which Gregor had chosen," the
family members grow into an independent purposiveness that Gregor
himself is never able to attain. The story may be said to end with
a second metamorphosis, focused in the image of Grete stretching her
young body -- almost like a butterfly newly emerged from her cocoon.

Gregor, left behind like the caterpillar whose demise releases her, is denied all but a premonitory glimpse of the sexual and repro- ductive fulfillment for which his sister seems destined.

QUESTIONS FOR DISCUSSION

1. Describe the effect of Kafka's matter-of-fact assertion of the bizarre incident with which the story begins. Are you very interested in how it came to pass? How does Kafka keep that from becoming an issue in the story?
2. What are Gregor's concerns in section I? To what degree do they differ from what would matter to him if he had <u>not</u> been transformed into an insect?
3. When Gregor is trying to get out of bed, he considers calling for help but then dismisses the idea. Why?
4. What seems most important to the members of Gregor's family as he lies in bed? His health?
5. Describe the reaction of Gregor's parents to their first view of the metamorphosed Gregor. What circumstances in ordinary life might elicit a similar response?
6. Discuss the view from Gregor's window.
7. Trace Gregor's adaptation to his new body. In what ways do the satisfactions of his life as an insect differ from the satis- factions of his life as a traveling salesman?
8. When Gregor's father pushes him back into his room at the end of section I, Kafka calls it "literally a deliverance." Comment on the possible implications of the term.
9. Describe Grete's treatment of Gregor in section II. Is Gregor ill?
10. What are Gregor's hopes for the future? Is there anything wrong with those hopes?
11. For a time, Gregor is ashamed of his condition and tries to hide from everyone. In what way might this be called a step forward for him?
12. Discuss the conflicting feelings Gregor has about having the furniture taken out of his room. Why does he try to save the picture? What might Kafka's intention be in stressing that it is on this occasion that Grete calls Gregor by his name for the first time since his metamorphosis?
13. "Gregor's broken loose." What does Gregor's father do? Why? Explain the situation that has developed by the end of section II.
14. How does the charwoman relate to Gregor? Why is she the one who presides over his "funeral"?
15. Compare the role of the lodgers in the family with that of Gregor. Have they supplanted him? Why does Gregor's father send them away in the morning?
16. Why does Gregor, who previously did not like music, feel so attracted to his sister's playing? What change has taken place in his attitude toward himself? What might Kafka mean by "the unknown nourishment he craved"?
17. Comment on Grete's use of the neuter pronoun <u>it</u> to refer to Gregor.

554-590 (text pages)

18. What is the mood of the final passages of the story?

TOPICS FOR WRITING

Critical Essays

1. How Kafka gains the reader's "willing suspension of disbelief."
2. Gregor Samsa's metamorphosis -- a triumph of the self.
3. Kafka's "The Metamorphosis" as a study of sublimated incest.
4. Kafka is known to have admired Tolstoy's "The Death of Ivan
    Ilych". Compare and contrast the two works as studies of
    dying.

Exercise for Reading

1. Study the excerpt from Gustav Janouch's Conversations with
    Kafka (in Part Two, p. 1169), together with the headnotes to
    both the story and the excerpt. Reread "The Metamorphosis"
    with an eye to its autobiographical implications. To what
    extent can Gregor be considered a version of the artist? What
    truth, what "personal spectre of horror," might the story's
    ending reflect?

Related Subject

1. Consider Kafka's use of apparently symbolic images whose com-
    plete meaning seems impossible to state in abstract terms --
    the apples, the fur muff, or the hospital beyond the window, for
    example. Write a vignette in which symbolic objects play a role
    without becoming counters in a paraphrasable allegory. Some
    examples of symbols: a candle, a cup, the sea, broken glass,
    ants.

SUGGESTED READINGS

Greenberg, Martin. "Kafka's 'Metamorphosis' and Modern Spiritual-
    ity," Tri-Quarterly, No. 6 (1966), 5-20.

Kafka, Franz. The Metamorphosis. Translated and edited by Stanley
    Corngold. New York: Bantam, 1972. (Contains notes, docu-
    ments, and ten critical essays.)

Moss, Leonard. "A Key to the Door Image in 'The Metamorphosis,'"
    Modern Fiction Studies, 17 (1971), 37-42.

Nabokov, Vladimir. Lectures on Literature. New York: Harcourt
    Brace Jovanovich, 1980. Pp. 250-283.

Taylor, Alexander. "The Waking: The Theme of Kafka's 'Metamorpho-
    sis,'" Studies in Short Fiction, 2 (1965), 337-342.

Wolkenfeld, Suzanne. "Christian Symbolism in Kafka's 'The Metamorphosis,'" <u>Studies in Short Fiction</u>, 10 (1973), 205-207.

D. H. Lawrence

"The Primrose Path" (page 592)

Daniel Sutton's character is a paradox that the story resolves.
In appearance and reputation -- and in fact -- he is a "great coarse
bully," godless, a devourer of women, domineering and sexually
powerful. But he is also a timorous coward, terrified of death and
unable to look directly at himself or others. As he stands tormented
with guilt and fear at the bedside of the dying wife he has abandoned,
Sutton clings to childish fantasies of innocence and escape, but in
the taxi speeding home his impulse to unconsciousness takes on a more
violent quality. Sutton's passionate relationship with his child
mistress Elaine (for although he says she is twenty-one, she is
described as merely adolescent) combines both his longing for youth
and his desire to lose himself in mindlessness. But in recoiling
from death and the responsible compassion for others that an
acknowledgment of death entails, Sutton condemns himself to a
repetition of the cycle from which he wants to escape. If the
poison he imagines his former mistress put in his coffee frightened
him as a hint of mortality, when Elaine (in Daniel Berry's phrase)
will "hate him like poison," will he be any more at ease with
himself?

Lawrence uses an omniscient point of view for this largely
autobiographical tale, but Berry provides a central consciousness
on which the story registers itself just as it does on the reader.
Many passages report Sutton's state of mind directly, but Lawrence
draws no conclusions that Berry, were he to write the story in
retrospect, might not have been able to deduce. That Sutton is his
uncle not only provides credible access to such background information as Lawrence sees fit to supply; it also provides the reader
with an inducement to regard with some sympathy a most unsympathetic
character. Most important, Daniel Berry's sense of kinship with
Daniel Sutton, whom he uneasily perceives as "an older development
of himself," suggests that Sutton's fears and impulses are not
foreign to any of us. When Sutton sees "a sort of <u>danse macabre</u> of
ugly criminals" walking the streets, the reader recognizes that his
desire to join in by "running the cab amuck among 'em" expresses
what he has in common with those he despises.

In <u>Hamlet</u>, Ophelia says to Laertes:
> Do not, as some ungracious pastors do,
> Show me the steep and thorny way to heaven,
> Whiles, like a puffed and reckless libertine,
> Himself the primrose path of dalliance treads,
> And recks not his own rede.
>   (I. iii. 47-51)

Readers can hardly deny their own susceptibility to choosing the primrose path taken by Sutton, and should find in the story -- to use Lawrence's phrase, quoted in the headnote -- "a mine of practical truth."

QUESTIONS FOR DISCUSSION

1. Define our first impression of Daniel Sutton. Is it consistent with the statement that he has an "uneasy conscience"?
2. Evaluate Sutton's response to the news that his sister Anna has died. What is his primary concern?
3. Why is Sutton so much more affectionate to pigeons and dogs than to people?
4. As Berry and his uncle ride toward Watmore in the cab, Berry observes that "The elder man had evidently something pressing on his soul." What is it? What might it be that it is not?
5. Describe Sutton's reaction to seeing his dying wife. Why does he respond so strongly to the picture of birds?
6. Why does Sutton invite Berry to dinner and then ignore him?
7. Elaine speaks with a "twang" in her voice. Who else in the story does that? What does it imply?
8. Of Sutton's brightening as he becomes aroused by Elaine, Lawrence remarks, "It was life stronger than death in him." Evaluate the relationship between Sutton and Elaine. What are its positive aspects?

TOPICS FOR WRITING

Critical Essays

1. The role of Daniel Berry in "The Primrose Path."
2. Lawrence's use of atmosphere and setting.
3. Lawrence's control of the omniscient point of view.

Exercise for Reading

1. Locate the likely source of Lawrence's title. Then review the story and explain its implications.

Related Subject

1. Write an essay about a relative or acquaintance of your own whose life would conventionally be considered reprehensible. Try to account for his or her behavior. What are its implications? (Be careful not to preach.)

SUGGESTED READINGS

Pinion, F. B. A D. H. Lawrence Companion: Life, Thought, Works.
New York: Barnes & Noble, 1979. P. 228.

Tedlock, E. W., Jr. D. H. Lawrence, Artist and Rebel: A Study of
Lawrence's Fiction. Albuquerque: University of New Mexico
Press, 1963. Pp. 106-107.

Widmer, Kingsley. The Art of Perversity: D. H. Lawrence's Shorter
Fictions. Seattle: University of Washington Press, 1962. Pp.
25-26.

D. H. Lawrence

"The Rocking Horse Winner" (page 603)

Lawrence's masterful technical control wins the reader's assent
to the fantastic premise on which the story is built; without that
assent, the thematic statement the story propounds would lack
cogency. Rather than confronting us boldly with his improbable
donnée, as Kafka does in "The Metamorphosis," Lawrence edges up to
it slowly. The whispering voices in the house that drive Paul to
his furious rocking begin as a thought in the mother's mind and then
become a figure of speech that crystallizes imperceptibly into a
literal fact -- or rather, into an auditory hallucination heard by
the children that expresses their perception of their mother's
unquenchable need for funds. Paul's ability to pick a winner by
riding his rocking horse to where he is lucky requires even more
circumspect handling. Like the family members, we learn about it
after the fact, putting together bits of information to explain a set
of peculiar but at first not at all implausible circumstances --
Paul's claim, "Well, I got there!", his familiarity with race
horses, Bassett's reluctance "to give him away" to Oscar, Paul's
giving Oscar a tip on a long shot that comes in a winner, and only
then, with Oscar's skepticism always preempting that of the reader,
the revelation of how much he has won. It is not until the very end
that we, with his astonished mother, actually witness Paul in the
act of receiving revelation -- just as he slips beyond the world of
everyday probability for good and into the uncharted supernatural
realm from whence his "luck" seems to emanate.

Although no explanation, supernatural or otherwise, is necessary
to account for good fortune at the race track, Lawrence persuades the
reader that Paul's success is caused by his exertions and therefore
has a moral meaning. In Paul's household the lack of love is per-
ceived as a lack of money and the lack of money is attributed to a
lack of luck. Since luck is by definition something that happens to
one, to blame one's troubles on luck is to deny responsibility for
them and to abandon any effort to overcome them. As the event makes
clear, Paul's mother will never be satisfied, no matter how much

money falls her way, because no amount of money can fill the emptiness left by the absence of love. The "hard little place" in her
heart at the beginning of the story has expanded until, at the end,
she feels that her whole heart has "turned actually into a stone."
Paul sets out by the force of will to redefine luck as something one
can acquire. He places belief before evidence and asserts, "I'm a
lucky person. . . . God told me," and then makes good on his promise
by riding his rocking horse to where luck comes from. "'It's as if
he had it from heaven,'" Bassett says, "in a secret, religious
voice."

In his singleminded devotion to winning money for his mother at
the race track by riding his rocking horse (which W. D. Snodgrass
has likened to masturbation as Lawrence understood it), Paul diverts
his spiritual and emotional forces to material aims, and Lawrence
symbolically represents the effect of this materialization in the
process of petrification by which the mother's heart and Paul's
blue eyes, which have throughout the story served as an emblem of
his obsession, turn to stone. At the end Oscar states the case with
epigrammatic precision: Hester's son has been transformed into
eighty-odd thousand pounds -- a tidy sum, but of course it will not
be enough.

QUESTIONS FOR DISCUSSION

1. How is Paul's mother portrayed at the outset? Does Lawrence
   suggest that she is blameworthy? Why or why not?
2. Explain the family's "grinding sense of the shortage of money."
   Why do the voices become even louder when some money becomes
   available? What would it take to still the voices?
3. Discuss the implications of Paul's confusing luck with lucre.
   How accurate is his mother's definition of luck? What would
   constitute true good luck for him?
4. Explain Paul's claim to be lucky. In what sense is he justified? In what sense is he very unlucky?
5. What function do Oscar and Bassett play in the story, beyond
   providing Paul with practical access to the race track and the
   lawyer?
6. "Bassett was serious as a church." Is this a humorous line?
   Does it suggest anything beyond the comic?
7. What is the effect on the reader of the episode in which Oscar
   takes Paul to the track and Paul's horse Daffodil wins the
   race?
8. Explain the mother's response to her birthday gift. What is
   its effect on Paul? Why?
9. Before the Derby, Paul does not "know" for several races. Can
   this dry spell be explained? What brings it to an end?
10. Analyze Paul's last words in the story. What does he mean by
    "get there"? Where, in fact, does he go? Is absolute certainty
    possible? How? Why is Paul so proud to proclaim that he is
    lucky to his mother? Finally, comment on her reaction.
11. Evaluate Oscar's remarks that end the story. Was Paul a "poor
    devil"? Why? In what senses?

TOPICS FOR WRITING

Critical Essays

1. The handling of the supernatural in "The Rocking Horse Winner" and Kipling's "The Wish House."
2. The religious theme of "The Rocking Horse Winner."
3. Luck, will, and faith in "The Rocking Horse Winner."
4. Realistic elements and the social theme of Lawrence's supernatural tale.
5. Luck, lucre, and love.

Related Subject

1. Look up a newspaper story about some unexplained phenomenon, ghost, or poltergeist, and work it into a narrative whose meaning is finally not dependent on an interest in the supernatural.

SUGGESTED READINGS

San Juan, E., Jr. "Theme versus Imitation: D. H. Lawrence's 'The Rocking Horse Winner.'" D. H. Lawrence Review, 3 (1970), 136–140.

Snodgrass, W. D. "A Rocking Horse: The Symbol, the Pattern, the Way to Live." In D. H. Lawrence: A Collection of Critical Essays. Edited by Mark Spilka. Twentieth Century Views. Englewood Cliffs, N.J.: Prentice-Hall, 1963. Originally published in The Hudson Review, 11 (1958).

Widmer, Kingsley. The Art of Perversity: D. H. Lawrence's Shorter Fictions. Seattle: University of Washington Press, 1962. Pp. 92–95, 213.

Isak Dinesen

"The Old Chevalier" (page 617)

The image of the danse macabre, with its alternating personifications of youthful desire and of death dancing in a ring, provides the basic structure for Dinesen's tale. In one permutation, youth is juxtaposed with age: The old chevalier tells his tale to the young narrator, remembering now at the end of his life the experiences of "the young man who had been so unhappy that long time ago." Just as the interweaving of skeletal and living dancers in the danse macabre states a profound truth, so the chevalier's comparison of the past with the present -- manners, styles, and attitudes toward the sexes -- turns the experience he reports into an embodiment of deep wisdom, whose meaning lies embedded in a rich context of literary allusion and philosophical speculation.

The narrative progress of the story imitates the alternations of the danse macabre as well. The chevalier's first mistress, though "pale, colorless, all through," possesses "unrivaled energy." She devotes it, however, to a thoroughly selfish competition with her husband, taking "her lovers as she took her fences, to pile up more conquests than the man with whom she was in love." For the chevalier, her vitality bodes death, the taste of which in the poisoned coffee she offers him still lingers on his lips. Appropriately, this dangerous young woman, whom he has already imagined as a werewolf and a witch, is suddenly transformed before his eyes "into a very old woman" when he foils her murderous intent.

With breathless haste, the story swings back again. As the chevalier sits, his life in ruins, "sick to death with horror and humiliation," he is accosted by Nathalie, whose youthful perfection of beauty emerges from the shell of her soggy black garments like life out of death, truth out of delusion. Contemplating this "greatest masterpiece of nature" causes the chevalier -- whose previous disquisition on "the idea of Woman" and "the mystery of life" prepares us for it -- to experience a neoplatonic vision of divine beauty: "She was so young that you felt, in the midst of your deep admiration, the anticipation of a still higher perfec-tion. . . ." Inevitably this transport must end. Nathalie the goddess woman is a projection of the chevalier's youthful self-centeredness ("No miracle was incredible to me as long as it happened to myself"); Nathalie the human woman extends her hand for twenty francs and slips away into the bleak chaos of the city -- like Eurydice, never to be retrieved. The meaning of her visitation for the old chevalier, and for the reader, comes into final focus in the fantasie macabre of the beautiful skull that might have been hers, which is as close as he can come to holding her in his hands again.

With the wisdom he has gleaned from his danse macabre life, the old chevalier has achieved resignation and the power to accept the "horror and humiliation" that weighed on him so heavily before. He can look upon his erstwhile poisoner seated contentedly with her great-granddaughters in a box at the opera, and he can find satisfaction in the ruin of a forest he sold to his neighbors because in his remorse he hears the Furies pursuing him and feels himself, as he did as a young man, at grips with the transcendent powers.

QUESTIONS FOR DISCUSSION

1. What is a chevalier? Why does Dinesen select such a quaint title for the old Baron von Brackel?
2. Study the second paragraph. What hints does it give about the story that ensues?
3. The chevalier says that the story of the woman who tried to poison him "has nothing to do with what I was going to tell you." Does it? If so, why does Dinesen have him enter this disclaimer?
4. Describe the relationship between the chevalier and his first mistress. Does he deserve the treatment he gets from her?

5. Comment on the chevalier's attitude toward the emancipation of
    women. Where, exactly, does he stand on this issue? Where
    does Dinesen stand?
6. At various points in the story, allusions are made to the
    Odyssey, Hamlet, Othello, several Greek tragedies, the legend
    of Joan of Arc, Genesis and the apocryphal story of Adam and
    Lilith, medieval philosophy, Darwin, Don Giovanni, the Arabian
    Nights, Romeo and Juliet, and the myth and the opera of
    Orpheus, not to mention a dozen other works, artists, poets,
    and historical events. What is the general effect of this
    broad context of allusion? What is the specific relevance of
    the material invoked?
7. What does the chevalier believe were the purpose and effect of
    the unnatural clothing styles worn by women in his youth? What
    disastrous confusion results for him?
8. Examine Dinesen's rendering of the night the chevalier and
    Nathalie spend together. What techniques do you find most
    effective in communicating a sense of the young man's rapture?
9. When the chevalier tries to account for his loss of Nathalie,
    he considers his moment of fear -- during which he wondered, "I
    am to pay for this; what am I to pay?" -- as a moment of weak-
    ness, a hamartia for which, like a tragic hero, he is being
    hounded by Nemesis. What is the explanation for his fear? In
    what sense has it caused him to lose Nathalie? Is he justified
    in regarding his experience in these terms?
10. When Nathalie asks for twenty francs, the chevalier says,
    "reality was shown to me, waste as a burnt house. This was the
    end of the play." Explain this response. Is it accurate? In
    this context, what is his reason for paying her?
11. For a time the chevalier is desolate, but "All this is now a
    long time ago." How does he now regard his youthful sufferings?

TOPICS FOR WRITING

Critical Essays

1. Dinesen's use of two narrators.
2. The function of the digressions in "The Old Chevalier."
3. "The Old Chevalier" as a study of old age.
4. The presence of death in Dinesen's "The Old Chevalier" and in
    Joyce's "The Dead."

Exercise for Reading

1. Study the literary allusions and references to history, philo-
    sophy, and religion that abound in the story. Select one or
    more that interest you and write a paragraph on each showing as
    many meaningful parallels and contrasts to the story of the old
    chevalier as you can.

617-647 (text pages)

Related Subject

1. Narrate Nathalie's encounter with the chevalier from her point
   of view, perhaps as she might have reported it to Marie the
   next day, perhaps as she might have recalled it years later.

SUGGESTED READINGS

Johannesson, Eric O. The World of Isak Dinesen. Seattle: University of Washington Press, 1961. Pp. 29, 41-42, 95-99.

Langbaum, Robert. The Gayety of Vision: A Study of Isak Dinesen's
Art. New York: Random House, 1965. Pp. 77-81.

Thurman, Judith. Isak Dinesen: The Life of a Storyteller. New
York: St. Martin's Press, 1982. Pp. 89, 149, 261-264, 301,
341.

Katherine Mansfield

"Bliss" (page 637)

The life that blooms in Bertha Young presses against the
restraints of "idiotic civilization" like a blossom bursting out of
its bud case. Through all of the incidents leading up to the
devastating revelation of the liaison between Harry and Pearl, Mansfield develops Bertha's flowerlike vulnerability. We are attracted
by her tolerant and amused appreciation of her husband and guests,
the delight she takes in her "absolutely satisfactory house and
garden," and her love for her Little B. But at the same time we
must feel a growing anxiety for this young woman who herself knows
that she is "too happy -- too happy!" She is so little in command
of her life that she must beg Nanny for a chance to feed her own
daughter; her catalogue of the wonderful things in her life dwindles
off into trivia ("their new cook made the most superb omelettes");
and her husband and "modern, thrilling friends" look to the skeptical
eye of the reader more like poseurs and hypocrites than the charming
and sincere eccentrics Bertha takes them for.

Mansfield defines Bertha's condition and the danger to which
it exposes her in the explicit symbol of the pear tree in bloom, to
which Bertha likens herself, and in the unsettling glimpse of the
cats, a grey one and its black shadow, that creep across the lawn
beneath it. On the telephone to Harry, Bertha tries and fails to
communicate her state of bliss, but she hopes that her fascinating
new "find," Pearl Fulton, with whom she feels a mysterious kinship,
will somehow be able to understand. In the moonlight the pear tree
resembles the silvery Pearl, just as in the daylight it matched
Bertha's green and white apparel, and as the two women gaze at it
together, Bertha feels that the ecstatic communion she has desired
is taking place. And in a sense it is, for the moment seems to

release in Bertha for the first time a passionate sexual desire for her husband that, as she too soon learns, is likewise shared by Pearl.

The reader winces as the long-anticipated blow falls at last, and Eddie Warren intones the line that might end a more cynical version of the story: "'Why Must it Always be Tomato Soup?' It's so <u>deeply</u> true, don't you feel? Tomato soup is so <u>dreadfully</u> eternal." But Mansfield will not leave it there. As the grey cat Pearl and the black cat Eddie slink off into the night, Bertha returns to the window to find the pear tree, an embodiment of the same energy and beauty that wells up within herself, standing "as lovely as ever and as full of flower and as still."

QUESTIONS FOR DISCUSSION

1. Define the impression of Bertha given by the opening section. What is the source of her bliss?
2. What is the function of the scene in which Bertha feeds Little B.? Comment on the way the section ends.
3. What does Bertha try and fail to say to Harry on the telephone?
4. What explains Pearl Fulton's limited frankness?
5. Do you agree that Harry's use of phrases like "liver frozen, my dear girl" or "pure flatulence" is an endearing, almost admirable quality?
6. Comment on the juxtaposition of the cats and the pear tree.
7. Can one be "too happy"? Explain.
8. Evaluate Bertha's summary of her situation. Does she indeed have "everything"?
9. Explain the line, "Her petals rushed softly into the hall. . . ."
10. What techniques does Mansfield use to characterize the Knights and Eddie Warren? What do you think of these people?
11. Comment on the possible implications of Harry's delayed arrival, followed shortly by Pearl Fulton.
12. Why is Bertha eager for Pearl to "give a sign"?
13. What transpires as Bertha and Pearl look at the pear tree?
14. Explain Harry's way of offering a cigarette to Pearl, and Bertha's interpretation of it.
15. Why does Bertha feel "that this self of hers was taking leave of them forever? as she bids farewell to her guests?
16. What is the effect of Eddie Warren's quoting a poem about tomato soup while the climax of the story takes place?
17. What <u>is</u> going to happen now?

TOPICS FOR WRITING

Critical Essays

1. Names in "Bliss."
2. The rebirth of Bertha Young.
3. Mansfield's use of light and color.

637-653 (text pages)

Exercise for Reading

1. The story is divided by white spaces into a number of sections.
   On your first reading, stop at each one of these spaces and
   write a few sentences addressed to Bertha Young. What would
   you say to her at each of those moments? When you have finished
   the story, review your previous advice and write one more
   letter to Bertha in response to her concluding question.

Related Subject

1. Study the way Mansfield characterizes Harry, the Knights, Eddie,
   and Pearl. Then write a character sketch of your own using
   some of the same techniques and devices.

SUGGESTED READINGS

Berkman, Sylvia. Katherine Mansfield: A Critical Study. New Haven,
    Conn.: Yale University Press, 1951. Pp. 156, 164, 180, 186-
    187, 192, 195.

Daly, Saralyn R. Katherine Mansfield. Twayne's English Authors
    Series, No. 23. Pp. 23, 80-81, 88, 120.

Katherine Mansfield

"The Doll's House" (page 647)

Mansfield's story is so masterfully constructed that it may at
first seem impenetrable to discussion. But, like the doll's house
itself, it swings open easily at the first question, revealing its
inner riches. It is enough to ask what happens and trace the plot.
Our Else, whom nobody has ever seen smile and who "scarcely ever
spoke," is caused to smile and speak. It is her glimpse of the
lamp in the doll's house that stirs her to do so, and her responsive-
ness to it reflects her recognition of Kezia's difference from the
other Burnells and from the rest of the community that has made
scapegoats out of the Kelveys. Kezia's forbidden desire to show the
doll's house to the Kelveys arises from the same sensitivity that
causes her to single out the little lamp as the only "real" thing in
the jerry-built and foul-smelling doll's house, which no more
deserves the admiration it receives than the unfortunate Kelveys
deserve the scorn that is heaped upon them.

The doll's house aptly reflects the kind of community Mansfield portrays. Most of the people in it seem as stiff as the dolls,
"sprawled . . . as though they had fainted in the drawing room."
Like Kezia looking at the doll's house, the hovering narrative
consciousness singles out the one "real" thing in view in the story,
the Kelveys, whose unpretentiousness and love for each other contrast sharply with the egotistical pride and selfishness that

characterize the other girls and the adults in the story. Mansfield
does not place Kezia in the role of protagonist or heroine, but
through the eyes of Our Else she sees in her recognition of the
Kelveys as fellow human beings and in her generous impulse to open
her house to them a "little lamp" in an otherwise dark society.

QUESTIONS FOR DISCUSSION

1. Is the doll's house a piece of good quality work? Explain the
   girls' reaction to it. Why does Kezia single out the lamp?
2. What is the main value of the doll's house for Isabel? Why are
   the Burnell girls so highly favored among their schoolmates?
3. Explain the position of the Kelveys in the society of the story.
   Why does "the line [have] to be drawn somewhere"?
4. Comment on the younger Kelvey's name, "Our Else." Characterize
   the behavior of the Kelvey girls to each other and with the
   other girls.
5. What prompts Kezia to ask her mother if she can show the doll's
   house to the Kelveys? What prompts her finally to do so?
6. Why does Lena expect Lil Kelvey to be upset by her asking if
   she plans to be a servant when she grows up? Why does Lil
   just smile?
7. Explain the girls' behavior after Lena has "hissed, spitefully"
   at the Kelveys, "Yah, yer father's in prison!"
8. Comment on the passage in which Kezia watches the Kelveys grow
   from "two little dots" in the road as they come toward her.
9. What does the paragraph about Aunt Beryl reveal about her
   attitude toward the Kelveys? Is she representative of the
   society portrayed in the story?
10. What has been the result of Kezia's invitation for the Kelveys?
    What other possible conclusions might the story have arrived at?

TOPICS FOR WRITING

Critical Essays

1. Why there is no central character in "The Doll's House."
2. Mansfield's use of foreshadowing and repetition.
3. The lamp and the pear tree -- symbols of the self in "The Doll's
   House" and "Bliss."
4. Mansfield's narrative technique in "The Doll's House."
5. What Kezia has in common with the Kelveys.

SUGGESTED READINGS

Berkman, Sylvia. _Katherine Mansfield: A Critical Study_. New Haven,
    Conn.: Yale University Press, 1951. Pp. 19, 88-89, 156, 195,
    201.

Daly, Saralyn. _Katherine Mansfield_. _Twayne's English Authors
    Series_, No. 23. New York: Twayne, 1965. Pp. 100-101.

647-669 (text pages)

Delany, Paul. "Short and Simple Annals of the Poor: Katherine Mansfield's 'The Doll's House.'" Mosaic, 10 (1976), 7-17.

Katherine Anne Porter

"María Concepción" (page 655)

This story will inevitably give rise to debates over the justice of the ending and over Porter's attitude toward her subject. Their futility may lead a class to confront some of the story's more basic issues. Juan's escape from execution as a deserter is no more deserved than María Concepción's escape from imprisonment for murdering María Rosa, but the reader may be inclined to feel indulgent in the former case and to be shocked at the latter. Juan's decision to quit the army is just as casual as his enlistment, and because the war itself is presented as pointless and grotesque, it seems hardly appropriate that he should lose his life for such a minor transgression. María Concepción, on the other hand, murders the young and attractive new mother in a considered, intentional way, fully conscious of the magnitude of her crime.

The tolerant, worldly Givens bails Juan out as he has bailed him out many times before. Givens laughs at the childlike irresponsibility and posturing of his head digger, but he stands somewhat in awe of María, whose nerve with her butcher knife gives him "the creeps." Givens's "fatherly indulgence," however, reinforces Juan's "primitive childish ways." Givens may be taken as a representative of modern civilization and hence as a potential surrogate for the reader, but his sympathy for Juan contributes to the disruption of social order in the village. María Concepción embodies that order. She grounds it in her relationship to her husband, which she has solemnized by a church wedding. María Concepción is bound to Juan Villegas on a level much deeper than love, and that bond enables her to forgive him everything while at the same time mercilessly destroying María Rosa, whom she blames for having violated it. In murdering her rival, María Concepción sets a value on her marriage that awakens first Juan and eventually the villagers to a sense of what is truly important. As he realizes what his wife has done, "for the first time in his life Juan was aware of danger" -- the danger that his wife, whom he was all too happy to have deserted before, will be taken away from him. In the inquest before the gendarmes, María Concepción is silently tried before the jury of her community, which closes ranks around her, affirming not her innocence of the murder but the preemptive importance of the principles that have driven her to commit it. At the end, providing milk from her goat for a baby who, though she did not bear him, is incontrovertibly hers, María Concepción becomes a powerful symbol of the interdependence that enables human life to continue in spite of death.

QUESTIONS FOR DISCUSSION

1. Describe María Concepción as she is first introduced. What are her concerns? Do you find her attractive? Admirable?
2. Explain María Concepción's attitude toward her fowls. Is she cruel? Callous?
3. Why has María Concepción insisted on a church wedding? What does that insistence contribute to the meaning of the story? Is María Concepción a good Christian?
4. Contrast María Rosa with María Concepción. What is their difference in ages? Why does Juan Villegas leave his wife for María Rosa?
5. Can María Concepción's "careful sense of duty" be reconciled with her desire to "cut the throats of her man and that girl"?
6. Why does María Concepción find Givens "diverting"? What effect do Givens and his excavations actually have on the society of the village?
7. Can you explain why María Concepción's anger against Juan dies, while her anger against María Rosa grows?
8. Evaluate Juan's military "adventure" with María Rosa.
9. Explain María Concepción's behavior and the attitude of the villagers toward her during the months Juan is away. Does she have anything to learn?
10. Why does Juan strut and swagger so after Givens releases him from the military authorities? Why does he return to María Concepción?
11. Why does Porter withhold the information that María Concepción is going to kill María Rosa until well after she has done so? How would the reader's response differ if Porter were more explicit sooner?
12. Why does Juan Villegas sense danger "for the first time in his life" when he realizes what María Concepción has done? Explain his behavior and feelings from that point to the end of the story.
13. Why does María Concepción no longer feel fear after she sees Maria Rosa's corpse?
14. Why do the villagers cover for María Concepción? Are they right to do so?
15. María Concepción has been called (by M. M. Liberman) "the very type of unevolved femaleness, as much of the earth as on it, carrying within her the future of race and sex." If María Concepción symbolizes the female in some fundamental way, what do you think Porter is implying about woman, man, and human life?

TOPICS FOR WRITING

Critical Essays

1. María Concepción and María Rosa -- Porter's two Marys.
2. The clash between primitive and modern civilization in "María Concepción."

655-679 (text pages)

3. Kipling's Gracie Ashcroft ("The Wish House"), Anderson's Mrs.
   Grimes ("Death in the Woods"), and Porter's María Concepción.

Related Subject

1. Research the topic of justifiable homicide. Are there or have
   there been any societies whose legal code would acquit María
   Concepción?

SUGGESTED READINGS

Johnson, James William. "Another Look at Katherine Anne Porter."
In Katherine Anne Porter" A Critical Symposium. Edited by
Lodwick Hartley and George Core. Athens: University of
Georgia Press, 1969. Pp. 83-96, especially p. 92. Originally
published in Virginia Quarterly Review, Autumn 1960.

Liberman, M. M. Katherine Anne Porter's Fiction. Detroit: Wayne
State University Press, 1971. Pp. 63-69.

Katherine Anne Porter

"Flowering Judas" (page 670)

From its title onward, "Flowering Judas" lends itself all too
readily to the kind of explication that leaps from allusion or
symbol to abstract interpretation and leaves the story's literal
narrative and the reader who strives to respond to it out of the
action. To avoid this process, which is mystifying to students and
reductive to the text, try to direct discussion first of all toward
character and situation.

Laura's three suitors are variously repellent. The revolutionary hero, ridiculous in his machismo and strings of silver buttons,
is as childish as the schoolchildren with whom Laura vaguely
confuses him. The young man to whom she throws a rose in the
mistaken intention of dismissing him is equally stereotypical and
contemptible in his mournful, dogged pursuit. Braggioni himself is
more complex but even less attractive. He is a "professional lover
of mankind," but Porter is at pains to show that he is cruel to his
followers, devious, egotistic, self-indulgent, and insofar as he
seems animated by any sincere revolutionary vision, fixated entirely
on the violent destruction of the old order rather than the creation
of a new society. Laura has little reason to love any of these men,
but could she do so, as the remarkable reunion between Braggioni and
his wife suggests, she would find them, and herself, transformed.

Laura, however, despite her swelling breasts and programmatic
dedication, can love no one, not even the children who bedeck her
desk with flowers. Out of fear of the nameless violent disaster
that she feels awaiting her, she says no to everything and closes

94

herself away from the world in her "not purposely nun-like" clothing
and demeanor. While Laura feels "that she has been betrayed irre-
parably" by the failure of her life as a revolutionary to live up to
her expectations, she may justly be accused of causing her own
disillusionment by repressing her desires at every stage. At the
start of the narrative we see her "avoiding her own house" and
entertaining Braggioni when she does not wish to. She has put herself in "the uniform of an idea" and, uninvited, "promised herself
to this place." But the natives "cannot understand why she is in
Mexico," and Braggioni himself "cannot understand why she works so
hard for the revolutionary idea unless she loves some man who is
in it."

Laura is at home neither in her chosen country nor in the
revolutionary faith that she has substituted for her former religion;
for she has, as she realizes at the outset of her dream, confused
love with revolution, supplanting one with the other. Those who need
to draw upon her -- the suitors and the schoolchildren no less than
the incarcerated revolutionaries -- become prisoners, and since she
deals with them out of policy rather than love, the only help she can
bring them is negation. The dream, however, reveals that Laura is
the true "poor prisoner," locked within herself and in deep need of
communion. When she partakes of the refreshing blossoms, however,
the meaning of the sacrament bursts into her mind, and for a final
time she denies it. For Laura, to devour the human body and blood
represented by the blossoms of the Judas tree would be to acknowledge
her need for love and for forgiveness of her betrayal, of others and
of herself, as a purveyor of lies, pills, and death in loveless
service to a phony cause.

Porter's invocation of Judas Iscariot's betrayal of Jesus in the
New Testament, of the legend of the Judas or redbud tree into which
Judas is said to have been metamorphosed, of the theological doctrines of the Crucifixion and Holy Communion, and of T. S. Eliot's
"Gerontion" (from which she takes the title out of a context of
similar concerns), provides a perspective on Laura's situation that
defines its meaning and broadens its implications. Rather than just
a frightened gringita entangled in the incomprehensible politics of
revolutionary Mexico, Laura comes to represent the human soul
paralyzed in the face of a world whose only reality appears to the
disillusioned eye to be death. When Laura cries "No!" to Eugenio's
declaration in her dream, she rejects participation both in that
enactment of death and in the life it stems from. While it is easy
enough to remark that Judas should have overcome his fear with faith
and love, a survey of Laura's predicament, or of Gerontion's, suggests how hard it may be to do so.

QUESTIONS FOR DISCUSSION

1. Define the relationship between Laura and Braggioni. Why does
    she tolerate his attentions? Why does he tolerate her refusal
    of his advances?

2. Describe Braggioni physically. What do his body and appearance reveal about the revolution he leads?
3. List the "romantic errors" of which Laura is guilty. In what "set of principles" has she "encased herself"?
4. Laura confuses the prisoners she visits with the schoolchildren she teaches. Why?
5. To what extent does Laura's physical attractiveness contribute to her malaise?
6. Explain why Laura rejects "knowledge and kinship" and why saying no gives her strength and a feeling of safety.
7. Why is Laura "waiting for tomorrow with a bitter anxiety as if tomorrow may not come"?
8. What is the effect of the reunion scene between Braggioni and his wife on our impression of Laura?
9. What does Laura's dream suggest about her attitude toward Eugenio?

TOPICS FOR WRITING

Critical Essays

1. Laura's "notorious virginity": Why she will not surrender to love.
2. Christ parallels and Christ parodies in "Flowering Judas."
3. Laura and Maria Concepcion as representatives of contrasting cultures.
4. Porter's use of flashbacks and telescoped chronology in "Flowering Judas."

Exercise for Reading

1. As you read, make a list of questions that do not seem to have immediate answers, such as "Why is Laura tolerant of Braggioni?" or "Why does she have no lover?" or "Why is she in Mexico?" When you encounter a potential or partial answer, note it under the appropriate question. When you finish, read over your questions and answers. Did your center of interest shift? Are any questions left unanswered? Are they important?

Related Subject

1. Study a notorious traditional villain or failure -- from the Bible, from classical epic or tragedy, or from Shakespeare, for example. Imagine him or someone like him in a modern setting, and try to understand his motives. Does his behavior take on new dimensions of meaning?

SUGGESTED READINGS

Liberman, M. M. Katherine Anne Porter's Fiction. Detroit: Wayne State University Press, 1971. Pp. 70-79.

West, Ray B., Jr. "Symbol and Theme in 'Flowering Judas.'" In Katherine Anne Porter: A Critical Symposium. Edited by Lodwick Hartley and George Core. Athens: University of Georgia Press, 1969. Pp. 120-128. Originally published in Accent, Spring 1947.

James Thurber

"The Secret Life of Walter Mitty" (page 681)

Like a good joke, a successful comic story may be easy to enjoy but hard to explain. Thurber has rendered his hero so convincingly that Walter Mitty has long since entered the popular vocabulary as a shorthand term for a certain personality type. The triumph of the story does not comes, however, at the expense of the henpecked and bullied daydreamer. Stephen A. Black rightly points out that Mitty's escapism risks a denial of the self in its retreat from reality, but it is important to note that Mitty's fantasy life, despite its dependence on pulp fiction cliches, is just as real on the page as his (equally stereotypic) impatient and condescending wife, the officious policeman, and the insolent parking-lot attendant. Thus the reader may respond with admiration to Mitty's imaginary competence, courage, and grace under pressure. Throughout the story Thurber uses things from the real environment to trigger Mitty's fantasies, but he also shows that the fantasies can have an impact on his actual life. The phrase "You miserable cur" reminds Mitty of the forgotten puppy biscuit. Near the end, after the sergeant tells "Captain Mitty" that "It's forty kilometers through hell, sir," Mitty has his life in Connecticut in mind when he musingly replies, "After all, . . . what isn't?" In his fantasy, "the box barrage is closing in," but Mitty is just as courageous in standing up to the salvo of questions and criticism launched moments later by his wife, which elicits his vague remark, "Things close in." As he stands against the drugstore wall in the Waterbury rain to face the imaginary firing squad, the reader can agree that he is "Walter Mitty the Undefeated" -- because his inner life remains, for his banal tormentors, "inscrutable to the last."

QUESTIONS FOR DISCUSSION

1. What is Walter Mitty actually doing in the first paragraph of the story?
2. Explain Mitty's attitude toward his wife. Why does she insist that he wear gloves and overshoes?
3. How familiar is Walter Mitty with medical terminology? What is the purpose for Mitty of his medical fantasy?
4. Do Mitty's fantasies help or hinder him in dealing with reality?
5. Explain Mitty's words, "Things close in."
6. Where do you think Walter Mitty gets his ideas of heroism? Is there any sense in which his real life can be called heroic?

681-689 (text pages)

TOPICS FOR WRITING

Critical Essays

1. Walter Mitty's final wish.
2. The romantic and the banal: The basis of Thurber's humor in
   "The Secret Life of Walter Mitty."

Exercise for Reading

1. Find as many connections as possible between Mitty's actual
   experiences and his fantasies. How are they related? What do
   you think will be the consequence, if any, of Mitty's imaginary
   execution?

SUGGESTED READING

Black, Stephen A. James Thurber -- His Masquerades: A Critical
    Study. The Hague: Mouton, 1970. Pp. 15, 18-19, 32, 42-43,
    49-50, 54, 56, 119.

Morseburger, Robert E. James Thurber. Twayne's United States
    Authors Series, No. 62. New York: Twayne, 1964. Pp. 18-19,
    44-48, 123, 151-152.

Isaac Babel

"My First Goose" (page 687)

The narrator is an outsider, a lonely and hungry intellectual
who wins a meal and the acceptance of the Cossacks by killing the old
peasant woman's goose. He does it roughly, demonstrating that he
will "get on all right" at the front. The act is portrayed partly
as a rape, partly as a crucifixion. The quartermaster tells him,
"you go and mess up a lady, and a good lady too, and you'll have the
boys patting you on the back," and that is what he does, trampling
her goose under his boot and plunging his sword into it while she
repeats, "I want to go and hang myself," and he says, "Christ!"
But the narrator recoils from his self-debasement: The night that
enfolds him resembles a prostitute, the moon decorating it "like a
cheap earring." Lenin says there is a shortage of everything, and
though Surovkov believes that Lenin strikes straight at the truth
"like a hen pecking at a grain," the narrator uses the spectacles of
his learning to discern "the secret curve of Lenin's straight line,"
the hidden purpose of the speech. The narrator, too, has taken an
apparently bold and forthright step in killing the goose, but the
secret curve of his straight line has been to gain acceptance by
the Cossacks and a share of their dinner, which reminds him of his
home. As he sleeps with his new friends he dreams of women, just as
he saw female beauty in the long legs of Savitsky; but in taking his

first goose he has messed up a good lady and stained his heart with
bloodshed, and his conscience is not at peace.

QUESTIONS FOR DISCUSSION

1. Describe Savitsky. What is the narrator's attitude toward him?
   Why does Babel begin the story with this character, who never
   reappears?
2. What advice does the quartermaster give? Does the narrator
   follow it?
3. Why are the narrator's "specs" an object of derision? Who else
   in the story wears glasses?
4. Why does the Cossack throw the narrator's trunk out at the gate?
5. When the narrator first tries to read Lenin's speech he cannot
   concentrate. Why?
6. How does the narrator win the respect of the Cossacks?
7. Explain the difference between Surovkov's understanding of
   Lenin's speech and the narrator's.
8. Explain the last sentence. What is the narrator's feeling about
   himself? About the situation he is in?
9. "Lenin writes that there's a shortage of everything." Of what
   is there a particular shortage in the story?

TOPICS FOR WRITING

Critical Essays

1. The function of sexual imagery in "My First Goose."
2. Why Babel's narrator stains himself.
3. The effect of Babel's extreme brevity in "My First Goose," and
   the way it is achieved.

Exercise for Reading

1. Before beginning to read "My First Goose," write your prediction
   of what its subject might be on the basis of its title alone.
   Write a second guess as well. After reading the story, review
   your predictions. To what extent were the expectations aroused
   by the title -- even if they were not confirmed -- relevant to
   an understanding of Babel's narrative?

SUGGESTED READINGS

Carden, Patricia. The Art of Isaac Babel. Ithaca, N. Y.: Cornell
    University Press, 1972. Pp. 97, 100, 110, 130-131.

Falen, James E. Isaac Babel: Russian Master of the Short Story.
    Knoxville: University of Tennessee Press, 1974. Pp. 142-145.

Isaac Babel

"Guy de Maupassant" (page 690)

Direct attention to the brief remark on this story included in the headnote on page 686. Students will readily locate many of the reminders of his own mortality to which the narrator is oblivious, from the first sentence on. Not only is he "half-starved" and given to spending time at the morgue looking for news, he also refuses a safe job as a clerk, which could sustain him. He prefers instead the attractions of the Bendersky household, which is built on war profits and haunted by the "high-breasted maid" whose air of "petrified lewdness" combines sex and death in a remarkable paradox.

Raïsa Bendersky herself is hardly petrified, but her passion for Maupassant leads the narrator ever closer to the recognition that ends the story. It is no accident that Babel cites "Miss Harriet" (a story whose similar theme is discussed earlier in this manual, on page   ), as the first one to be translated. Maupassant's works look to the narrator like a "magnificent grave," and Raïsa's charms become entwined for him with images of violence and death: He sees scars on her back, and as she spreads her arms in surrender he imagines a crucifix. Even his dreams and fantasies speak the darker truth to him. At the beginning of his collaboration with Raïsa the narrator dreams of the washerwoman: "We almost destroyed each other with kisses." When he visits her in the morning he sees a sexless, aged woman. After making love with Raïsa, the narrator walks home in self-willed drunkenness through a fog that "amputated the legs. . . ."

The fog serves as one token of the illusions the narrator not surprisingly prefers to the dark truth that will finally dawn on him. Other indications are supplied by Bendersky, whose dependence on death for his profits has driven him entirely out of touch with reality forever; and by Kazantsev, who lives in a Spain of his imagination, despite the grim wartime St. Petersburg that surrounds him, some of whose hungry victims he takes into his home. But Kazantsev's romanticism has some of the dignity and wisdom of Don Quixote, with whom he is associated in the last scene, and he feels not only admiration but also horror at the narrator's recklessness in turning down the clerk's job. By contrast, until the grim facts of Maupassant's fate begin to instruct him, the narrator's attitudes are callow posturing. Only one who has not yet become aware of death could berate Tolstoy so vehemently for his fear of it.

QUESTIONS FOR DISCUSSION

1. What is the narrator's condition at the beginning of the story?
2. To what extent can the narrator take credit for the good fortune he experiences?
3. What do Kazantsev and Don Quixote (whose adventures Kazantsev has fallen asleep reading at the end of the story) have in common?

4. Explain Kazantsev's dual response to the narrator's refusal of a job as a clerk.
5. What impression is the Bendersky house intended to convey? What is the truth about it?
6. Discuss the narrator's comments on literary style. Is his military imagery appropriate? Comment on Raïsa's reaction, and the maid's.
7. Of his description of his childhood to Raïsa, the narrator remarks, "To my amazement the story turned out to be very sordid." Explain.
8. When Raïsa brings out the Muscatel '83, she says, "My husband will kill me when he finds out." Discuss the implications of that remark.
9. How does Maupassant's story "L'Aveu" contribute to the progress of relations between the narrator and Raïsa?
10. What effect does the narrator's clumsiness as he lurches toward Raïsa's armchair have on the tone of the passage? Why can he nonetheless report that "the white mare of my fate went on at a walking pace"? Where will that mare eventually lead him?
11. Comment on the implication of the term Babel uses to describe Raïsa's response: "'You are funny,' growled Raïsa."
12. After living out a parallel to one of Maupassant's stories, the narrator, who prides himself on his ability to recapture the great master's style, learns some facts about his life. What is their effect on him? Why do you think Babel chooses to quote, "Monsieur de Maupassant va s'animaliser"?

TOPICS FOR WRITING

Critical Essays

1. Babel's use of literary allusions.
2. Maupassant's "Miss Harriet" and Babel's "Guy de Maupassant."
3. Babel's control of tone in "Guy de Maupassant."

Exercise for Reading

1. Read Babel's story in conjunction with Maupassant's "Miss Harriet" and Tolstoy's "The Death of Ivan Ilych." Specify their similarities of theme.

Related Subject

1. Write a narrative about an occasion when you tried to imitate some fictional character, legendary author (Kerouac? Hemingway?), or film star. What did you learn from the experience?

SUGGESTED READINGS

Carden, Patricia. The Art of Isaac Babel. Ithaca, N. Y.: Cornell University Press, 1972. Pp. 115, 207-210.

Hallett, R. W. _Isaac Babel_. Russian Literary Profiles, No. 2.
    Letchworth, England: Bradda Books, 1972. Pp. 29, 119-121.

F. Scott Fitzgerald

"Babylon Revisited" (page 697)

"Babylon Revisited" develops a paradox about the past: It is
irretrievably lost, but it controls the present inescapably.
Charlie Wales revisits the scenes of "the big party" carried on by
stock-market rich Americans in Paris during the 1920s -- a party at
which he has been one of the chief celebrants -- and shakes his head
over how much things have changed. His memories of those times come
into focus only gradually, and as they do his nostalgia modulates to
disgust. His guilt-ridden desire to repudiate his past behavior
reaches a peak _not_ when his negotiations to get his daughter back
remind him that he brought on his wife's pneumonia by locking her out
in the snow, but only when Lorraine's _pneumatique_ reminds him that
for several years his life was given over to trivial foolishness.
For a man trying to reestablish himself as a loving and responsible
father, the memory of harming his wife in wild anger at her flirtation with "young Webb" is less embarrassing than the memory of
riding a stolen tricycle all over the Étoile with another man's wife.

The problem for Charlie Wales is that his past -- for the
moment embodied in the pathetic relics Duncan and Lorraine -- clings
to him despite his efforts to repudiate it. The reader (like Marion)
is inclined to fear that Charlie might return to his past ways, but
Charlie is not tempted by Lorraine or by the lure of alcohol. His
lesson has been learned, but that does not prevent the past from
destroying his plans for the future. Or perhaps, as David Toor
argues, it is Charlie who clings to the past; perhaps he ambivalently
punishes himself out of a guilt he refuses to acknowledge, as when he
sabotages his campaign to get Honoria from the Peterses by leaving
their address for Duncan with the bartender at the Ritz. As the
story ends, history is repeating itself. Just as Charlie caused
Helen's sickness, the inopportune arrival of his old friends has
sickened Marion. As a result he loses Honoria, at least for six
months of her fast-waning and irretrievable childhood -- just as he
has lost Helen for good.

QUESTIONS FOR DISCUSSION

1. Why does Fitzgerald begin the story with what seems to be the
    end of a conversation that then begins when Charlie walks into
    the bar in the next paragraph?
2. As Charlie rides through Paris on his way to see his daughter,
    he thinks, "I spoiled this city for myself." What reason might
    Fitzgerald have for treating this subject so mildly and in such
    vague terms here?

3. Characterize the Peters family. To what extent are we to approve of their attitudes?
4. What is the effect of Charlie's repeatedly taking "only one drink every afternoon"? Does the reader expect him to regress into alcohol abuse?
5. What does Charlie's brief encounter with the woman in the brasserie contribute to the story?
6. Why does Charlie identify the fine fall day as "football weather"?
7. Discuss the impact of the appearance of Duncan and Lorraine after Charlie's lunch with Honoria.
8. Why is Marion reluctant to release Honoria to her father? Why is Charlie able to win her consent, temporarily?
9. When Marion suggests that Charlie may have caused Helen's death, "an electric current of agony surged through him," but Lincoln says, "I never thought you were responsible for that." Was he? What does Charlie himself think? Explain his reaction.
10. Explain Charlie's reaction to Lorraine's pneumatique. Why does he ignore it? Why does that tactic fail?
11. Why does Fitzgerald introduce the arrival of Duncan and Lorraine precisely where he does, and in the way he does?
12. What does Paul mean when he supposes that Charlie "lost everything [he] wanted in the boom" by "selling short"? What does Charlie mean when he replies, "Something like that"?
13. Explain the irony of Charlie's present financial success, apparently unique among his old friends.
14. What does the title mean?

TOPICS FOR WRITING

Critical Essays

1. Fitzgerald's use of recurring motifs and foreshadowing.
2. Charlie Wales -- a study of remorse.
3. Techniques of characterization in "Babylon Revisited" -- the secondary characters.
4. Charlie's daughter's name as the key to his underlying motives.

Exercise for Reading

1. After reading each of the five sections of the story, write a paragraph giving your assessment of Charlie Wales and your prediction of what will happen in his future life. Is there consistency, or a progression, in your judgments?

SUGGESTED READINGS

Gallo, Rose Adrienne. F. Scott Fitzgerald. Modern Literature Monographs. New York: Ungar, 1978. Pp. 101-105.

Gross, Seymour. "Fitzgerald's 'Babylon Revisited.'" College English, 25 (1963), 128-135.

694-722 (text pages)

Male, Roy R. "'Babylon Revisited': The Story of the Exile's
    Return." Studies in Short Fiction, 2 (1965), 270-277.

Toor, David. "Guilt and Retribution in 'Babylon Revisited.'" In
    Fitzgerald/Hemingway Annual, 1973. Edited by Matthew J.
    Bruccoli and C. E. Frazer Clark, Jr. Washington, D.C.:
    Microcard Editions, 1974. Pp. 155-164.

William Faulkner

"A Rose for Emily" (page 715)

Few stories, surely, differ more on a second reading than does
"A Rose for Emily," which yields to the initiate some detail or
circumstance anticipating the ending in nearly every paragraph. But
Faulkner sets the pieces of his puzzle in place so coolly that the
first-time reader hardly suspects them to fit together into a picture
at all, until the curtain is finally swept aside and the shocking
secret of Miss Emily's upstairs room is revealed. Faulkner makes it
easy to write off the episodes of the smell, Miss Emily's denial of
her father's death, the arsenic, and the aborted wedding (note the
shuffled chronology) as the simple eccentricities of a pathetic old
maid, to be pitied and indulged. The impact of the final scene
drives home the realization that the passions of a former generation
and its experience of life are no less real or profound for all their
being in the past -- whether we view them through the haze of sentimental nostalgia, as the Confederate veterans near the end of the
story do, or place them at an aesthetic distance, as the townspeople
do in the romantic tableau imagined in section II.

    In his interviews with students at the University of Virginia
(excerpted in Part Two, p. 1180), Faulkner stressed Miss Emily's
being "kept down" by her father as an important factor in driving
her to violate the code of her society by taking a lover, and he
expressed a deep human sympathy for her long expiation for that sin.
In the narrative consciousness of the story, however -- the impersonal "we" that speaks for the communal mind of Jefferson -- Miss
Emily Grierson is a town relic, a monument to the local past to be
shown to strangers, like the graves of the men slain at the battle
of Jefferson or the big houses on what long ago, before they put the
sidewalks in, used to be the "most select street." Because all
relics are to a degree symbolic, one should not hesitate to take up
the challenge found in Faulkner's ambiguous claim, quoted in the
headnote, that "the writer is too busy . . . to have time to be
conscious of all the symbolism that he may put into what he does or
what people may read into it." Miss Emily, for example, may be
understood to express the part of southern culture that is paralyzed
in the present by its inability to let go of the past, even though
that past is as dead as Homer Barron, and even though its reality
differed from the treasured memory as greatly as the Yankee paving
contractor -- "not a marrying man" -- differs from the husband of
Miss Emily's desperate longings. Other details in Faulkner's

104

economical narration fit this reading: the prominence of Miss
Emily's iconic portrait of her father; her refusal to acknowledge
changing laws and customs; her insistence that the privilege of
paying no taxes, bestowed on her by the chivalrous Colonel Sartoris,
is an inalienable right; her dependence on the labors of her Negro
servant, whose patient silence renders him an accomplice in her
strange crime; and not least, her relationship of mutual exploitation
with Homer, the representative of the North -- a relationship that
ends in a morbid and grotesque parody of marriage. In this context,
the smell of death that reeks from Miss Emily's house tells how the
story judges what she stands for, and the dust that falls on everything brings the welcome promise of relief.

But Faulkner will not let it lie. Seen for what she is, neither
romanticized nor trivialized, Miss Emily has a forthright dignity
and a singleness of purpose that contrast sharply with those representatives of propriety and progress who sneak around her foundation
in the dark spreading lime or knock on her door in the ineffectual
effort to collect her taxes. And as the speechless townsfolk tiptoe
aghast about her bridal chamber, it is Miss Emily's iron will,
speaking through the strand of iron-gray hair that lies where she has
lain, that has the final word.

QUESTIONS FOR DISCUSSION

1. The story begins and ends with Miss Emily's funeral. Trace the
   chronology of the intervening sections.
2. Emily is called "a fallen monument" and "a tradition." Explain.
3. Why does the narrator label Miss Emily's house "an eyesore among
   eyesores"?
4. Define the opposing forces in the confrontation that occupies
   most of section I. How does Miss Emily "vanquish them"?
5. Discuss the transition between sections I and II. In what ways
   are the two episodes parallel?
6. Apart from her black servant, Miss Emily has three men in her
   life. What similarities are there in her attitudes toward them?
7. Why is Homer Barron considered an inappropriate companion for
   Miss Emily?
8. Consider Faulkner's introduction of the rat poison into the
   story in section III. What is the narrator's avowed reason for
   bringing it up?
9. At the beginning of section IV, the townspeople think Emily
   will commit suicide, and they think "it would be the best
   thing." Why? What is the basis of their error regarding her
   intentions?
10. Why do you think Miss Emily gets fat and develops gray hair
    when she does?
11. Why does Miss Emily's servant disappear after her death?
12. Describe Miss Emily's funeral before the upstairs room is
    opened. In what way does that scene serve as a foil to set off
    what follows?

13. Discuss the role of dust in the last few paragraphs of the
    story.
14. Why does Faulkner end the story with "a long strand of iron-
    gray hair"?

TOPICS FOR WRITING

Critical Essays

1. Various attitudes toward the past in "A Rose for Emily."
2. The meaning of time and Faulkner's handling of chronology.
3. Emily Grierson -- criminal, lunatic, or heroine?
4. The title of "A Rose for Emily."
5. "A Rose for Emily" and the history of the South.
6. Who is the narrator of "A Rose for Emily"?

Exercise for Reading

1. Were you surprised by the ending? On a second reading, mark
   all passages that foreshadow it.

Related Subjects

1. Imitate Faulkner by telling the events that lead up to a climax
   out of chronological order. What new effects do you find it
   possible to achieve? What problems in continuity do you
   encounter?

SUGGESTED READINGS

Hall, Donald. To Read Literature: Fiction, Poetry, Drama. New
    York: Holt, Rinehart and Winston, 1981. Pp. 10-16.

Heller, Terry. "The Telltale Hair: A Critical Study of William
    Faulkner's "A Rose for Emily.'" Arizona Quarterly, 28 (1972),
    301-318.

Howe, Irving. William Faulkner: A Critical Study. Second edition.
    New York: Vintage, 1962. P. 265.

Leary, Lewis. William Faulkner of Yoknapatawpha County. Twentieth-
    Century American Writers. New York: Thomas Y. Crowell, 1973.
    P. 136.

William Faulkner

"Dry September" (page 723)

Students' first responses to the story may focus on the horror
of lynching and the prejudiced mentality that precipitates and
condones it, which Faulkner so neatly portrays in the barbershop
and in the satisfied observation of Minnie's friends that there are
no Negroes on the square. The unlikely theoretical possibility that
Will Mayes is in fact guilty of something can find no substantiation
in the text, but it is worth discussing long enough to reach a sense
of how futile is any inquiry into what actually happened, in face of
the irrefutable a priori principle enunciated by McLendon: "Happen?
What the hell difference does it make? Are you going to let the
black sons get away with it until one really does it?"

In their bullish determination to lynch Will Mayes, McLendon
and his mob roll over the feeble resistance put up by Hawkshaw,
leaving him tumbled in the brush at the side of the road. Their
rage cannot have been triggered by the shock of a horrible crime,
since no clear report of any such crime has been made, so it must
arise from other sources. To find them, it is necessary to attend
to other elements of Faulkner's narrative.

The one overriding reality in the world of the story is the
drought: Two months of oppressive heat and no rain have built up a
tension in the town that has reached its breaking point. The rumor
of something happening spreads "like a fire in dry grass." To the
men in the barber shop, suffocating in their own breath that is
blown back on them by the fan, it offers a chance to burst out of
their stagnation and take some purposeful action. To those who do
not join the mob, it provides a juicy bit of salacious speculation.
The dead, drought-stricken landscape reflects another kind of
sterility in Jefferson. Hawkshaw remarks that women who never marry
get strange notions. They are not alone, the town as Faulkner
presents it is full of voyeurs. They may follow the movements of
women's hips with their eyes, but when they issue forth from their
male bastions of barbershop and front porch to do something, their
repressed sexuality emerges as violence.

The most unfortunate voyeur of all is Minnie Cooper, now
entering her own sexless September, who through years of frustration
and disappointment has been confined to watching a fantasy of life
unfold on the silver screen and in the streets around her. The
horrible irony that sets her off into a fit of hysterical laughter
is that, when the rumor has made her a sex object worth ogling once
again, the men of Jefferson who never knocked on her door are eager
to kill to defend her honor. The titillating speculations indulged
in by the town gossips become obscene when their relationship to
the lynching is revealed, but the hypocrisy of a whole system that
puts "white womanhood" on a pedestal in order to keep from having to
address the needs of individual women becomes clearest in the final
section, when McLendon returns to his buttoned-up home to berate his

defeated and brutalized wife for crossing his line of vision. His
night's escapade has brought him no relief, and the story closes in
an atmosphere of enraged paralysis even more uncomfortable than the
one in which it began.

QUESTIONS FOR DISCUSSION

1. The story begins in "the bloody September twilight." Explain
   the image and then trace the coordinate descriptions of the
   landscape, moon, and stars that punctuate the story. To what
   is the physical world being compared?
2. Characterize the quality of the argument that takes place in
   section I. What is the effect of all the uncompleted statements? Why does Butch exclaim, "Facts, hell!"? Explain
   McLendon's notorious question.
3. How does McLendon differ from the other identifiable men in the
   story? How does he manage to get the others to follow him?
4. Explain Minnie Cooper's disappointing life as surveyed in
   section II. Why has she ended up alone?
5. Why does Hawkshaw join the others in striking Will? Discuss
   the implications of this event.
6. Why does Minnie Cooper dress in "her sheerest underthings" for
   her trip to the movies? Why do the men now tip their hats and
   give her the eye as she walks past?
7. Explain Minnie's laughter.
8. What reasons might McLendon have for insisting that his wife
   not wait up for him?
9. Does this story have a central character? If not, what alternative techniques does Faulkner use to give it unity and focus?
10. A good story is supposed to have a beginning, a middle, and an
    end, or a complication, climax, and resolution. Apply these
    terms to the stories of Hawkshaw, Minnie, and McLendon respec-
    tively. What parallels do you notice?

TOPICS FOR WRITING

Critical Essays

1. "Dry September" -- Faulkner's waste land.
2. "Jees Christ, Jees Christ" -- the lynching of Will Mayes as a
   sacrificial rite.
3. Protecting white womanhood: The dehumanizing effect of the
   chivalric code in "Dry September."

Exercise for Reading

1. The parts of the story that are not told invite speculation.
   Imagine several possible ways the rumor might have got started.
   Would the differences change the main theme and effect of the
   story? Imagine the particulars of the lynching. Why might
   Faulkner have excluded them?

Related Subject

1. Imitating Faulkner's style as well as you can, write an episode
   about Hawkshaw's return to the barbershop that might be added
   to the story.

SUGGESTED READING

Faulkner, Howard. "The Stricken World of 'Dry September.'" Studies
   in Short Fiction, 10 (1973), 47-50.

Ernest Hemingway

"The Snows of Kilimanjaro" (page 734)

It should be easy to trigger the two simple symbolic recognitions that are necessary for a meaningful discussion of this story,
if they do not occur to students unprompted. To resolve the issues
raised by that discussion may, however, be somewhat harder.
Rereading the epigraph makes it clear where Harry is going, or
thinks he is going, in his final dream. Similarly, the passage about
a third of the way through the story in which Harry avows that his
reason for coming to Africa was "to work the fat off his soul," like
an athlete in training, should lead without difficulty to the notion
that the moral gangrene of Harry's soul is showing up in the physical
rotting of his body. Whether we respond more strongly to the irony
or the apotheosis of the ending, it is certain that Harry, when
confronted with imminent death, recognizes his debasement. Despite
the temptation to escape into comfort and oblivion, he does what he
can to go back to work by running over in his mind a series of
vignettes from his past that he has heretofore neglected to write.
The material he imagines is no escapist pulp, either. Most of his
memories confront him with instances of loss or death that relate to
his present situation, and all of them recall the times of his life
when he was coming to grips with his experiences -- of war and love,
of places and people and struggle -- firsthand, not insulated from
reality by the comforting ministrations of his rich wife.

It is the recognition of mortality that drives Harry forward in
the story. Whenever his affection for his wife (whether hypocritical
or sincere) lets him sink into the illusion that all may yet be well,
the vultures, the hyena, or the disembodied hallucinations of death
renew his awareness. That awareness reveals what is wrong with
being unproductive and merely comfortable, and it spurs Harry to
the best "writing" of his career.

The story begins with a quarrel, the true substance of which is
Harry's effort to remain in touch with the reality of what is
happening to him in the face of his wife's efforts to deny it. She
ignores the smell coming from his leg, expresses confidence that
help is on the way, and assures him, "You're not going to die."

Harry keeps his eye on the vultures. Surveying his life with new clarity of vision, he responds with self-contempt: He is a cock on the dunghill of love, making his living by a lie, and he is dead -- "already over." Further contemplation modifies these conclusions. He makes his living "with something else instead of a pen or a pencil," and he decides that it is "vitality" that he has sold, "in one form or another, all his life." This recognition helps him to a more balanced assessment of his marriage, which serves a serious purpose for his wife and, if destructive, involves "good destruction." But just as "he could feel the return of acquiescence in this life of pleasant surrender," the hyena reappears. Harry's next reverie takes his discovery of how he should live a crucial step forward. "He had been in it and he had watched it and it was his duty to write of it; but now he never would." He tries, however. Resolving that "the one experience that he had never had he was not going to spoil now," he spends the rest of lis life writing in his mind, ending with his supreme fiction, the fantasy of escape that turns into a flight to the pure, "square" snow-cap of Kilimanjaro, far above the teeming plain where things kill to eat, rot, and are devoured. Like the leopard in the epigraph, Harry has given the slip to the vultures and hyenas and made it to a place where no decay occurs, physical or moral.

But perhaps he has not, merely deluding himself with the trite dream of a narrow-escape ending while rotting to death in his cot. Who will read his latest works, his final effort to fulfill his duty as a writer? His wife does not take dictation, so the world will never get to see his splendid description of the African plain from aerial perspective, his profoundly shocking accounts of brutality, stupidity, and suffering in war, his evocations of the bittersweet postwar experience, his reminiscence of the melted weapons in a heap at his grandfather's ranch, his realization of life among the Paris poor, or his parable of the half-wit chore boy, whose fate eerily reflects what life may be for all of us. Except that of course we do read all these things, thanks to Hemingway, who struggles with the temptation to which Harry succumbs and finds that it does not always require mortal wound to resist.

QUESTIONS FOR DISCUSSION

1. What are the sides in the opening quarrel? What deeper needs lead Harry and his wife to take up the positions they do?
2. Discuss the causes of Harry's illness. Where should the blame be placed for his death? Should Harry and his wife have come to Africa?
3. Analyze the first italicized passage. Why does Harry remember these events? What lends the passage coherence?
4. Why does Harry emerge from this reverie in such a bitter mood? What important stage in the process of dying has Harry completed by the time he falls asleep? What step toward regeneration might he be said to have made? Trace his subsequent steps along both paths through the remainder of the story.

5. Evaluate the relationship between Harry and his wife. What are its bases? Summarize Harry's life before his present marriage as it is revealed in his reveries and recollections. In what ways does it resemble his wife's life?
6. Analyze the sequence of perceptions and recognitions that lead up to Harry's memories of Constantinople. Why does Harry realize he is going to die at the moment he does, rather than when he sees the hyena?
7. Why does Harry ask his wife if she can take dictation?
8. What is the import of the story of Williamson, the bombing officer?
9. Why does Hemingway narrate Harry's dying fantasy in such a vivid and realistic style? Why do you think he doesn't use italics? What peculiarities of the passage mark it as a dream?
10. Discuss the last section of the story. What is in store for Harry's widow?

TOPICS FOR WRITING

Critical Essays

1. Harry's reveries -- contrasts and parallels to his present experience.
2. The story of the half-wit chore boy: Harry's masterpiece.
3. The experience of dying in "The Snows of Kilimanjaro" and London's "To Build a Fire."

Exercise for Reading

1. Reread all the italicized segments in a block. Summarize the general tenor of Harry's experience before he sold out to his wife. Can we blame him? Then reread the section of the story that summarizes her experience. What are its similarities to Harry's? What does the Memsahib have left to learn?

Related Subject

1. Study Hemingway's descriptions of animals -- the vultures, hyenas, and game. Describe with similar accuracy an animal you can observe, but in such a way that it evokes a strong emotion.

SUGGESTED READINGS

Benson, Jackson J. Hemingway: The Writer's Art of Self-Defense. Minneapolis: University of Minnesota Press, 1969. Pp. 130-134.

Dussinger, Gloria R. "'The Snows of Kilimanjaro': Harry's Second Chance." Studies in Short Fiction, 5 (1967), 54-59.

Grebstein, Sheldon Norman. Hemingway's Craft. Crosscurrents/Modern Critiques. Carbondale: Southern Illinois University Press, 1973. Pp. 15-16, 21-22, 164.

MacDonald, Scott. "Hemingway's 'The Snows of Kilimanjaro': Three
    Critical Problems." Studies in Short Fiction, 11 (1974), 67-
    74.

Walz, Lawrence A. "'The Snows of Kilimanjaro': A New Reading."
    In Fitzgerald/Hemingway Annual 1971. Edited by Matthew J.
    Bruccoli and C. E. Frazer Clark, Jr. Washington, D.C.:
    Microcard Editions, 1971. Pp. 239-245.

Vladimir Nabokov

"First Love" (page 754)

Nabokov published "First Love" (also known as "Colette") both
as a short story and as a chapter of his autobiography, Speak,
Memory. This generic ambiguity is characteristic of the author,
whose fictions continually reveal the personal presence of Vladimir
Nabokov creating, sustaining, and participating in their imagined
worlds and whose major interest in "real experience" is the conscious
awareness of it that can shape it into a work of art. The process of
imaginative construction by which the mind orders the chaos of perception and salvages the beauty it conceives from the flux of time
is Nabokov's great theme; and since that process is also what his
writing does, his works mirror themselves, just as the world
apprehended mirrors the mind that apprehends it. "First Love" is a
story about the triumph of the narrator's memory in its effort to
imprison within the glass (or mirror) of words, like "the rainbow
spiral in a glass marble," the swirl of images associated with
Colette.

Colette herself does not appear, however, until section III.
Sections I and II bring us to her. In section I, Nabokov not only
takes the reader on a train trip from St. Petersburg to Biarritz,
he also takes his memory on a journey back in time toward its as yet
unspecified goal. From the outset he also explores the various
interpenetrations of reality and reflected or created images of it.
The model railroad car, an object of desire and admiration, is "not
for sale" and cannot be possessed, but to the boy riding in such a
car, the world flowing by outside -- which he can enter only
through "optical amalgamations" -- appears a toy, an image, a
reflection. Rolling through the "illegible" night, the narrator
finds repose by imagining himself the driver of the train whose
motion has nauseated him in the dining car, but the images of his
subsequent involuntary dream negate his sense of control: The
upended toy engine's wheels spin on, the glass marble rolls out of
reach.

The briefer section II marks our safe arrival in the recon-
structed past. The line of "maddening details" that began on
Nevski Avenue ends with some quaint snapshots of Biarritz, summer
1909. A butterfly, Nabokov's recurrent symbol of evanescent beauty
pursued and sometimes captured (the reader of Lolita will find other

familiar matter as well), floats along the beach and is caught, to be "preserved ever since in a glass cell of memory" as a piteous word -- legible, nonetheless -- in the Basque of Nabokov's remembering.

"My passion for Colette all but surpassed my passion for butterflies," the narrator recalls in section III, and that passion is based in part on pity. The narrator's efforts to protect Colette and to salvage her from her life by eloping with her and his butterfly net to the cinema reveal the same impulses in the child that stir the mature rememberer. With the shift to the present tense at the end of the idyll, the past seems to have been retrieved from time. When, surveying the toys he kept as souvenirs of the summer, the narrator recalls the "almost symbolic" penholder with its tiny window onto "a miraculous photographic view" of Biarritz, he is so delighted with what he (a penholder himself as he writes) has been able to accomplish that he celebrates with one more feat of memory, grasping the last maddening detail that has escaped him, the name of Colette's dog, which fills up his memory as the reflective water fills up the footprints on the beach.

But to seize a memory is at the same time to recognize the pastness of what is remembered. The stock symbolism that ends the next-to-last paragraph prepares the way for the definitive formulation of Nabokov's theme of memory with which the story ends. Changed now, a proper Parisienne as out of reach as if she inhabited a town glimpsed out the window of a moving train, Colette whirls by with her hoop and her sugared almonds -- even those delivered through an intermediary -- describing circles around a forceful symbol of the passage of youth into time, "a fountain choked with dead leaves." Although the narrator holds in his memory (a butterfly-like) "wisp of irridescence," Colette "dissolves among the slender shadows cast on the graveled path by the interlaced arches of its low looped fence" -- a less painful version of the earlier image of telegraph wires beaten down from their "triumphant swoop of pathetic elation" by the passage of time as revealed in motion through space.

QUESTIONS FOR DISCUSSION

1. Why are the details of the model railroad car "maddening"?
2. In the first four paragraphs, how does Nabokov convey the pastness of the era he is recalling?
3. Who are the "discarnate gamblers"? Explain other instances of the illusionary interpenetration of the world inside and outside the train.
4. The narrator loses his dinner because of motion sickness. Does his illness have an intellectual as well as a physical component?
5. Explore the implications of the term illegible as applied to the "headlong rush of the outside night."
6. Interpret the narrator's dream on the train.

7. Define the tone of section II.
8. When the narrator meets Colette, he knows "at once that this was the real thing." What are his motives for loving her?
9. What does it imply that the narrator and Colette make their romantic escape to the cinema, where they watch a film of a bullfight at San Sebastian?
10. The meerschaum penholder "now seems almost symbolic." What does it almost symbolize?
11. Why does the narrator think of footprints filling with "sunset water" as he remembers Floss?
12. Discuss the narrator's last meeting with Colette. What images and motives that were present earlier in the story recur here? Comment on the condition of the fountain. Dissolve is a technical term in cinematography. Is such a meaning relevant here?

TOPICS FOR WRITING

Critical Essays

1. Toys, souvenirs, and memory in "First Love."
2. Under glass -- Nabokov's effort to preserve beauty.
3. Maddening details -- "the diving details" in Nabokov's narrative art.

Exercise for Reading

1. "First Love" contains a network of recurrent or related images, patterns, and ideas. There are, for example, a real train, an imaginary train, a model train, and a toy train; a souvenir toy Eiffel Tower and a souvenir penholder with a window; a glass window, glass mirrors, a magnifying glass, and glass marbles. Reread the story and chart these and other recurrences and relationships on a large sheet of paper with lines showing interconnections. How much of the story can you work into your map? Revise and rearrange your diagram so that the elements most linked to others stand near the center of the paper. How accurate a representation of the story have you been able to design? What does it reveal about the story's structure and theme?

Related Subjects

1. Recall the sense images associated with an experience of your own. Write a reminiscence about that experience in which you proceed from image to image by means of associations, trying to circle in on the recollection that seems to you most important, saving it for last.

SUGGESTED READINGS

Stegner, Page. Escape into Aesthetics: The Art of Vladimir
    Nabokov. New York: William Morrow, 1966. Pp. 53-54.

Stuart, Dabney. Nabokov: The Dimensions of Parody. Baton Rouge:
    Louisiana State University Press, 1978. P. 186.

Williams, Carol T. "Nabokov's Dozen Short Stories: His World in
    Microcism." Studies in Short Fiction, 12 (1975), 213-222.
    Especially p. 216.

Jorge Luis Borges

"The End of the Duel" (page 762)

The particularly disquieting quality of this story derives from
the value-neutral framework in which it is presented. Neither the
narrative tone nor the structure of the plot allows the reader the
escape of outrage or even the release of laughter. Although the
narrator admits that the ending of the tale is "grim," that judgment
is counterbalanced by his pleasant memory of the circumstances under
which he heard it. And should the reader nonetheless be steeling
himself for an instance of that gothic horror which is made tolerable,
even delightful, by the very fact of its being extraordinary, Borges
hastens to introduce Juan Patricio Nolan, whose name and reputation
as a friendly rogue and prankster promise something to evoke a smile
of sentimental indulgence.

Silveira and Cardoso, too, tempt the reader's stock responses.
These colorful gauchos, caught up in the passion of their romantic
hatred, will surely, we suppose, demonstrate in meeting their fate
an innocent purity of motive or the dignity of the human heart; or
they may learn a profound lesson at the satiric hands of Nolan.
Such expectations are defeated. Not only does the feud, like most
feuds, lack adequate motive, it elicits no elevated behavior. Their
mutual hatred lends the only meaning there is to the lives of
Silveira and Cardoso, and nothing else in the story has any meaning
at all. Love does not conquer hatred here. Relations with La
Serviliana are casual and sordid compared to the gauchos' enduring
bond of animosity. Honor offers little more than love. The war
between the Reds and the Whites, explained in a foreign language,
is meaningless to Silveira and Cardoso. Killing a man is like
killing a cow, and they are capable of feeling only whispers of
fear. So limited are both men in imagination that as they line up
for their final competition they are "eager." Cardoso, however, has
previously expressed curiosity about "what it was like" to cut a
man's throat, and for this, perhaps, he is rewarded with victory --
though he is dead before he can savor it.

To summarize the gauchos' limitations, however, is to impose an unjustifiable scale of values on the story, for no one in it is any more sensitive. The executions are "expected"; the "understanding" Nolan gives in to the prisoners' desire to watch the race; and although as they await execution some of the condemned seem to be expressing emotions that call for a sympathetic response, when we hear their conversation it turns out that they simply envy the gauchos and resent one another.

The most appalling insinuation of the story is that Borges's vision may be true. The executioner's remark about birth pangs invites us to liken the race to life itself, which we stagger through already irrevocably doomed, no less than if our throats were slit, struggling for no permanent reward, in a world where, as Borges says of the feud, it is impossible to be sure "whether the events . . . are effects or causes." "This is what always happens," the author remarked of his story's ending in the interview quoted in Part Two (p. 1182): "We never know whether we are victors or whether we are defeated." The only hope Borges holds out for the reader who wishes to reject the universe portrayed in the story is that the narrative may be inaccurate, "since both forgetfulness and memory are apt to be inventive." To clutch at this straw, however, is to exchange absurdity for total indeterminacy, a bargain of questionable merit.

QUESTIONS FOR DISCUSSION

1. How appropriate are the memories the narrator associates with this anecdote?
2. What kind of man do we expect Juan Patricio Nolan to be on the basis of the description given in the second paragraph. Are our expectations confirmed?
3. Do the narrator's remarks on the provenance and uncertainty of the tale make the reader more or less receptive?
4. Why are Silveira and Cardoso such loyal enemies?
5. What impels the gauchos to join the Blancos' army?
6. Discuss Cardoso's request to his superior. Does he "handle himself like a man"?
7. The "proceedings" for the "expected" executions have been "arranged down to the last detail." Comment on Borges's diction.
8. Why do the other prisoners want to watch the race?
9. Why does Borges have the executioner mention birth pangs?

TOPICS FOR WRITING

Critical Essays

1. The tone of "The End of the Duel."
2. The race of Cardoso and Silveira as a symbol of human existence.
3. Is there a political theme in "The End of the Duel"? (See the interview with Borges in Part Two, p. 1182.)

Related Subjects

1. Revise the story so that it becomes comic. Then revise it again
   so that it becomes inspiring. Change it only as much as is
   necessary to achieve the desired effect. What changes do you
   find essential for each purpose?

SUGGESTED READING

McMurray, George R. Jorge Luis Borges. Modern Literature Mono-
    graphs. New York: Ungar, 1980. Pp. 21-23, 179, 189.

Jorge Luis Borges

"Borges and I" (page 765)

It is a nice challenge to read this piece, usually called a
sketch or a parable, as a short story. The narrator may be identi-
fied as the time-bound ongoing consciousness of Jorge Luis Borges.
His essence, like everyone's is change; his existence is flight;
and he is "destined to perish" because he lives only in an instant.
The problem for this narrative consciousness is that all his efforts
are expropriated by the accruing public identity known as "Borges,"
the imagined composite entity projected from his known works, past
and present. Because "Borges" is the sum of previous accomplishments, he cannot be identical with the subjective narrative
consciousness, locked as it is within the present moment. This
relationship of difference provides the story's conflict. By
writing, the subjective consciousness produces something lasting,
but as soon as this is written it becomes a work of the other
"Borges." Even the successful efforts of the writer to achieve
literary immortality, then, contribute to his extinction. And since
Borges believes that works of literature arise from and dissolve
into a vast impersonal tradition, the expropriation is complete: "I
lose everything." The resolution, however, involves a paradoxical
counterstatement. That it is impossible to tell whether "Borges"
or the personal consciousness is writing implies an identity between
the two that may be as comforting to the reader as it is disquieting
to Borges.

QUESTIONS FOR DISCUSSION

1. Why does the narrator learn about "Borges" through outside
   sources?
2. What is Borges's opinion of his public image?
3. Is Spinoza right? Explore the implications of that possibility.
4. Why did the stratagem of changing his interests fail?
5. Explain how the last sentence can be true.

765-779 (text pages)

TOPICS FOR WRITING

Critical Essays

1. "Borges and I" and Shakespeare's Julius Caesar.
2. Borges and every writer's dilemma.

Related Subject

1. Exchange a small collection of your writing, including a
   personal essay, with a fellow student. Write a short sketch
   defining the personality of the colleague whose writings you
   have read. Exchange these sketches. Do you recognize yourself?

SUGGESTED READINGS

Christ, Ronald J. The Narrow Act: Borges's Art of Allusion. New
   York: New York University Press, 1969. P. 93.

McMurray, George R. Jorge Luis Borges. Modern Literature Monographs. New York: Ungar, 1980. Pp. 113-114.

Sean O'Faolain

"How to Write a Short Story" (page 768)

     Some of the difficulties that the obtuse and self-preoccupied
Morgan perceives in making a short story out of Frank's experience
do pose serious problems for the writer. O'Faolain solves them by
the clever expedient of inventing Morgan, whose inquiries provide a
way to unify a narrative with its prologue and four sequels, and
whose misinterpretations and sentimental distortions prevent the
reader from falling into similar errors. Morgan's interest is first
aroused by an attraction to the same little boy that Bruiser loved,
and throughout the conversation he keeps wanting to write the story
with Bruiser as its romantic hero. His various failures to find a
literary cliché suitable to swallow up the experience of life
(C'est la vie"!) that Frank is confiding in him reveal the blindness
of this twenty-four-year-old innocent to the reality of the human
being sitting across the room from him. His inability to appreciate
the meaning of what Frank is telling him parallels his misappre-
hension of Maupassant as "a besotted Romantic at heart." One need
only glance at O'Faolain's critical commentary on Maupassant (in
Part Two, p. 1156) to recognize, for example, how tone-deaf Morgan
is to the irony in the title "An Idyll." In his innocence he
imagines that Frank's story will make an idyll, too, and when it
turns out instead to concern the homosexual rape of a child by his
trusted friend and the devastating consequences of that rape,
Morgan continues undeterred in his speculations about how to
transform the unpleasant event into "Art, Frank! Art!" -- something
comfortable and pretty, unthreatening and unreal.

"I wish I was a doctor," says the aspiring writer at one point, and he goes on to list a few doctors who have written well. In this story, too, the only good literary mind belongs to the doctor. Perhaps his profession has brought him into much closer contact with actual human suffering than the young librarian, but neither is Frank ignorant of books, as his allusion to Hamlet makes clear; he simply knows how to read them rather than to hide in them. Morgan listens to Frank's story in an entirely egocentric way, considering what he can use it for, assuming that Frank will be delighted if he does use it and disappointed if he does not, and projecting his own sentimentality onto the material. Only after the main events have been told does he recognize in Bruiser, with whom he has wanted to identify himself, "a character of no human significance whatever." When he allows that "the story becomes your story," Frank gently admits that he has always thought so. But Frank's powers of compassion justify his angelic appearance as a youth. He hopes that Bruiser knew a woman before he died; he spares Bruiser's posthumous reputation and his mother's feelings; and he even makes the best of Morgan's insensitivity and misguided enthusiasm by appreciating him as "a marvelous young fellow." It is this quality of compassion (empathy, "negative capability"), more than details, documents humaines, well-made plots, or Art, that makes for good fiction.

QUESTIONS FOR DISCUSSION

1. The story concerns a conversation between a young librarian and an elderly doctor. How important are their ages and occupations in their characterization?
2. Explain the doctor's response to Morgan's line, "It's not possible, Frank." Relate this gesture to the image with which the story ends.
3. How good a reader is Morgan of the books he treasures?
4. Trace references to imprisonment, walls, and canes throughout the story. Then trace references to women. How are the two sequences related?
5. Contrast O'Faolain's line, "The doctor rose and stood with his back to the fire staring fixedly in front of him," with Morgan's effort to narrate the same gesture. What does Morgan have to learn as a stylist? Is O'Faolain's sentence merely factual, devoid of emotion or symbolic import?
6. Why is "Bruiser" a better name than "Cyril" for the character who bears it?
7. Morgan remembers that Frank is a bachelor and thinks he may be a virgin. Why is he so wide off the mark? What reasons does the story offer for Frank's remaining a bachelor?
8. When Bruiser first kissed him, Rosy "thought I'd choke." What other references to eating and nausea appear in the story? Do they form a pattern?
9. What is the effect on the reader of Morgan's repeated intrusions into Frank's narrative with erroneous anticipations and comments?

10. Why does Morgan so badly misapprehend Maupassant's "An Idyll"? Does the answer to that question explain his responses to Frank?
11. What reasons apart from literary theory may Morgan have for disliking sequels? Why are the sequels so important to Frank?
12. Evaluate Morgan's efforts to place Frank at his ease by confessing his virginity and by offering to romanticize Frank's relationship with Brigitte.
13. Is Morgan's last erroneous description of Maupassant an accurate description of Morgan himself?
14. What does Frank gain from the evening?

TOPICS FOR WRITING

Critical Essays

1. Misunderstanding Maupassant: O'Faolain's "How to Write a Short Story" and Babel's "Guy de Maupassant." (See also Maupassant's "The String" and "Miss Harriet" and the commentary by O'Faolain on p. 1156.)
2. "He did not cane me" -- the imagistic unity of "How to Write a Story."
3. Morgan's role in the telling of Frank's story.

Exercise for Reading

1. Outline the plot of "How to Write a Short Story," showing that the unities of time, place, and action are observed.

Related Subject

1. Eavesdrop on a conversation, transcribing or making notes as much as you can. As soon as possible thereafter, write out what you remember in full. Study your transcription and your recollections of intonation, rhythm, and the like, and try to deduce the unstated attitudes, concerns, and objectives of each interlocutor. Sharpen your material into a sketch that reveals two different characters through their differing understandings of the subject or subjects about which they are conversing.

SUGGESTED READINGS

Bonaccorso, Richard. Review of Foreign Affairs and Other Stories, by Sean O'Faolain (1976). Eire/Ireland, 13 (Summer 1978), 135-136. (General commentary applicable to "How to Write a Short Story.")

Core, George. Review of Foreign Affairs and Other Stories, by Sean O'Faolain (1976). Sewanee Review, 84 (Winter 1976), ii-iv. Especially p. iv.

Langston Hughes

"Conversation on the Corner" (page 781)

Be sure to have students read the excerpt from Hughes's introduction to The Best of Simple (in Part Two, p. 1185), because it
defines Simple and the narrator (elsewhere named as Boyd, a writer)
as representatives of differing social conditions, recurrently
voicing appropriate attitudes, rather than individualized characters
whose unique fates are developed in the story. A fair analogy might
be the static personages of a comic strip or situation comedy, whose
behavior in any situation is predictable and who never seem to learn
from their experiences. Dagwood will always seek refuge in the
bathtub, oblivious to decades of interruptions. Likewise, the
narrator in "Conversation on the Corner" keeps asserting societal
rules and regulations that Simple repeatedly shows to be irrelevant
to the conditions under which he lives. Boyd can always be counted
on for a stock legalism or a bit of conventional wisdom -- "if you
go in for bigamy, you will end up in the arms of justice" -- while
the irrepressible Simple never lacks a rejoinder that, however
amusing, strikes the props from under Boyd's pieties and confronts
the reader with real values and real problems: "Any old arms," says
the impoverished and lonely Jesse, "are better than none."

In revealing the conditions under which Jesse B. Simple lives
as a neglected victim of a white society that has failed to educate
him, failed to pay him, and expropriated his labor for inscrutable
purposes of its own, Hughes turns his story to an evident political
end. But by demonstrating that the shiftless alcoholic and gambler
is entangled in a complex web of circumstances whose knots and
catches are beyond his power -- or anyone's -- to unravel, and that
despite his bravado, wit, and rationalizations he feels "lonesome
inside myself," Hughes strikes a firm blow for his cause. Jesse's
scandalous behavior and opinions express a much more persuasive
humanity than the narrator's obtuse interrogations and the pious
fantasy that stands behind them.

QUESTIONS FOR DISCUSSION

1. What is the relevance of the opening paragraph to the story's
   eventual theme?
2. The narrator claims to be "observing life for literary purposes." How does this activity compare with what Simple is
   doing?
3. Jesse says, "You don't see me out here hustling off nobody, do
   you?" Do we? Should Jesse make a greater effort to gain
   funds?
4. Why is Jesse lonesome? Trace the events that have alienated
   him from three women. What has he learned? What have we?

781-796 (text pages)

TOPICS FOR WRITING

Critical Essays

1. "Conversation on the Corner" as satire.
2. The conversation as vaudeville, and as blues.

Related Subject

1. Retell this episode from a third-person limited-omniscient point
   of view that reveals Jesse's thoughts to the reader as well as
   what he says and does. What changes in character and event do
   you feel compelled to invent?

SUGGESTED READINGS

Emanuel, James A. Langston Hughes. Twayne's United States Authors
     Series, No. 123. New York: Twayne, 1967. Pp. 154-150.
     (General remarks on tales of Simple.)

Jemie, Onwuchekwa. Langston Hughes: An Introduction to the Poetry.
     Columbia Introductions to Twentieth-Century American Poetry.
     New York: Columbia University Press, 1976. Pp. 141-143.
     (General remarks on tales of Simple.)

Mintz, Lawrence E. "Langston Hughes's Jesse B. Simple: The Urban
     Negro as Wise Fool." Satire Newsletter, 7 (Fall 1969), 11-21.
     (General discussion of tales of Simple and traditions of Ameri-
     can humor.)

Frank O'Connor

"Guests of the Nation" (page 787)

O'Connor's story draws exceptional power from its concern with
a betrayal of the most primitive basis of human society, the host-
guest relationship. The English prisoners, billeted with their
guards in a cottage so thoroughly rooted in the land that its
occupant still bears traces of indigenous paganism, earn the status
of guests and come to feel at home. Belcher's contributions to the
household chores call attention to the simple satisfactions of the
peaceful, cooperative labor that is disrupted by the war, and
Hawkins's learning Irish dances implies the underlying brotherhood
of men, in contrast to which the scruples of "our lads" who "at that
time did not dance foreign dances on principle" seem absurd -- and
ominous. The futility of Hawkins's debates with Noble on theology
calls further into question the reality of the issues that divide
the English from the Irish, and his international socialist politics
provide a hint that there are issues of at least equal importance
that would not polarize the two pairs of men but unite them against
a common enemy.

The inhumanity of the conflict that orders Belcher and Hawkins to be executed by their "chums," their brothers, appears clearer for O'Connor's skillful portrayal of the prisoners as distinct from each other, individualized and consistent in their personalities. Further, by opening the story with a plunge into what seems an ongoing state of affairs, O'Connor shows that it is the war that interrupts the natural friendly interaction among the men rather than their fellowship interrupting a "normal" condition of bitter hostility between the English and the Irish. Even Jeremiah Donovan, who eventually brings down the cruel warrant and carries it out, forms part of the circle around the card table and scolds Hawkins for poor play "as if he were one of our own."

Bonaparte, the narrator, embraces the Englishmen as comrades and chafes at his official duties as their guard. With Noble, he imagines that the brigade officers, who also "knew the Englishmen well," will treat them as men rather than as enemies. But when the moment of decision arrives, Noble's resistance only extends to accepting the secondary role of gravedigger, and Bonaparte, though he hopes the prisoners will run away, finds himself powerless to aid them. Belcher and Hawkins are most fully themselves at the moment of their deaths, Hawkins talking on about his larger cause, Belcher finally revealing the fullness of his loving and generous nature. To Bonaparte and Noble the execution conveys a shock of revelation that changes the world for them. As Noble prays with the old woman in the doorway of the cottage, now become a shrine to the communion that took place within it, the only holy place in a world that seems to Noble composed entirely of the grave of his friends, Bonaparte, made profane in the literal etymological sense ("outside the shrine") and figuratively as well by his participation in the killing, feels himself cast out, alone, cut off from all atonement.

QUESTIONS FOR DISCUSSION

1. Describe and explain the pacing of the story. Contrast the movement of sections II and III with that of section IV.
2. What is the effect of the abrupt beginning of the story? Why does O'Connor introduce the characters before specifying that they are prisoners and guards in a war?
3. Why does O'Connor trouble to introduce the message from Mary Brigid O'Connell about her brother's socks?
4. Distinguish between the two Englishmen. Are they more different from the Irishmen or from each other?
5. Explore the significance of the old woman's superstitions about Jupiter Pluvius and "the hidden powers." Compare her interest in religion with that of Noble and Hawkins.
6. Why is Bonaparte so shocked when he learns what may happen to the hostages?
7. What is the relevance to the story of Hawkins's political beliefs? Do we think less of him when he volunteers to become a traitor and join the Irish cause?

8. What is the effect of Belcher's last-minute confidences? Of his apparently sincere repetition of the word <u>chum</u> throughout his ordeal?

9. Discuss Bonaparte's role in the execution. Is he culpable? Does he feel guilty?

10. Define the symbolic implications of the final scene. Why do Noble and Bonaparte have contrasting visions? Do their visions have anything in common? Why does Bonaparte burst out of the cottage where Noble and the old woman are praying?

TOPICS FOR WRITING

Critical Essays

1. The meaning of the old woman and her cottage.
2. "Guests of the Nation" and Babel's "My First Goose" -- introductions to war.
3. Executions in "Guests of the Nation" and Borges's "The End of the Duel."

Exercise for Reading

1. Summarize the conflict and the action of this story on personal, public (national, historical, political), and eternal (philosophical, religious, mythical) levels. Could these levels be reconciled so the polarities of value would be parallel?

SUGGESTED READINGS

Bordewyk, Gordon. "Quest for Meaning: The Stories of Frank O'Connor." <u>Illinois Quarterly</u>, 41 (Winter 1978), 37-47. Especially pp. 38-39.

Prosky, Murray. "The Pattern of Diminishing Certitude in the Stories of Frank O'Connor." <u>Colby Library Quarterly</u>, 9 (June 1971), 311-321. Especially pp. 311-314.

Frank O'Connor

"My Oedipus Complex" (page 796)

O'Connor derives the delightful comic effect of this story primarily from his control of the point of view. As a retrospective narrator, Larry knows as well as the reader the various mistaken assumptions that he has made as a child, but he never points them out explicitly. The reader is thus left to discover the incongruities between Larry's ideas and what is actually the case. These discoveries would not elicit laughter, however, if they merely measured the distance between childish innocence and adult sophistication. What makes the story funny is the secure confidence in

his own sophistication, in his profound insight into his mother's
feelings, for example, that the child Larry expresses at the very
moments of his greatest misunderstandings.

Because he has experienced an abnormal set of circumstances,
growing up in a home where his father appears only on occasion,
mysteriously, like Santa Claus, and where his mother has in many
ways turned to her son to take his place, Larry's paradigm for
normalcy is badly distorted: "The war was the most peaceful period
of my life." From this Edenic state, whose only defect he considers,
ironically, to be the lack of a baby like the ones other families in
the terrace have, Larry is catapulted by the Armistice into a war
with his father for his mother's attention and the right to her bed.
The reader, reminded of a different sort of paradigm by O'Connor's
title, chuckles at the comically inverted version of the Oedipal
conflict that ensues, and may be inclined to fear that a not-so-
comic primal scene is in store. O'Connor's narrative mocks the
reader's misguided assumptions as well as Larry's, however, when the
baby Larry has thought he wanted arrives to give father and son a
common enemy and, moreover, an occasion to understand the true
nature of their former rivalry. Both driven out of the featherbed
by the squalling Sonny, they must make do with such comfort as they
can provide each other, and Father hears no objection from Larry when
he takes up his role as Santa Claus once again.

QUESTIONS FOR DISCUSSION

1. In what ways do the first two paragraphs help to prepare us for
   the ultimate reconciliation of father and son?
2. What is Larry's life like before his father comes home? How
   does O'Connor convey a sense of it to the reader?
3. What does O'Connor accomplish by mentioning Larry's desire that
   his mother buy a baby for seventeen and six at such an early
   point in the story?
4. Describe the difficulties Larry has adjusting to Father's
   presence.
5. How well does Mother handle the situation? How sensitive is
   Father?
6. Tabulate Larry's various misconceptions. Which ones does he
   assert with the greatest confidence?
7. Explain Father's response to overhearing Larry's declaration,
   "If another bloody baby comes into this house, I'm going out."
   Does Larry make a similar recognition?

TOPICS FOR WRITING

Critical Essays

1. Oedipus complex or sibling rivalry?
2. A well-made story -- O'Connor's use of foreshadowing in "My
   Oedipus Complex."

125

3. The importance of "Daddy's toys."
4. How O'Connor draws a laugh -- the comic techniques of "My Oedipus Complex."

Related Subject

1. Try transposing sections of the story into different narrative points of view, such as stream-of-consciousness, first-person from the mother's perspective, narration by the child Larry shortly after the fact (as in Huckleberry Finn), or third-person limited-omniscient. What is lost or gained in these modes? Do you think O'Connor chose the best point of view for his story? Why?

SUGGESTED READING

Bordewyk, Gordon. "Quest for Meaning: The Stories of Frank O'Connor." Illinois Quarterly, 41 (Winter 1978), 37-47. Especially p. 45.

Isaac Bashevis Singer

"A Crown of Feathers" (page 807)

"A Crown of Feathers" may remind students of folk tales or fairy tales -- and not without reason. Not only is the setting, in a premodern world of villages, castles, and archaic customs and superstitions, reminiscent of traditional oral tales and their literary adaptations for children; Singer also draws his characters in the same bold lines and traces their fortunes over vast expanses of time. Akhsa is superlatively beautiful, loving, and wise, and her fate leads her to a series of unparalleled miseries, losses, and disappointments. Zemach, her destined mate, is more repulsive than the frog of any fairy-tale princess. Ludwik, her ill-chosen husband, is an unmitigated cad. Each of the characters exists in the story, like the characters in folklore, as a one-dimensional projection of some emotional problem or danger that a person may confront in passing through the stages of life, and like the protagonists of many fairy tales, Akhsa resorts to supernatural aid in order to find her way.

But the expectations aroused by these familiar elements in the story are repeatedly and significantly disappointed. Most fairy tales, like myths and dreams, develop solutions to the problems of life, and thus ease the anxieties of their readers and help them proceed in a healthy fashion through the transitions from infancy to childhood, maturity, and death. Singer, however, confronts Akhsa and the reader with one equivocation after another. Just as there is no way to resolve the contradictions between the antithetical voices of her two grandparents, so we can never be sure whether Akhsa is right to convert, right to return, right to reject

126

Zemach, or right to seek him out. The manifestations of the supernatural, which customarily have the reassuring last word on such
issues in fairy tales, are here the essence of ambiguity. Not only
do the voices that speak to her from beyond directly contradict each
other; Singer also takes great care to leave open the skeptical
possibility that these manifestations arise from Akhsa's troubled
imagination, and he provides a naturalistic psychological rationale
for her experience of them and for the actions she decides to take
under their influence. The disjunction between Akhsa's preparation
for life and what actually happens to her leads to frustration and
deprivation more than sufficient to engender both the guilt that
leads her to one self-destructive deed after another (for is she not
always being punished?) and the distorted sexual longings that bring
the devil to her bed and lead her to indulge in orgies of asceticism
and self-abasement with Zemach.

Fairy-tale heroines and saints have suffered as much, but for
them in the end a sign appears, a flower grows, an angel bends down
from above, and everything is justified. The sign Akhsa receives
comes not only at the end but also at the beginning of her troubles,
and may be credited with causing them. The crown of feathers is no
more substantial than her other contacts with the supernatural (or
her fantasies and hallucinations), and offers uncertain recompense
for years of suffering and finally death. Singer leaves the reader
to decide if Akhsa is being rewarded or mocked by her visions of
such an "intricate and hidden" symbol of the unfathomable truth of
things; but how much more delicate, beautiful, and evanescent --
how much more like Akhsa -- is the sparkling wreath of feathers with
which she begins and ends than the spider-web devil she encounters
in between. This devil expresses the story's paradoxical theme in
self-negating terms: "The truth is that there is no truth." Akhsa
dies praying for yet another miracle, but Singer, unwilling to end
with the devil's conundrum, brings the story to rest on a note of
acceptance and appreciation.

QUESTIONS FOR DISCUSSION

1. Comment on the way Akhsa is introduced to the reader. How does
   Singer manage to convey such a positive impression?
2. Why is Akhsa so strongly influenced by the voices first of her
   grandmother and eventually of her grandfather as well?
3. Give a naturalistic explanation for what happens when Akhsa
   tries to sign the contract to marry Zemach. Does it matter how
   we explain her behavior?
4. Why is Akhsa susceptible to conversion after her grandfather
   dies? Can the debate between the shades of her dead grandparents be understood as a conflict within Akhsa herself?
5. What implications may be derived from the fate of the first
   crown of feathers?
6. What stages does Akhsa pass through between her conversion to
   Christianity and her decision to seek out Zemach? Do they
   follow each other in a meaningful sequence of causes and
   effects?

7. What is the first place Akhsa visits when she returns to Krasnobród? Describe Zemach's house. How is the hut in which Zemach and Akhsa live decorated? Do the common elements of these places cast any light on the meaning of Akhsa's quest?
8. Why do Akhsa and Zemach reject the forms of contrition suggested by Reb Bezalel?
9. Why is Akhsa not content with the second appearance of the crown of feathers?
10. How can Zemach's disappearance be explained?
11. What is our final estimate of Akhsa?

TOPICS FOR WRITING

Critical Essays

1. "A Crown of Feathers" -- Singer's modern legend of a saint.
2. The presentation and effect of the seemingly supernatural in "A Crown of Feathers" and Hawthorne's "Young Goodman Brown."
3. Akhsa's death wish -- motivation and result.
4. A comparison and contrast of the central characters and themes of "A Crown of Feathers" and Flaubert's "A Simple Heart."
5. The meaning of the symbolic crown of feathers.
6. What "A Crown of Feathers" and Borges's "The End of the Duel" have in common.

Exercise for Reading

1. On a first reading, stop at each of the eight white spaces that divide the story and write one or two sentences saying what you are hoping will happen to Akhsa. After you have completed the story, review each of your comments and compare your hopes (or expectations) with what actually ensues. What would the story mean if it worked out as you had hoped? What does it seem to mean as is?

Related Subjects

1. Rewrite "A Crown of Feathers" as a children's story. Why did you make the changes you did?
2. Select a folk tale, a fairy tale, or a saint's life that you know and retell it so that its implications are in harmony with those of Singer's story -- as phrased, for instance, in the concluding line. Why did you make the changes you did?

SUGGESTED READING

Hernández, Frances. "Isaac Bashevis Singer and the Supernatural." CEA Critic, 40 (January 1978), 28-32.

Richard Wright

"The Man Who Was Almost a Man" (page 827)

Dave Saunders dislikes being laughed at, and his discomfort at becoming an object of amusement for accidentally shooting old Jenny, the mule, precipitates his final step into manhood. Although the anecdote around which Wright builds the story is comical enough, the reader probably should accede to Dave's wish to be taken seriously, for the fate that lies ahead of this young man as he rolls toward his unknown destination atop a boxcar with nothing in his pocket but an unloaded gun is likely to be grim.

At the same time, however, Dave's self-esteem and independence deserve respect. At the beginning of the story he dissociates himself from the field hands and fixes on his ambition to declare his manhood by owning a gun. Throughout the story the idea that boys do not have guns recurs, and Dave not only wants a gun but also chafes at being called "boy" by his parents and at being treated as a child. Just before he goes out to master the gun and hop a freight, Dave grumbles, "They treat me like a mule, n then they beat me." His resolution to escape his inferior status will involve not only leaving home but taking potshots at the facade of white society just as he wants to shoot at "Jim Hawkins' big white house" in order "t let im know Dave Saunders is a man." The question Wright leaves hanging for the reader as his story trails off into ellipses is whether Dave has killed the mule in himself or whether he himself, like Jenny, may become the victim of his own wild shots.

QUESTIONS FOR DISCUSSION

1. Explain the pun in the last sentence of the first paragraph.
2. Define our first impression of Dave. What resons do we have to admire him? To laugh at him? To pity him?
3. What does it take to be a man in the world of the story? Is a gun enough? How does one get a gun?
4. What is ironic about the way Dave gets the money to buy his gun?
5. How is Dave treated by his father? Why does Ma say of the gun, "It be fer Pa"?
6. With the gun under his pillow, Dave feels "a sense of power. Could kill a man with a gun like this. Kill anybody, black or white." What does Dave still have to learn before he can be called a man? How does the story bring it home to him?
7. Explain what happens the first time Dave fires the gun. What does he do differently the next time?
8. Why does Wright describe the death of the mule in such detail?
9. Explain why being laughed at is so painful for Dave. What might enable him to join in and laugh at himself?

10. Comment on the possible implications of Dave's remark, "They treat me like a mule, n then they beat me," both within the story and in a broader social and historical context. Does Dave's killing the mule have a symbolic significance?
11. Where might Dave be headed as he hops the Illinois Central? What might he find at the end of his journey?
12. Why is the title not "The Boy Who Was Almost a Man"?

TOPICS FOR WRITING

Critical Essays

1. The tone of Wright's story.
2. "The Man Who Was Almost a Man" and Frank O'Connor's "My Oedipus Complex."
3. "A Man Who Was Almost a Man" and Wright's social themes. (See the headnote, p. 826.)

Related Subjects

1. Write a sequel to Wright's story, another episode in the life of Dave Saunders -- something that happens on the train ride or when he arrives in New Orleans or Chicago or wherever. Try to sustain and develop as many themes and motives already present in Wright's story as you can, but make the material your own by imagining what you think happens, not necessarily what you guess Wright might have written. Decide whether to adopt Wright's style and point of view or to employ a different mode of narration. Remember that the story is set during the Great Depression.

SUGGESTED READINGS

Felgar, Robert. Richard Wright. Twayne's United States Authors Series, No. 386. Boston: G. K. Hall, 1980. P. 156.

Margolis, Edward. The Art of Richard Wright. Crosscurrents/Modern Critiques. Carbondale: Southern Illinois University Press, 1969. Pp. 75-76.

Eudora Welty

"Petrified Man" (page 839)

Students in the age of the unisex hair salon may need to be reminded that Welty's beauty parlor is a female bastion in the same way that Faulkner's barbershop in "Dry September" is an exclusively male preserve. Such a recognition may help to explain why the story ends as it does, and it may also constitute a necessary first step toward grasping the thematic dimensions of these two trivial

conversations between two insignificant women whose fates are left
largely unknown to the reader. The issue in Leota's shop is not
race relations but the battle of the sexes, and it is the women's
conflicts over their sex roles and their position in relation to men
that cause their discomfort and their strange behavior.

In Fred's terms, the story, despite Welty's perfect comic
pacing, is less "funny-haha" than "funny-peculiar" -- or even funny-
grotesque, for it is impossible to laugh at these spiteful, envious,
hypocritical ladies without at the same time feeling some of their
pain. The real freak show, of course, is not next door at all, but
right here in the beauty parlor (or chamber of horrors), where
women's faces are plastered and their hair is wound on rollers,
baked, and permanently set. The supposed purpose of these operations
is to become more attractive to the opposite sex, but the customers'
actual goal is more likely to excel one another. The conversation
between Leota and Mrs. Fletcher reveals that the women prefer to
dominate men rather than to attract them. Mr. Fletcher, though he
is "five foot nine and one-half," can easily be mastered by the sick-
headache ploy; Fred and Mr. Pike are nicely under control because
they are unemployed, so Fred can be rusticated to Vicksburg when it
suits the whim of Leota or her fortune-teller; and the men who arouse
the most interest are the pygmies and the petrified man. What brings
the women the most discomfort is the idea of fulfillment of their
biological roles in pregnancy and motherhood. Mrs. Fletcher seeks
to conceal her condition; Mrs. Mountjoy scandalizes everyone by
coming to be beautified while actually in labor; and the unfortunate
Billy Boy, consigned by his mother to the care of the beauticians,
is kept strictly subjugated.

With their fortifications against the opposite sex in place,
the women must deal with one another. Although alliances are sometimes necessary and convenient, the keynote here is competition and
the struggle for advantage. In the first section of the story,
Leota uses her friendship with Mrs. Pike, whom she values as a prize
possession and likes because she can patronize her by helping her,
to gain the upper hand on the snobbish Mrs. Fletcher, whose only
recourse is to make her sarcastic exit just before the white space.
In the second section the alignments are reversed, and Leota and
Mrs. Fletcher can join in spiteful envy of Mrs. Pike's good fortune,
which somehow seems to come at their expense. Mrs. Pike has won the
$500 reward for the same powers of observation that spied out Mrs.
Fletcher's pregnancy, and she used Leota's magazine to accomplish
the feat. Her success represents a major victory in the bitter
competition among women that the story explores.

Mrs. Pike's discovery of the rapist inside the petrified man
threatens the ladies in another way as well, for it suggests the
bankruptcy of their strategy in the war against men and reminds them
in a painful way of their vulnerability. So frightened are they,
however, that compassion for the rapist's victims is out of the
question. Leota speaks of them as sexual commodities easily
converted into cash: "Four women. I guess those women didn't have
the faintest notion at the time that they'd be worth a hundred an'

twenty-five bucks apiece some day to Mrs. Pike." This failure of
compassion marks the limitations of Welty's grotesque characters.
It is parallel to their reaction to the pickled Siamese-twin fetuses.
Although they are "kinda pathetic," they are too repulsive to contem-
plate and need not concern anyone who does not marry a relative.
The only kind of sisterhood possible to such insensitive women
involves participation in the ritual that ends the story, where they
all gather round to watch Billy Boy get paddled. His crime, eating
some stale peanuts purchased by his mother, hardly merits such
punishment, except that his invasion of Leota's purse reenacts Mrs.
Pike's triumph and embodies, in symbolic form, rape -- the very
source of the fears that have hardened these women's hearts.

QUESTIONS FOR DISCUSSION

1. Comment on the narrative method Welty uses for the story. What
    special demands does it place on the reader?
2. What parallels and differences are there between the two
    conversations?
3. Compare the opening and concluding incidents in the story.
    What other unifying devices does Welty use?
4. What does Leota think of Mrs. Pike during the first conver-
    sation? Why?
5. Has Mrs. Fletcher caught dandruff from Mr. Fletcher? What
    problem with her hair has he caused? What is the effect of her
    blurring the two considerations together?
6. Discuss what is on display at the freak show, and explain the
    women's reactions. Would they like to be married to a pygmy
    or a petrified man?
7. Explain Mrs. Fletcher's exit at the end of the first conver-
    sation.
8. Why does Mrs. Mountjoy stop by the beauty shop on her way to
    the hospital? Why does it upset everyone so?
9. Why does Leota feel that Mrs. Pike's good luck is her own bad
    luck?
10. "'Not really petrified at all, of course,' said Mrs. Fletcher
    meditatively." What might she be thinking?
11. Discuss Billy Boy's role in the story. Why is his punishment
    a suitable ending for the story. Explain the appropriateness
    of his parting shot.

TOPICS FOR WRITING

Critical Essays

1. Mississippi Medusae.
2. Sex, money, and competition in "Petrified Man."
3. Who is Welty's protagonist?
4. "Funny-haha or funny-peculiar" -- Welty's tone in "Petrified
    Man."

Related Subject

1. People's idle conversations, like their dreams, sometimes
   reveal their deepest concerns. Write a vignette in which two
   characters pass the time of day by discussing items in the news
   or similar topics. Try to let their attitudes express their
   distinct personalities.

SUGGESTED READINGS

Jones, Alun R. "The World of Love: The Fiction of Eudora Welty."
   In Women Writers of the Short Story: A Collection of Critical
   Essays. Edited by Heather McClave. Englewood Cliffs, N. J.:
   Prentice-Hall, 1980. Pp. 96–111. Especially pp. 100–101.
   (Originally published in 1963.)

Kreyling, Michael. Eudora Welty's Achievement of Order. Baton
   Rouge: Louisiana State University Press, 1980. Pp. 8–9.

Eudora Welty

"A Worn Path" (page 850)

Try not to force the Christian or mythological schemes of
allegory the story supports until you encourage the students to
savor the beauty of the literal narration. Phoenix Jackson is an
embodiment of love, faith, sacrifice, charity, self-renunciation,
and triumph over death in herself, quite apart from the typological
implications of her name or the allusions to the Stations of the
Cross in her journey. Phoenix transcends her merely archetypal
significance just as she transcends the stereotype of old black
mammies on which she is built. Welty accomplishes this act of
creation by entering fully into the consciousness of her character.
There she discovers the little child that still lives within the
old woman and causes her to dream of chocolate cake, dance with a
scarecrow, and delight in a Christmas toy. Phoenix is right when
she says, "I wasn't as old as I thought," but she does not merit
the condescension of the hunter's exclamation, "I know you old
colored people! Wouldn't miss going to town to see Santa Claus!"
Even in her greatest discomfort, lying in the weeds, losing her
memory, getting her shoes tied, "stealing" a nickel, or taking one
as a handout, Phoenix retains her invincible dignity, an essential
component of the single glimpse we receive of her triumphant home-
ward march, bearing aloft the bright symbol of life she has retrieved
through her exertions.

In her comments on the story (included in Part Two, p. 1187),
Welty implies that the meaning of Phoenix's journey is that of any
human exertion carried out in good faith despite the uncertainty of
the outcome: "The path is the thing that matters." In keeping with
this theme, Welty repeatedly shows Phoenix asserting life in the

face of death. Her name itself, taken from the mythical bird that
periodically immolates itself and rises reborn from its ashes,
embodies the idea. (She even makes a noise like "a solitary little
bird" in the first paragraph.) Phoenix makes her journey at the
time of the death and rebirth of the year; her own skin is like the
sun bursting through darkness; she overcomes discouragement as she
tops the hill; she extricates herself from a thorn bush (of which
much may be made in a Christian allegorical interpretation); she
passes "bid dead trees" and a buzzard; she traverses a field of
dead corn; she sees a "ghost" that turns out to be a dancing scarecrow; she is overcome by a "black dog" but rescued by a death-
dealing hunter whose gun she faces down and whom she beats out of
a shiny nickel; and she emerges from a deathlike trance in the
doctor's office to return with the medicine her grandson needs to
stay alive. Phoenix's strength lies in the purpose of her journey,
and her spirit is contagious. The hunter, the woman who ties her
shoes, and the doctor's attendant all perform acts of charity toward
her, and lest the reader overlook the one word that lies at the
heart of Welty's vision, the nurse says "Charity" while "making a
check mark in a book."

QUESTIONS FOR DISCUSSION

1. Notice Phoenix's identification with "a solitary little bird."
    What other birds does she encounter on her journey? Explain
    their implications.
2. What techniques does Welty use to suggest the laboriousness of
    Phoenix's trip?
3. Before she crosses the stream, Phoenix says, "Now comes the
    trial." Does she pass it? How? To what extent is this event
    a microcosm of the whole story? Are there other microcosmic
    episodes?
4. What effect do Phoenix's sequential reactions to the scarecrow,
    the abandoned houses, and the spring have on the reader's view
    of her?
5. What is your opinion of the hunter? What conclusion might be
    drawn from the fact that even though he kills birds and
    patronizes Phoenix, he helps her in a way he does not know?
6. Interpret the passage that begins with Phoenix bending for the
    nickel and ends with her parting from the hunter.
7. Describe Natchez as Phoenix perceives it. Is it a worthy
    culmination for her journey?
8. In her comments reprinted in Part Two (p. 1187), Welty remarks
    that Phoenix's victory comes when she sees the doctor's diploma
    "nailed up on the wall." In what sense is this moment the
    climax of the story? What is different about the ensuing
    action from the action that leads up to this moment? Are there
    any similarities?
9. How does Phoenix describe her grandson? What is Welty's
    reason for using these terms?
10. Explain the irony in the way the nurse records Phoenix's visit.

TOPICS FOR WRITING

Critical Essays

1. Why readers want to think that Phoenix Jackson's grandson is really dead.
2. Phoenix and the other birds in Welty's "A Worn Path."
3. What "Petrified Man" and "A Worn Path" have in common -- style and theme.

Exercise for Reading

1. After your first reading of "A Worn Path," write a paragraph giving your opinion of Phoenix Jackson. Then study some symbolic interpretations of the story (such as those by Keys, Isaacs, and Ardelino, cited below). Reread the story and write another assessment of the central character. Does she bear up under the freight of symbolic meaning the critics ask her to carry? Does her relationship to these archetypes help to account for your original response?

Related Subject

1. Read Welty's account of how she came to write "A Worn Path" (Part Two, p. 1188). Following her example, write an account of what you imagine to be the day's experience of someone you catch a glimpse of who strikes your fancy. Use the intimate interior third-person limited-omniscient point of view that Welty employs for Phoenix Jackson.

SUGGESTED READINGS

Ardelino, Frank. "Life out of Death: Ancient Myth and Ritual in Welty's 'A Worn Path.'" Notes on Mississippi Writers, 9 (Spring 1976), 1-9.

Isaacs, Neil D. "Life for Phoenix." Sewanee Review, 71 (1963), 75-81.

Keys, Marilynn. "'A Worn Path': The Way of Dispossession." Studies in Short Fiction, 16 (Fall 1979), 354-356.

Phillips, Robert L., Jr. "A Structural Approach to Myth in the Fiction of Eudora Welty." In Eudora Welty: Critical Essays. Edited by Peggy Whitman Prenshaw. Jackson: University Press of Mississippi, 1979. Pp. 56-57. Especially p. 60.

John Cheever

"The Enormous Radio" (page 858)

The goal of this story is to explode the placid stereotype out-
lined at the start. Cheever implies that it is an illusion that such
people exist, and that anyone who pretends to be living such a life
must be guilty of hypocrisy or self-delusion. The instrument
Cheever uses to puncture the bubble in which Irene Westcott has
sealed herself off from life is the fantastic radio, which comes into
her home with its "malevolent green eye" like "an aggressive
intruder" to unleash "the violent forces that were snared in its ugly
gumwood cabinet." The plot of the story traces Irene's reactions to
what the radio reveals about the world and about herself, and it
leaves her stripped of her facade and her illusions, painfully
confronting with the reader a reality anyone would rather ignore.

Irene's education begins almost as punishment for her having
"made her peace with the radio," convincing herself that she could
accommodate the thing in her living room and thus avoiding a conflict
with Jim over his selection. From that point on, the radio pours
forth a steady stream of revelations. First the unpleasant sound
effects of modern life are thrust upon Irene, who understandably
prefers to wall them out or drown them with music. When the voices
of the neighbors begin to come through, Irene is fascinated and
delighted. Significantly, however, she worries that the radio may
be broadcasting her own conversations with Jim, though at this point
she seems to have nothing to hide.

Further revelations are more shocking, and it becomes apparent
that the innocent Irene, whose life "was nearly as simple and shel-
tered as it appeared to be," is at last learning the score. Irene's
penultimate attempt to insulate herself from the life of venality
and suffering that the radio parades before her is to affect pity.
She endorses the Salvation Army and quotes Shakespeare's sainted
Portia, but Jim has little patience for her "Christly" attitude. He
urges her to shut out the voices and pretends to agree with her when
she asks, "Our lives aren't sordid, are they, darling?" Jim has
needs of his own, however, and when Irene tries to get him to hide
his feelings from the radio, he bursts out with an indictment of
Irene that jolts her as much as it does the reader, though of
course she is already aware of the truth of what he says. Irene
rushes to the radio for comfort, but what she hears is a noncommittal
report of a disaster, an act of heroism, and the weather. Life is a
rich mixture of good and evil, pain and pleasure, but the Westcotts
have attempted to live it as the newscaster reads his script, without much awareness of either.

QUESTIONS FOR DISCUSSION

1. Why does Cheever pointedly introduce his characters as stereotypes?
2. Is it appropriate that the instrument of their enlightenment
   should be the radio, their one unusual enthusiasm?
3. Describe the radio as Cheever presents it. Are we surprised
   when it begins receiving such strange programs?
4. Comment on the phrase, "the lamentation of a vacuum cleaner."
   What does it contribute to the passage from which it is taken?
   Are there other instances of similarly effective stylistic
   choices elsewhere in the story?
5. Why does the radio first bring in the sounds of appliances and
   only later the voices of the neighbors?
6. Irene's first worry is, "Maybe they can hear us." Why?
7. Why does Irene get hooked on the "demonstrations of indigestion,
   carnal love, abysmal vanity, faith, and despair" that she
   overhears? What else does Irene hear? How does Irene's
   interest in these broadcasts compare with an addiction to soap
   operas?
8. Explain Irene's view of the Salvation Army. Explain her
   quotation from Shakespeare.
9. Contrast Jim's and Irene's positions in the last part of the
   story. Why does Jim at first comfort her and then later blow
   up?
10. What is our final assessment of Irene?

TOPICS FOR WRITING

Critical Essays

1. "The Enormous Radio" -- satire or parable?
2. The radio as a device and as a symbol.

Exercises for Reading

1. On a second reading, note all anticipations of the final
   revelations about Irene. Were you nonetheless surprised?
   Explain.

Related Subject

1. Write a sketch or a story based on a "what if" idea. Concentrate on the effects of the imaginary condition on one or two
   realistic characters.

SUGGESTED READINGS

Coale, Samuel. John Cheever. New York: Ungar, 1977. Pp. 40-43.

Waldeland, Lynne. John Cheever. Twayne's United States Authors
    Series, No. 335. Boston: G. K. Hall, 1979.

867-876 (text pages)

John Cheever

"The Swimmer" (page 867)

One way to reconstruct a naturalistic time scheme for the story, so Neddy's "misfortunes," the awareness of which he seems to have repressed, can be dated with regard to the other events in the narrative, is to imagine a gap in time covered by the line, "He stayed in the Levys' gazebo until the storm had passed." The authoritative point of view in the opening paragraphs seems to preclude placing the misfortunes before Neddy begins his swim, while the gathering clouds and circling de Haviland trainer assert the continuity of the first phase of his journey. After the storm, however, signs of change appear, and it is possible to reconcile Neddy's subsequent encounters with the proposition that he is continuing his swim on another day or days under quite different circumstances. Before the storm, he visits the Grahams and the Bunkers, who greet him as the prosperous and popular Neddy Merrill described at the beginning of the story, but after the storm Neddy visits only the empty houses of the Lindleys and the Welchers, the public pool where any derelict may swim, the peculiar Hallorans, who mention his troubles, the Sachses, who have problems of their own and who refuse him a drink, the socially inferior Biswangers, who snub him, and his old mistress Shirley, who implies that this call is not the first he has paid in this condition.

But Cheever is not interested in a realistic time scheme. If he were, he would not have burned the 250-page novelistic version of the story (mentioned in the headnote, p. 858) that presumably filled in the blanks. Instead, he has constructed the story so Neddy's recognition of his loss strikes the reader with the same impact it has on Neddy. By telescoping time, Cheever thrusts us forward into a state of affairs, that exists only as a dim cloud on the horizon on the day the story begins and at first seems to be entirely taking place.

What accounts for the reversal in Neddy's life? Surely it is possible to tax Neddy for irresponsibility and childishness in turning his back on his friends and family and so casually setting off on an odyssey from which he returns far too late. Neddy's own view of his adventure is considerably more attractive. The only member of his society who seems free from a hangover on this mid-summer Sunday, Neddy simply wishes to savor the pleasures of his fortunate life: "The day was beautiful and it seemed to him that a long swim might enlarge and celebrate its beauty." Although he has been (or will be) unfaithful to his wife with Shirley Adams, and although he kisses close to a dozen other women on his journey, Neddy does not construe his departure as infidelity to Lucinda. Rather, to swim the string of pools across the suburban county is to travel along "the Lucinda River." As "a pilgrim, an explorer, a man with a destiny," Neddy plunges into this river of life aware of the gathering storm on the horizon but regarding it with pleasurable anticipation. When it finally breaks over the Levys' gazebo he savors the exciting release of tension that accompanies the arrival of a thunder shower, but with the explosion of thunder and the smell

of gunpowder that ensues, Neddy finds his happy illusions, his world
of "youth, sport, and clement weather" lashed by a more unpleasant
reality, just as the "rain lashed the Japanese lanterns that Mrs.
Levy had bought in Kyoto the year before last, or was it the year
before that?"

What Neddy now confronts, though he tries gamely to ignore it,
are the twin recognitions that his youth is not eternal and that the
pleasant society on the "bonny and lush . . . banks of the Lucinda
River" is unstable, exclusive, and cruel. Grass grows in the
Lindleys' riding ring, the Welchers have moved away, and the sky is
now overcast. Crossing Route 424 in his swimming suit, Neddy is
subjected to the ridicule of the public, and at the Recreation Center
he finds that swimming does not convey the same sense of elegance,
pleasure, and freedom that it does in the pools of his affluent
friends. The validity of the society Neddy has previously enjoyed is
called further into question by the very existence of the self-
contradictory Hallorans, whose personal eccentricity is matched by
their political hypocrisy. Neddy's visits to the Biswangers and to
Shirley Adams complete the destruction of his illusions, but it is
Eric Sachs, disfigured by surgery and (with the loss of his navel)
symbolically cut off from the human community, who embodies the most
troubling reflection of Neddy's condition. "I'm not alone," Shirley
proclaims, but Neddy is, and as this man who "might have been
compared to a summer's day" recognizes that his summer is over, it
is not surprising that for "the first time in his adult life" he
begins to cry. While the reader may relish Cheever's indictment of
a society whose values have so betrayed Neddy, it is hard not to
feel some admiration for a man who, by executing his plan to swim
the country through the now icy autumn waters, has indeed become a
legendary figure, an epic hero of a sort.

QUESTIONS FOR DISCUSSION

1. Who is referred to by the word everyone in the opening sentence?
   Who is not?
2. How does Neddy Merrill relate to the world in which he moves?
   Why does he decide to swim home?
3. Why does Neddy name his route "the Lucinda River"? The Levys
   live on the "Alewives Lane." Alewives are a kind of fish that
   swim up rivers to spawn. Is there a sexual component to Neddy's
   journey?
4. Is the storm that breaks a surprise? How does Neddy feel about
   the beginning of the rain?
5. What differences can be noticed between what Neddy experiences
   before and after the storm? How might they be explained?
6. What new elements enter the story when Neddy crosses Route 424?
   Why do the drivers jeer at him?
7. Before he dives into the unappealing public swimming pool,
   Neddy tells himself "that this was merely a stagnant bend in the
   Lucinda River." How characteristic is this effort to assuage
   his own doubts and discontents?

8. Based on what the Hallorans, the Sachses, the Biswangers, and Shirley Adams say to Neddy, what is the truth about himself and his life of which he is unaware?
9. Cheever has his hero discover the season by observing the stars. What effect does that choice among various possibilities have on our attitude toward Neddy?
10. It is not difficult to say what Neddy has lost. What has he gained?

TOPICS FOR WRITING

Critical Essays

1. "The Swimmer" and "The Enormous Radio" -- Cheever's consistency of theme and technique.
2. Why Neddy Merrill talks only with women.
3. Rusty Towers, Eric Sachs, and Neddy Merrill.
4. Neddy Merrill's voyage of exploration and discovery.
5. Cheever's attitude toward the swimmer.

SUGGESTED READINGS

Coale, Samuel. John Cheever. New York: Ungar, 1977. Pp. 43-47.

Waldeland, Lynne. John Cheever. Twayne's United States Authors Series, No. 335. Boston: G. K. Hall, 1979. Pp. 94-95.

Tillie Olsen

"I Stand Here Ironing" (page 878)

One way to begin discussing this story is to look at the ending. "I will never total it all," the narrator affirms, and then proceeds to pronounce the summary whose inadequacy she has already proclaimed. The summarizing passage clarifies and organizes the impressions the reader may have gleaned from the preceding monologue. It is so clear that if it stood alone or came first in the story the validity of its interpretation of Emily could hardly be doubted. But since it follows her mother's "tormented" meditations, the summary seems incomplete in its clinical precision and must give way to a final paragraph of comparatively obscure and paradoxical requests focused in the startling but brilliantly adept image of the "dress on the ironing board, helpless before the iron," which links the story's end to its beginning and directs attention to the true central character.

What is mainly missing from the summary is the love and under-standing that Emily's mother feels for her daughter as a result of living through the experiences bracketed by the orderly generaliza-tions. Just as much as Emily, her mother has been the victim "of

depression, of war, of fear." By virtue of having had to cope with
those circumstances, she can respect Emily's response to them. Doing
so enables her to counter the suggestion that "she's a youngster who
needs help" with "Let her be." A good deal of the help Emily and
her mother have received so far has put them in separate prisons --
as when Emily was incarcerated at the convalescent home -- and cut
them off from love. To let Emily alone is at least to allow her
some freedom to grow at her own slow pace.

Her mother is tempted to blame herself for the deficiencies in
Emily's childhood, since she learned things about being a mother with
her second family that she did not know with Emily. But her
consideration of a characteristic incident early in the narrative
suggests a crucial qualifying factor: When she parked Emily at
nursery school at the age of two, she did not know what she was
subjecting her daughter to, "except that it would have made no
difference if I had known. . . . It was the only way we could be
together, the only way I could hold a job." As much a victim of
rigid and unfavorable economic and historical circumstances as her
daughter, Emily's mother can speak her concluding line with feeling.
In pleading that Emily somehow be made to know "that she is more
than this dress on the ironing board, helpless before the iron,"
Emily's mother asks that her daughter be spared a condition to which
she herself has been subjected. But Emily's mother, unlike
Whistler's, does not sit for her portrait passively in a rocking
chair; she stands there wielding the iron, controlling the very
symbol of the circumstances that have not yet flattened her, painting
her own self-portrait, and calling for help not in adjusting Emily
to the world but in making the world a place in which Emily can
thrive.

QUESTIONS FOR DISCUSSION

1. Who is _you_ in the first sentence? What is the mother's first
   response to the request to unlock the mystery of Emily? Does
   her position change?
2. Does Emily's mother feel guilty about how she has cared for
   Emily? Why? What factors have affected her dealings with her
   daughter?
3. Why is the passage in which Emily throws the clock so effective?
4. Discuss the "help" Emily gets at the convalescent home. How
   does it compare to the help her mother calls for at the end?
5. Emily has suffered from the absence of her father, the exuaus-
   tion of her mother, poverty, asthma and other diseases,
   sibling rivalry, and unpopularity, among other complaints.
   What is the effect of these hardships on the young woman she
   has become? What is the effect of her discovery of a talent?
6. What has her mother learned from Emily?
7. Does Emily's mother love her daughter? How can we tell?

878-897 (text pages)

TOPICS FOR WRITING

Critical Essays

1. Like mother, like daughter -- Emily's talent and her mother's.
2. The function of the interruptions in "I Stand Here Ironing."
3. "I will never total it all" -- the importance of indeterminacy
   in Olsen's analysis of Emily.
4. The politics of "I Stand Here Ironing."

Related Subject

1. Write a summary statement in general terms about the personality of a sibling, relative, or friend you have known closely
   for a long time. Put it aside and cast your memory back to
   three or four specific incidents involving your subject.
   Narrate them briefly but in specific and concrete terms. Read
   over your sketches and compare the personality of your subject
   as it emerges with what you wrote in your generalized summary.
   Do you still think your summary is accurate? What are its
   limitations?

SUGGESTED READING

Frye, Joanne S. "'I Stand Here Ironing,': Motherhood as Experience
   and Metaphor." Studies in Short Fiction, 18 (Summer 1981),
   287-292.

O'Connor, William Van. "The Short Stories of Tillie Olsen." Studies
   in Short Fiction, 1 (Fall 1963), 21-25. Especially pp. 21-22.

Ralph Ellison

"Battle Royal" (page 886)

In the headnote to his comments on "Battle Royal" reprinted in
Part Two (p. 1190), Ellison is quoted expounding on the importance
of "converting experience into symbolic action" in fiction. One of
the major triumphs of "Battle Royal" (and of Invisible Man as a
whole) is Ellison's success in the realistic rendering of experiences
that are in themselves so obviously significant of larger social,
psychological, and moral truths that explication is unnecessary.
From the small American flag tattooed on the nude dancer's belly to
the "rope of bloody saliva forming a shape like an undiscovered
continent" that the narrator drools on his new briefcase, Ellison's
account of the festivities at the men's smoker effectively symbolizes
the condition of blacks in America while at the same time remaining
thoroughly persuasive in its verisimilitude. Both the broader
structure of the evening and the finer details of narration and
description carry the force of Ellison's theme. The young blacks
are tortured first by having the most forbidden of America's riches

dangled before them, then by being put through their paces in a melee in which their only victims are their fellows and the whites look on with glee, and finally by being debased into groveling for money (some of it counterfeit) on a rug whose electrification underlines their own powerlessness. In one brief passage, the nightmare of such an existence appears in a strange subaqueous vision of primitive life: "The boys groped about like blind, cautious crabs crouching to protect their mid-sections, their heads pulled in short against their shoulders, their arms stretched nervously before them, with their fists testing the smoke-filled air like the knobbed feelers of hypersensitive snails."

Because his actual experience forms itself into such revealing images, the narrator's dream of his grandfather seems all the more credible as a statement of his position. "Keep this Nigger-Boy Running," he dreams the message of his briefcase says -- not far from "You've got to know your place at all times." The narrator's grandfather knew his place and played his role, but he never believed a word of it. It is this assurance of an inner being quite different from the face he turned toward the world that makes him so troubling to his descendants. In his effort to please the white folks and in so doing to get ahead, the narrator seeks alliance rather than secret enmity with his antagonists. As a result he subjects himself to the trickery and delusions the white community chooses to impose on him. Dependent for his sense of himself on his ability to guess that they want him to do, the narrator finds himself groping in a fog deeper than the swirls of cigar smoke that hang over the scene of the battle royal. When the smoke clears and the blindfold comes off, he will recognize, as he puts it at the start, that he is invisible to the whites and may therefore discover his own identity within himself.

This first episode of a long novel does not accomplish the narrator's enlightenment, but it constitutes his initiation into the realities of the world he must eventually come to understand. Ellison says (in the commentary in Part Two, p. 1191) that the battle royal "is a ritual in preservation of caste lines, a keeping of taboo to appease the gods and ward off bad luck," and that "it is also the initiation ritual to which all greenhorns are subjected." This rite of initiation bears a revealing relationship to the primitive initiation ceremonies known to anthropologists. The battle royal, for example, separates the boys from their families, challenges them to prove their valor, and subjects them to instruction by the tribal elders in a sort of men's house. The boys are stripped and introduced to sexual mysteries. But the hazing of women that is a frequent feature of such initiations is not carried on here by the boys but by the gross elders, whose savagery is barely under control; the ritual ends not with the entry of the initiates into the larger community but with their pointed exclusion; and the sacred lore embodied in the narrator's recital of his graduation speech makes explicit the contradictions inherent in the society it describes. To cast down his bucket where he is forces him to swallow his own blood. The narrator is delighted with the scholarship to "the state college for Negroes" that he wins by toeing the line and knowing his place, and he does not object that the "gold coins" he groveled for are fraudulent. His education in the meaning of his grandfather's troubling injunctions will continue, but the reader has already seen enough to recognize their validity.

QUESTIONS FOR DISCUSSION

1. In the opening paragraph the narrator says, "I was naive." In what ways is his naiveté revealed in the story that follows?
2. Why does the narrator feel guilty when praised?
3. What is the message to the narrator behind the suggestion "that since I was to be there anyway I might as well take part in the battle royal"? Explain his hesitation. What is the most important part of the evening for the whites?
4. Who is present at the smoker? Discuss the role of the school superintendent.
5. What techniques does Ellison use to convey to the reader the impact that seeing the stripper has on the boys?
6. What does the stripper have in common with the boys? Why are both a stripper and a battle royal part of the evening's entertainment?
7. During the chaos of the battle, the narrator worries about how his speech will be received. Is that absurd or understandable?
8. Does the deathbed advice of the narrator's grandfather offer a way to handle the battle royal?
9. Why does Tatlock refuse to take a dive?
10. Explain the narrator's first reaction to seeing the "small square rug." In what sense is his instinct correct?
11. What is the meaning of the electric rug to the whites? What do they wish it to demonstrate to the blacks?
12. Explain Mr. Colcord's reaction when the narrator tries to topple him onto the rug.
13. Analyze the narrator's speech. What is the implication of his having to deliver it while swallowing his own blood?
14. Why is the school superintendent confident that the narrator will "lead his people in the proper paths"?
15. Why does the narrator stand in front of his grandfather's picture holding his briefcase? Who gets the better of this confrontation?

TOPICS FOR WRITING

Critical Essays

1. Seeing and understanding in "Battle Royal."
2. Sex, violence, and power in "Battle Royal" and Faulkner's "Dry September."
3. The battle royal and the black experience in America.
4. The "permanent interest" of "Battle Royal." (See Ellison's comment in Part Two, p. 1191.)
5. The blonde, the gold coins, and the calfskin briefcase.

Exercise for Reading

1. Select a passage of twenty lines or less for detailed explication. Relate as many of its images as possible to others in
   the story and to the general ideas that the story develops. To
   what extent does the passage you chose reflect the meaning of
   the story as a whole?

Related Subjects

1. Recall an experience in which you were humiliated or embarrassed. What motives of your own and of those before whom you
   were embarrassed put you in such a position? Narrate the
   incident so these underlying purposes become evident to the
   reader.
2. Write a description of a game or ceremony with which you are
   familiar. What set of principles or relationships (not
   necessarily malign) does it express?

SUGGESTED READINGS

Blake, Susan L. "Ritual and Rationalization: Black Folklore in the
Works of Ralph Ellison." PMLA, 94 (January 1979), 121-126.
Especially pp. 122-123.

Horowitz, Ellin. "The Rebirth of the Artist." In Twentieth-Century
Interpretations of "Invisible Man." Edited by John M. Reilly.
Englewood Cliffs, N. J.: Prentice-Hall, 1970. Pp. 80-88.
Especially p. 81. (Originally published in 1964.)

O'Meally, Robert G. The Craft of Ralph Ellison. Cambridge, Mass.:
Harvard University Press, 1980. Pp. 12-14.

Vogler, Thomas A. "Invisible Man: Somebody's Protest Novel." In
Ralph Ellison: A Collection of Critical Essays. Edited by
John Hersey. Englewood Cliffs, N. J.: Prentice-Hall, 1974.
Pp. 127-150. Especially pp. 143-144.

Aleksandr Solzhenitsyn

"Zakhar-the-Pouch" (page 899)

Solzhenitsyn's pretended artlessness masks the skill and
precision with which he steers between the perils of sentimental
patriotism and impermissibly bitter satire. In consequence he
manages to achieve both patriotic and satiric objectives, and thus
to arm his mildly chiding conclusion with a strength of conviction
to which his understatement lends credibility. The Battle of
Kulikovo accomplished little concrete except to kill a large part
of the population; two years later the Tartars were back in Moscow.

But from the perspective of history it struck the first blow in the Russian struggle for liberation, which took 150 years to complete. More through his evocation of the landscape in which it took place than through his vivid glimpses of the battle as he imagines it (guided in part by Aleksandr Blok's poem, "On the Battlefield of Kulikovo"), Solzhenitsyn conveys to the reader a sense of its importance. The present governing authorities, whose view of history confines their attention only to the western-front warfare of the last 150 years, have allowed the monument to fall into neglect. Their failure to appreciate the significance of Kulikovo redoubles the force of the impression Solzhenitsyn seeks to convey to the reader, and at the same time insinuates the relative transience of the political status quo, like the transience of the nineteenth-century cast-iron monument, in contrast to the Russian nation itself.

These serious concerns share the stage with the comical figure of Zakhar-the-Pouch, whose absurd appearance and behavior make him all the more acceptable a vehicle for Solzhenitsyn's major themes. For Zakhar Dmitrich, whose patronymic links him to Dmitry Donskoi and Dmitry Volinsky-Bobrok, the heroes of the Kulikovo, is not only the Keeper, the guardian of the national past against the depredations of time, neglect, historical ambiguity, and, as Rosette C. Lamont points out, the latter-day hordes of vandals who deface the monument; he is also the personification of that national history, of the nation itself. It has been Russia's fortune to suffer, to fall back, to give up everything, and yet to endure, to reemerge, to pop up from under a haycock on a frosty morning, undestroyed. At Kulikovo, "Our men were mown down like wheat, and we were trampled to death beneath their hoofs," and yet it was a victory, and a similar pattern has frequently held. Likewise Zakhar-the-Pouch, reduced to his overcoat and hatchet and twenty-seven roubles for pay, endures in his task with a passionate dedication at which it is finally no longer possible to smile: "Immediately our previous attitude of amused condescension vanished."

QUESTIONS FOR DISCUSSION

1. What expectations are aroused by Solzhenitsyn's informal opening?
2. Explain the tension that gives rise to the "even though" construction in the second paragraph. How important is this opposition?
3. Discuss the effect of the slow approach to the monument made by the bicyclists. Why does Solzhenitsyn interweave the facts about Kulikovo sporadically through the narration?
4. Why do the domes on the church suggest "something never seen except in fairy tales"?
5. Comment on Solzhenitsyn's use of the one-sentence paragraph beginning "Our men were mown down. . . ."
6. What period of history does the monument itself reflect? What characters in the story respond with most appreciation to the physical structure?

7. Explain the narrator's remark, "our invaders have not always come from the West."
8. Define the tone in which Zakhar is first presented. Why does Solzhenitsyn first introduce him as a colossus? What is the effect of the subsequent details?
9. Zakhar fusses that the monument is defaced with initials and dates, but he shrugs tolerantly over the theft of building materials. Why?
10. Solzhenitsyn favors us with glimpses of Zakhar smoking with "unalleviated grief," sprawled like a fallen warrior in the field, wearily dragging off to the village, and bursting out from under a haycock. What is the composite effect of these images?
11. When Zakhar says of his limp, "It's a souvenir from the war," the narrator thinks he is lying. Is he?
12. Was the Battle of Kulikovo a victory for the Russians? Explain.
13. What is our final assessment of Zakhar? How does he earn the narrator's esteem?

TOPICS FOR WRITING

Critical Essays

1. Zakhar's pouch.
2. The long and short views of Russian history in "Zakhar-the-Pouch."
3. The plot of Solzhenitsyn's narrative.
4. Defend the story against the charge of ethnocentrism.

Related Subject

1. Visit a historical site after first reading about the events that took place there. Note your reactions to the past events and the present circumstances, and write a personal essay about your visit. What would you need to add in order to turn your essay into a story like Solzhenitsyn's?

SUGGESTED READINGS

Grazzini, Giovanni. Solzhenitsyn. Translated by Eric Mosbacher. London: Michael Joseph, 1971. Pp. 131-133.

Kodjak, Andrej. Aleksandr Solzhenitsyn. Twayne's World Authors Series, No. 479. Boston, G. K. Hall, 1978. Pp. 120-121.

Lamont, Rosette C. "Solzhenitsyn's Nationalism." In Aleksandr Solzhenitsyn: Critical Essays and Documentary Materials. Edited by John B. Dunlop, et al. Second edition. New York: Collier, 1975. Pp. 94-116. Especially pp. 104-107. (Originally published in longer form in Review of National Literatures, 3 (Spring 1972), 153-182.)

Doris Lessing

"To Room 19" (page 912)

Lessing traces Susan's long slide into suicide in an ample, undramatic narrative that reflects Susan's personality and explores in their full complexity the reasons for her despair. If one factor is more significant than any other, it is the one Lessing announces at the start: "The Rawlings' marriage was grounded in intelligence." Matthew and Susan are known for "their moderation, their humor, and their abstinence from painful experience." Abstaining effectively from painful experience necessitates abstaining from all experience. Just as Susan does not "feel strongly about" her advertisements, she does not become fully engaged with anything else in her life. The establishment of a marriage and a family that depends on her is not her, and it has no purpose to which it is committed. Looking for a focal point, Susan fixes on her husband and "their love for each other," but that love is so reasonable, so well-chosen, so painless, that it leaves them feeling "dry, flat." Matthew's affair and Susan's tolerant, intelligent reaction to it devalue their love further without replacing it with anything. "Nothing is important," she feels. The marriage and the house and the children, to which she has given everything she has -- her soul -- come to seem merely a hiatus in her life. "In another decade, she would turn herself back into being a woman with a life of her own."

"The essential Susan," she supposes, has been "in abeyance, as if she were in cold storage," for twenty years, but when she is free to reemerge after the twins start school, Susan is surprised to find that there is only an emptiness that needs to be filled, an aimlessness that needs to be kept "occupied." Since she has already alienated herself from the things she has to do to fill up time, the intermittent demands placed on her by the children and the household now seem imprisoning. After trying several unsuccessful strategies to find an intelligent way to be alone, Susan finally turns her old life over to Sophie and retreats to Room 19 of Fred's Hotel. There she can get in touch with the "dark creative trance" or "dark fructifying dream" in which, if anywhere, the seeds of her new being may ripen and sprout. But when Matthew tracks her down and insists upon a reasonable discussion of the situation, Susan, to hide her last shred of privacy from his intrusions, invents a reasonable explanation. The fiction of Michael Plant, however, proves too exhausting to sustain, and she, for once animated by a clear purpose, has no recourse but to seek the repose of death.

QUESTIONS FOR DISCUSSION

1. Explain the phrase "abstinence from painful experience" as a way of characterizing the lives of Matthew and Susan before their marriage.
2. How important are their careers to Matthew and Susan?
3. Matthew and Susan are good at avoiding mistakes. Is it a mistake to do so?

4. Discuss the way Matthew and Susan handle Matthew's first infidelity. Explain what it would mean for Susan truly to forgive him.
5. Why does "Susan feel (though luckily not for longer than a few seconds at a time) as if life had become a desert"?
6. Comment on the idea that, "above all, intelligence forbids tears."
7. Why does Susan compare herself to a root that has been in cold storage?
8. Discuss Susan's reaction to the children's all going to school. What might have prevented her from having such difficulties?
9. If Susan's enemy is "emptiness," why does having the children and others call on her fill her with resentment? Why does she need to be alone?
10. Why does Susan feel imprisoned when given a room of her own?
11. Comment on Susan's vision of the devil. Assuming he is a hallucination, what needs or fears of Susan's may he be expressing? Why does he never reappear? What changes in Susan's behavior after his appearance?
12. Why does Susan want to hire an <u>au pair</u> girl? What is the result of Sophie's arrival? Consider the passage where Susan looks in through the kitchen window. What room does Sophie sleep in?
13. Explain what Susan derives from her hours in Room 19. Is she getting away from her "roles" and in touch with herself, or is she sinking away from herself into nothingness? What effect do her hours in Room 19 have on the rest of her life?
14. Comment on the images of the snail and the moth, which Lessing uses in describing Susan's feelings in Room 19 when she goes back after learning that Matthew has discovered it.
15. Why does Matthew, as Susan realizes, hope that she is having an affair? Why does she try to accommodate him by inventing Michael Plant? Explain her recoil from Matthew's suggestion that they make a foursome.
16. At what point does Susan decide to commit suicide? Evaluate her decision. Given her circumstances, is it an intelligent one?
17. Does it matter if we call Susan insane? Where should the blame for her death be laid? On Matthew? On Susan herself? On society, or her social position? Could Susan's death have been avoided, or was it in the cards from the beginning?

TOPICS FOR WRITING

Critical Essays

1. The imagery of dryness, moisture, and vegetation in Lessing's story.
2. "To Room 19" and Katherine Mansfield's "Bliss."
3. Lessing's analytical style.
4. "To Room 19" -- social criticism, psychological fiction, or horror story?

912-940 (text pages)

<u>Exercise for Reading</u>

1. Try to state the theme of Lessing's story as a piece of social criticism and as a piece of moral philosophy. How well do these themes reflect the story's impact on the reader?

SUGGESTED READING

Pruitt, Virginia. "The Crucial Balance: A Theme in Lessing's Short Fiction." <u>Studies in Short Fiction</u>, 18 (Summer 1981), 281-285.

Doris Lessing

"Homage for Isaac Babel" (page 938)

Lessing pays tribute to Babel, among other ways, by treating his theme of the self-destruction of innocence, but she does it with the French Impressionist painter Pierre Auguste Renoir in mind, so the pink and gold beauty of young Catherine's spirit shines through the portrait and dominates the reader's impression. In Philip and Catherine, Lessing paints two versions of innocence, both doomed in a world where even in the movies priests can only rescue some of the criminals, a world in which great writers are spirited away to concentration camps and murdered without compunction, a world that breeds bitterness like that of the movie doorman. Philip's notion that the cruelty of the world may somehow be prevented from just going on and on is no less naive, finally, than Catherine's enthusiastic sentiments, and no less poignantly destined to disappointment. The process of corrosion is already evident in Catherine's letter, where her affectation of a taste for Babel's "conscious simplicity of style" contrasts as markedly with the pure <u>unconscious</u> simplicity of her delightful postscripts as the white house in which she now lives contrasts with "the sweeping brown tides of the river" that await her below.

QUESTIONS FOR DISCUSSION

1. How would our opinion of Catherine be changed if the allusion to Renoir were omitted?
2. Comment on Catherine's preference in living quarters. What does this have to do with the theme of the story?
3. As a secondary character, Philip receives concise handling. How effectively does Lessing portray him?
4. What is the narrator's attitude toward Philip and Catherine, as expressed, say, in the view of them walking together at the school?
5. Explain what the film contributes to the story.
6. Account for Catherine's first reaction to the news that Babel is dead and has been for twenty years.

7. Why does the narrator want "to protect this charming little person from Isaac Babel?" Is it necessary? Is it possible?
8. How good a job is Catherine doing in "endeavouring to emulate" Babel's "conscious simplicity of style"?
9. Comment on Catherine's postscripts, contrasting them with the rest of her letter.
10. To use Babel's phrase from "My First Goose," is there a secret curve to Catherine's straight line about Babel from the start?

TOPICS FOR WRITING

Critical Essays

1. Doris Lessing's homage to Renoir.
2. Why "Homage for Isaac Babel" is so short, and "To Room 19" so long.
3. Allusion and theme in "Homage for Isaac Babel."

Exercise for Reading

1. Read, or reread, "My First Goose," imagining what it would mean to Catherine, and to Philip. Do either of them understand Babel? Explain.

Related Subject

1. Write a sketch in which two characters discuss one of the stories in The Story and Its Writer. Show how their respective personalities affect their understanding of the story. If possible, let the outcome of your sketch embody your own response to the story under discussion.

SUGGESTED READING

Butcher, Margaret K. "'Two Forks of a Road': Divergence and Convergence in the Short Stories of Doris Lessing." Modern Fiction Studies, 26 (Spring 1980), 55-61. Especially pp. 60-61.

Shirley Jackson

"The Lottery" (page 942)

The interpretive suggestions in the headnote should guide students toward a recognition of the main themes of "The Lottery." The near universality of the ritual sacrifice of year-gods and scapegoats in primitive cultures to ensure fertility, the continuation of life, and the purgation of society has been a common assumption since the publication of James G. Frazer's The Golden Bough. Jackson does not explore the transmutations of these old ceremonies in the accepted religious practices and psychological

mechanisms of modern man; rather, she attempts to shock her readers
into an awareness of the presence of raw, brutal, and superstitious
impulses within us all. A fruitful approach for class discussion
might involve exploring how the story achieves its impact. Jackson's
comments (reprinted in Part Two, p. 1192) provide incontrovertible
documentation of the power of "The Lottery" to stir the dark
instincts dwelling below the surface of the civilized psyche,
perhaps the same regions from which the story emerged fully formed
-- as Jackson claims -- in the mind of the writer. No wonder
readers, from the author's agent on, have found "The Lottery"
disturbing.

But they have also found it compelling, fascinating, and
irresistible, and the reason may have partly to do with Jackson's
technical skill. For the inattentive first reader, the natural
suspense of any drawing, contest, or lottery provides strong motivation to hurry through to the ending, and when the realization of
what is at stake comes, it strikes with redoubled force because of
the reader's increased velocity. For the more careful reader, or
for the reader already aware of the ending, the subtle foreshadowing
-- the boys are gathering stones, the box is black, Tessie Hutchinson "clean forgot what day it was," -- trigger an uncomfortable
double awareness that also urges haste, a haste like that which
spurs Mr. Summers's final, horrible remark, "All right, folks. . . .
Let's finish quickly," and the cries of "Hurry up" and "Come on"
voiced by other villagers.

For Jackson has succeeded in gaining the vicarious participation
of the reader in the lottery. Even the backwoods New England
quaintness of the setting draws not the kind of condescending
laughter that would distance the reader but the warm sentimental
indulgence we reserve for the cutest Norman Rockwell illustrations.
Little boys are being little boys as they pick up the stones, the
villagers are walking clichés, and even Tessie Hutchinson, singled
out from the rest by her tardiness, is tardy for the most house-
wifely of reasons. (How different the story would be if she
appeared nervous and flustered, a few moments ahead of, say, a
disheveled Steve Adams!) The reader is drawn to sink into this warm
bath of comfortable stereotypes, illusions intact. Totally off
guard against the possibility that the good hearts of these neigh-
borly folks might beat in time with an ancient and brutal rhythm,
that superstitious fears of hunger and death might easily outweigh
feelings of friendliness and compassion, the reader may well recoil
from any previous fascination and, in an effort to deny involvement,
recoil from the story, too. Except that we do not reject it; "The
Lottery" continues to exert such power over the imagination of its
readers that it clearly must be providing a catharsis for instincts
similar to those that move the villagers to pick up stones.

QUESTIONS FOR DISCUSSION

1. What associations does the word <u>lottery</u> have for you? Are they relevant to the story?
2. Comment on the ending of the first paragraph.
3. On what other occasions might the people of the village gather in the same way they do for the lottery? Mr. Summers is in charge of "civic activities." Is the lottery one of these? Explain.
4. Discuss the degree to which the tradition of the lottery has been kept. Why does no one want to make a new box? Why is the whole institution not abandoned?
5. Examine the character of Tessie Hutchinson. She claims that her fate is not <u>fair</u>. Is there any reason why she should be singled out? Is she a tragic heroine? Consider her cry, "There's Don and Eva. . . . Make <u>them</u> take their chance!"
6. On your first reading, when did you begin to suspect what happens at the end of the story? How soon might it become evident? What are the most important hints?
7. One reason that the ending can surprise a reader is that the villagers never speak directly of what they are about. Why not? Are they ashamed? Afraid?
8. Comment on the conversation between the Adamses and Old Man Warner. What is the implication of Steve Adams's last appearance in the story?
9. Does the rhyme, "Lottery in June, corn be heavy soon," adequately explain the institution of the lottery? What other reasons might people have for such behavior? What is the social function of a scapegoat?
10. After her family has received the black spot, Tessie complains, but Mrs. Delacroix tells her, "Be a good sport, Tessie." Comment on Mrs. Delacroix's choice of words.
11. Discuss the reaction of the Hutchinson family. Why does the lottery single out a family first, then a victim?
12. Old Man Warner complains, "People ain't the way they used to be." Are they? What does he mean?
13. Why are the people in such a hurry to "finish"?
14. What is the implication of "someone gave little Davy Hutchinson a few pebbles"?

TOPICS FOR WRITING

Critical Essays

1. "The Lottery" and Faulkner's "Dry September."
2. Shirley Jackson's techniques for building suspense.
3. The usefulness of stereotypes in "The Lottery."

Related Subject

1. Examine the behavior of groups of people with which you are familiar. Can you find actual instances of formal or informal practices similar to the one described in "The Lottery" -- even

though they may not lead to such a brutal finale? Have you or has anyone you know been made a scapegoat? Write an essay showing how one such case reflects and confirms the implications of Jackson's story.

SUGGESTED READING

Freidman, Lenemaja. <u>Shirley Jackson</u>. Twayne's United States
    Authors Series, No. 253. Boston: G. K. Hall, 1975. Pp. 63-67.

Grace Paley

"A Conversation with My Father" (page 951)

The story the narrator writes in response to her father's request is so interesting that it is easy to forget for a while that it is only an element within the larger story Paley has to tell. Confronted with the inescapable fact of the father's imminent death, the narrator and her father respond in differing ways because of their differing needs. Both use gallows humor to make the situation less intolerable, as when the father remarks, "It so happens I'm not going out this evening"; but the narrator seeks that refuge much more often, and her father chides her repeatedly for doing so. Things <u>matter</u> to a dying man, and it is not surprising that he should prefer the straight line of tragedy -- in which failure and defeat are compensated for by a perception of the real value of what has been lost -- to the idea of "the open destiny of life" which, by holding out the hope of recovery from any disaster, implies that there is nothing indispensable, no absolute loss. A man on his deathbed knows better.

The narrator's first attempt to write a story that suits her father's taste reflects her discomfort with the assignment. Her "unadorned and miserable tale" remains so sketchy that it lacks verisimilitude and conviction, like meaningless statistics on high-way deaths or counterinsurgency body counts. Challenged to try again, she partly confirms her father's complaint that "with you it's all a joke" by writing a brilliantly comic and incontrovertibly realistic version of the story, whose merits even her father has to recognize: "Number One: You have a nice sense of humor." In a few deft strokes, Paley renders an incisive satiric portrait of two contemporary "lifestyles," their hypocrisy, and their destructiveness, focused neatly in the competing periodical titles, <u>Oh! Golden Horse!</u> (heroin) and <u>Man Does Live by Bread Alone</u>. The narrator knows as well as her father how thorough a perversion of true spiritual values is embodied in each of these titles, and she dramatizes her understanding in the destruction of the mother in her story. But she cannot quite "look it in the face," and she ends her tale with one last grim joke: "terrible, face-scarring, time-consuming tears." Her father spies out her desperate evasion: "Number Two: I see you can't tell a plain story. So don't waste

154

time." Ironically, the clarity of his disillusioned vision enables
the dying man to feel a purer sympathy for the mother in the story
than the narrator herself, who claims to care so much about her
characters that she wants to give them all a second chance. "Poor
woman," he says, "Poor girl, born in a time of fools, to live among
fools. The end. The end. You were right to put that down. The
end." Not necessarily, the narrator argues, and goes on to invent
the kind of future for her character that we always imagine for the
dying, in the probably misguided effort to ease their anxiety. But
her father, as usual, knows better: "How long will it be?' he asked.
'Tragedy! You too. When will you look it in the face?"

QUESTIONS FOR DISCUSSION

1. Describe the medical condition of the narrator's father. How
   important is it to understanding his position in the conversation?
2. Explain the phrase, "despite my metaphors," in the first
   paragraph. What other writerly tactics of the narrator does
   her father ignore?
3. The narrator says she would like to tell a story with the kind
   of plot she has always despised. Analyze her conflict.
4. What is the point of the first version of the story? What is
   wrong with it as a piece of fiction?
5. When her father asks for details, the narrator comes up with
   things he calls jokes. Are they? What makes them jokes rather
   than facts?
6. Why does the narrator's father consider that "it is of great
   consequence" whether the woman in the story is married or not?
   Is he simply old-fashioned?
7. What does the narrator add to her story in the second version?
   Does the point of the story remain the same? Does her father
   get the point?
8. The woman in the story "would rather be with the young."
   Consider that motivation and its results from the point of view
   of the narrator and of her father.
9. What techniques does Paley use to satirize the woman's son and
   his girlfriend?
10. Explain the term "time-consuming" at the end of the inset story.
11. The narrator's father makes three separate responses to the
    story. Account for each of them. Do they cohere?
12. What does the narrator's father mean by the statement he makes
    in various forms culminating in his final question?

TOPICS FOR WRITING

Critical Essays

1. Attitudes toward death and life in "A Conversation with My
   Father" and in Hemingway's "The Snows of Kilimanjaro."
2. Stories about writing stories -- Paley's "Conversation with My
   Father" and O'Faolain's "How to Write a Short Story."

155

3. Tragedy versus satire in "A Conversation with My Father."
4. Attitudes toward adolescents in "A Conversation with My Father" and in Lessing's "Homage for Isaac Babel."

Related Subject

1. Write your own version of the narrator's story. Start from her first version and elaborate upon it as you choose, without necessarily using the material the narrator includes in her second version and subsequent commentary.

Nadine Gordimer

"A Chip of Glass Ruby" (page 957)

Without portraying sensational horrors or indulging in sentimental glorification of her heroine, Gordimer makes a powerful political statement about the inhumanity of <u>apartheid</u> and portrays in Mrs. Bamjee a woman whose beauty of spirit is just barely suggested by the poor jewel that gives the story its title. In doing so, Gordimer seems to have drawn on what she learned from the three writers mentioned in the headnote as having influenced her. The dialogue, like the setting observed with Hemingwayesque precision, makes the Bamjee household as real to the reader as home; the sense of a Lawrencian life force, expressing itself equally in Mrs. Bamjee's motherly care, in her revolutionary politics, and in the burgeoning reproductivity that carries forward despite old age and the Special Branch, unifies the story's concerns into a single theme; and the decision to tell the story as a record of the impact of its events on the consciousness of Bamjee as a Jamesian "reflector" provides form and structure for the plot. The struggle of human life against poverty and oppression can hardly be concluded in the narrow confines of a story, but it can be realized and appreciated. By showing how Bamjee comes to understand the connection between his wife's political activities, which he has heretofore found unsettling but irrelevant, and the traditional female roles that she executes so well, and by showing how he simultaneously discovers the reason "why he desired her, the ugly widow with five children," Gordimer dramatizes such a realization within the confines of a concise and well-made story.

QUESTIONS FOR DISCUSSION

1. The duplicating machine seems out of place to Bamjee in his crowded home. Is it? Comment on the objects it displaces from the sideboard.
2. What role do the children play in the opening scene? Why are they so important in this story?
3. Mrs. Bamjee turns out leaflets "as if she might have been pounding chillies." Explain the implications of the simile.

4. Define Bamjee's political attitudes. Are they affected by the arrest of his wife? How?
5. Bamjee sees that his wife is "not like other people, in a way he could not put his finger on," and he cannot quite define "the attraction that led him to marry her." What does he learn about these subjects as the story unfolds?
6. What concerns are uppermost in the minds of Bamjee and Mrs. Bamjee respectively as she is taken away? What later causes the "lump of resentment" to rise in Bamjee's throat?
7. Why is it Girlie rather than Bamjee who takes the lead in tracing Mrs. Bamjee's whereabouts and goes to visit her?
8. Contrast Girlie's appearance and demeanor with that of her mother.
9. What is the role of Girlie's pregnancy in bringing about Bamjee's recognition? What other factors are important? Explain the potential symbolic significance of it being Bamjee's birthday.

TOPICS FOR WRITING

Critical Essays

1. Mrs. Bamjee's politics of love.
2. Two revolutionaries: Gordimer's Mrs. Bamjee and Katherine Anne Porter's Laura (in "Flowering Judas").
3. Why Mrs. Bamjee is the heroine but not the central character of "A Chip of Glass Ruby."

Exercise for Reading

1. Bamjee reaches an insight at the end of the story. Try to get forth that insight in clear, analytical language. Refer to the earlier parts of the story, including sections revealing Mrs. Bamjee's attitudes. Are you satisfied with the result? Does it take into account the very last image in the story?

SUGGESTED READING

Magarey, Kevin. "Cutting the Jewel: Facets of Art in Nadine Gordimer's Short Stories." Southern Review (Adelaide), 7 (February 1974), 3-28. (A general discussion of Gordimer's short fiction, with passing comments on "A Chip of Glass Ruby.")

Flannery O'Connor

"A Good Man Is Hard to Find" (page 967)

O'Connor's comments (reprinted in Part Two, p. 1196) direct
attention to the climax of her story and suggest how she intended
the central characters to be viewed and what she meant the story to
imply. Students may benefit, however, from struggling at first to
interpret the text unassisted by authorial explanation. The effort
should reveal dimensions of O'Connor's art that might otherwise be
overlooked.

The grandmother's reawakening to reality, which leads to her
gesture of grace as she reaches out to The Misfit as one of her own
children, may be triggered by the violence of the murders going on
just offstage and the extremity of her own case, but her conversion
has been carefully prepared for. Throughout the story this old
woman longs in various ways to go back <u>home</u> -- to Tennessee, to the
days of her youth, to the mansion with the imaginary secret panel,
which is as much in heaven as it is down a hilly back road in
Georgia. Death is seldom far from her thoughts, though for a long
time she does not apprehend its reality. Her initial worries about
The Misfit are disingenuous, but encountering him or returning to
east Tennessee comes to the same thing in the end. On the road, the
grandmother dresses up in nice clothes so that "anyone seeing her
dead on the highway would know at once she was a lady," observes a
graveyard, and remembers her mansion at a town named Toombsboro. The
Misfit and his men approach in a "hearse-like automobile"; the
family awaits them in front of the woods that "gaped like a dark
open mouth." The grandmother is at odds with present times. She
squabbles with the children (whose behavior even the reader may find
unusually improper), easily upstages the cabbage-headed, slacks-
wearing woman who is their mother, joins Red Sammy in deploring the
state of world affairs, and disastrously deludes Bailey by smuggling
the cat into the car. But she loves the world as well, in a
selfish, childish way. She <u>will</u> have the cat along; she admires the
scenery (including a picturesque "pickaninny" for whose poverty she
is not yet ready to feel compassion); she wishes she had married
Mr. <u>E</u>. <u>A</u>. Teagarden, who courted her with watermelon and would have
supplied all her worldly needs from the proceeds of his Coca-Cola
stock; and she even makes a play for Red Sammy, the only tycoon in
sight.

These desires may be misdirected, but just as it takes very
little to upset the valise, release the cat, flip the car off the
road, and carry the story into an entirely new set of circumstances,
so, under the intensifying presence of death, it takes only a
moment for the grandmother's selfish love for and alienation from
the world to flip over into the selfless love that leads her to
open her heart to The Misfit. After all, she at least rationalizes
bringing the cat to protect it; she supportively asserts that Red
Sammy is "a good man" in face of his own cynicism and despair; and
she offers the same praise to The Misfit from the moment she
recognizes him. Without a doubt the grandmother's motive in

158

insisting that The Misfit is "a good man" and in urging him to pray is to divert him from his evident intention and so to save her skin. But as the bullets ring out in the background and the grandmother's maternal instincts burst forth in her repeated cries of "Bailey Boy," she begins to act charitably in spite of herself. She offers The Misfit one of Bailey's shirts, listens to his confession (although she is the one who is about to die), and when he _is_ wearing Bailey's shirt, she reaches out to him in his anguish. A good man _is_ hard to find; Jesus may have been the only one who was intrinsically good. But when she loves and pities the radically fallen Misfit, the grandmother becomes for the moment a _good woman_ through her Christ-like action, as The Misfit himself acerbically recognizes.

As O'Connor mentions in her commentary, The Misfit has evoked widely differing responses from readers and critics, who have associated him with the devil, the modern agnostic existentialist, or "the prophet he was meant to become," in O'Connor's own phrase. Perhaps The Misfit's Daddy provides the best way of distinguishing him from the rest of the characters with his remark, "It's some that can live their whole life out without asking about it and it's others has to know why it is, and this boy is one of the latters." Unlike O'Connor, whose vision of the world was grounded in _belief_, The Misfit wants to _know_. With Faustian presumption, he seeks to comprehend the divine mysteries in terms of his own intellect and demands a kind of justice in life that he can understand. When he cannot find the answers to his questions, but only the implication of inexplicable guilt (like Original Sin) in the punishment he receives, The Misfit sees the world not as the charming place it has appeared to the grandmother but as a prison whose empty sky resembles the blank walls of his cell in the penitentiary. In his own calculus of guilt, The Misfit feels he has been excessively punished, and he seems to be going about the world committing crimes in order to right the balance. His most perverse principle, "No pleasure but meanness," is sustained surprisingly well by the world O'Connor portrays. (Is _this_ the reason for the story's lack of anything or anyone to admire and its unremittingly ironic tone?) But it gives way after he has been touched by the grandmother to his first true prophecy: "It's no real pleasure in life" -- no _real_ pleasure in _this_ life, though true goodness sometimes appears in those made conscious of death.

QUESTIONS FOR DISCUSSION

1. What is the grandmother's reason for bringing up The Misfit at the beginning of the story?
2. Describe "the children's mother." Why does O'Connor make her such a nonentity?
3. What about John Wesley and June Star? What would have been the result had O'Connor characterized them as something other than totally obnoxious?
4. Discuss the grandmother's reasons for her fatal decision to bring Pitty Sing on the trip.

5. Why does the grandmother dress so nicely for the trip?
6. Compare the grandmother's response to the scenery and the trip with that of the children. What does O'Connor accomplish by means of this distinction?
7. Just before the stop at the Tower, the grandmother reminisces about her old suitor, Edgar Atkins Teagarden. Specify the connections between the two episodes.
8. What tower might O'Connor have had in mind in choosing the name for Red Sammy's establishment? Why is there a monkey in a chinaberry tree feasting on fleas posted outside the Tower? What do we learn about the world at Red Sammy's?
9. Contrast the Tower with the mansion the grandmother awakens to remember "outside of Toomsboro."
10. What factors cause the accident? Consider its meaning as a consequence of the grandmother's choices and desires.
11. Describe the manner in which The Misfit arrives on the scene. What effect does his appearance have on the reader?
12. The grandmother's response to The Misfit's remark, "it would have been better for all of you, lady, if you hadn't of reckernized me," is "You wouldn't shoot a lady, would you?" Evaluate her question.
13. To what extent is the grandmother correct in her praise of The Misfit? In what ways is he a gentleman?
14. Describe the grandmother's reaction to Bailey's departure. Is her response consistent with her previous behavior?
15. Define The Misfit's experience of the world. To what extent can his criminality be blamed on the conditions of his life? Does The Misfit feel any more free outside the penitentiary than in it?
16. How can the logic of The Misfit's position that "the crime don't matter . . . because sooner or later you're going to forget what it was you done and just be punished for it" be attacked? To what extent does The Misfit's description of himself apply to everyone? Bear in mind that the whole family is being punished with death for no ascertainable crime.
17. Explain how, to The Misfit, "Jesus thown everything off balance."
18. What is the effect of O'Connor's comparing the grandmother to "a parched old turkey hen crying for water"?
19. Does The Misfit do or say anything to deserve the grandmother's gesture of concern?
20. Explain The Misfit's final evaluation of the grandmother: "She would of been a good woman . . . if it had been somebody there to shoot her every minute of her life."
21. Contrast The Misfit's remark, "No pleasure but meanness," with his last words in the story.

TOPICS FOR WRITING

Critical Essays

1. "A Good Man Is Hard to Find" and Tolstoy's "The Death of Ivan Ilych."

2. The function of tone in O'Connor's story.
3. Techniques of characterization in "A Good Man Is Hard to Find" and Welty's "Petrified Man."

Related Subject

1. Write a parable or short tale designed to illustrate a religious or philosophical truth. Following O'Connor's example, portray your characters ruthlessly as embodiments of what you want them to represent.

SUGGESTED READINGS

Asals, Frederick. Flannery O'Connor: The Imagination of Extremity. Athens: University of Georgia Press, 1982. Pp. 142-154.

Browning, Preston M., Jr. Flannery O'Connor. Crosscurrents/Modern Critiques. Carbondale: Southern Illinois University Press, 1974. Pp. 54-59.

Feeley, Sister Kathleen. Flannery O'Connor: Voice of the Peacock. New Brunswick, N. J.: Rutgers University Press, 1972.

Orvell, Miles. Invisible Parade: The Fiction of Flannery O'Connor. Philadelphia: Temple University Press, 1972.

Flannery O'Connor

"The Artificial Nigger" (page 980)

The next-to-last paragraph gives in explicit theological terms an interpretation of what has happened to Mr. Head, but these formal and serious cogitations are not likely to make much sense to a reader who has not been following the symbolic undercurrents that flow along with the comical narrative from the start. While critics correctly remark that "The Artificial Nigger" is one of the few stories by O'Connor to end with hope for a continued and better life for its characters in this world, O'Connor is no more tender in her treatment of Mr. Head and Nelson than in that of the grotesques in "A Good Man Is Hard to Find." She subjects them to the same devastating comic irony. Frederick Asals has discovered by studying her manuscripts that O'Connor's first interest was in the literal narration of a trip to the city by an old man and a boy from the country, and our first response as readers is bound to be laughter at their arrogant self-importance, their habitual one-upmanship, and their bumbling about in the city.

But Mr. Head's comic pomposity, despite being as illusory as the dignity the reflected moonlight lends to the appointments of the cabin in the opening scene, constitutes for O'Connor true spiritual pride, and his efforts to act as Nelson's moral guide are ironically

161

infecting the child with the same sin. Mr. Head takes advantage of
the absence of blacks in the country to gain the upper hand over
Nelson on the train ride, but in truth neither of them has really
seen a Negro, nor themselves, until they get to Atlanta.

Mr. Head imagines himself as Vergil summoned to guide Dante
through the underworld, and his trip to the city has definite
infernal dimensions: With Nelson he passes allusions to Cerberus
as they enter the train and leave the city, and as they wander along,
their roughly spiral route brings them face to face with manifestations of human sinfulness, not least of all their own. In his
effort to communicate to Nelson his fear of the city, the site of
his own previous humiliation, Mr. Head introduces his grandson to
the dark, sucking sewer system that lies beneath the streets, and
Nelson "connected the sewer passages with the entrance to hell and
understood for the first time how the world was put together in its
lower parts." It is his own lower parts -- those parts of his being
that dwell below the head -- that Nelson next becomes acquainted
with, however, as -- tired, hungry, and lost -- he asks the black
woman for directions. He feels "his breath drawn up" as he looks at
her, and as her motherly physical being awakens emotions long
dormant in the orphan, he feels "as if he were reeling down through
a pitchblack tunnel." Nelson abandons his pretense of independence
at this point and puts his hand in Mr. Head's.

But Mr. Head remains for the time unchanged, and chides Nelson
for "standing there grinning like a chim-pan-zee while a nigger
woman gives you direction." Unaware of his own lower nature, Mr.
Head betrays himself a moment later by squatting "like an old monkey
on the garbage can lid," waiting out of sight, in his most heartless
stratagem yet, for Nelson to wake up. The consequent action leads
Mr. Head to put his hostility toward the boy into terms so explicit
that even he can understand them, severing the bond between them.
Immediately "he felt Nelson's fingers fall out of his flesh," and
Mr. Head finds himself in his own lonely hell, a "hollow tunnel,"
with Nelson's eyes like pitchfork prongs in his back. Pride denies
the connectedness of men, asserting, in the words of The Misfit in
"A Good Man Is Hard to Find," that "I don't want no hep. . . .
I'm doing all right by myself."

Mr. Head knows well that he is not doing all right, and his
subsequent efforts are directed at regaining contact with Nelson.
Atonement is not available on demand, however, and Nelson cannot
be reached by Mr. Head's condescension as he proffers the false
sacraments of "Co-Cola" and of water from a low spigot. While
Nelson waits for the "black mysterious form" of love to melt his
frozen mind again, Mr. Head is ready to abase himself by throwing
himself down a sewer entrance. Suddenly the way out of hell comes
into view and Mr. Head has the grace to cry out "Oh Gawd I'm lost!"
But being instructed in the way home is not enough, for it is only
as they stand side by side facing the "artificial nigger," whose
symbolic suffering reflects and surpasses their own, that the two
lost souls find each other and themselves again. Feeling mercy for
the statue, they acknowledge their own need for mercy and feel it

for each other, and O'Connor describes all three -- old man, boy, and statue -- in similar terms. Back in the country with the speed of thought, they find themselves in a type of paradise, illuminated but not distorted by the transfiguring moon. From this garden the "frightened serpent" that has taken them on their harrowing journey disappears. The final line of the story reveals that the enlightenment Mr. Head sought to convey to his young charge has in fact reached him, but through the channel of the heart instead.

QUESTIONS FOR DISCUSSION

1. Examine the first three paragraphs carefully. Are the dignity of the room and the wisdom of Mr. Head with which it is associated real or imaginary?

2. What is the effect of comparing the "slop jar" to a "small personal angel" on our attitude toward Mr. Head's "moral mission"?

3. What is the real point at issue between Mr. Head and Nelson in their argument about previous trips to the city?

4. How do the foreshadowings about getting lost affect the reader's response to the unfolding narrative?

5. "They were grandfather and grandson but they looked enough alike to be brothers not too far apart in age. . . ." Discuss the importance of the similarity of appearance between Mr. Head and Nelson later in the story.

6. Define the meaning that having "ever seen a nigger" has for Mr. Head and Nelson at the outset. What further dimensions do their confrontations with black people take on? Mr. Head observes that "a six-month-old child doesn't know a nigger from anybody else." Why not? In what sense does the infant's perspective turn out to be valid?

7. Why are Mr. Head and Nelson "prepared to ignore the train if it passed them"? Is their attitude here characteristic?

8. On the train, "Mr. Head demonstrated the ice-water cooler as if he had invented it. . . ." Find other ways in which Mr. Head implies a proprietary stake in the things he shows to Nelson. Is he justified? What happened to Mr. Head on his previous trip to the city?

9. Explain Nelson's reaction to his failure to recognize the "coffee-colored man" as a Negro.

10. Why does it make Nelson uncomfortable to see his reflection in the train window?

11. How valid are the descriptions of themselves Mr. Head and Nelson receive from the "weighing machine"?

12. Why does Mr. Head show Nelson the sewer? Explain Nelson's dual reaction to it.

13. After seeing the sewer, Mr. Head and Nelson find they have come full circle back to the railroad station. Does Mr. Head have anything more to show? What happens next?

14. "We didn't come to look at niggers," says Mr. Head. What does it mean that they do mainly that?

15. Why does Nelson have such a strong reaction to the black woman? With what does he associate her? What feelings does she release in him? Why does he now hold Mr. Head by the hand?
16. What are Mr. Head's true reasons for leaving Nelson alone while he sleeps? What does this incident suggest about Mr. Head's whole "moral mission"? Why does his plan go so far awry?
17. Explain Mr. Head's denial of Nelson. Why does he disown the child? What do his feelings afterwards reveal?
18. Why does Mr. Head offer "Co-Cola" and then water? Why does he feel despair when Nelson rejects them?
19. What is Nelson waiting for as he keeps his distance from Mr. Head? How does it come to him?
20. What does it mean for Mr. Head to ask directions from the man with the bulldogs? Why does this incident have to precede the encounter with the "artificial nigger"?
21. Why does the broken down statue seem "some great mystery" to Nelson and Mr. Head? Does Mr. Head's explanation suggest the answer?
22. Does the statue function as an icon, a crucifix? Why is an "artificial nigger" particularly appropriate as a vehicle for the atonement of Mr. Head and Nelson?
23. Compare the effect of moonlight in the last scene with that in the first scene. Compare moonlight with the sunlight that dominates the day in the city, making the protagonists hot and thirsty and making everything look "like exactly what it was."
24. How can we tell that Mr. Head's sense of salvation is not just one more self-delusion?

TOPICS FOR WRITING

Critical Essays

1. The meaning of monkeys and apes in O'Connor's "A Good Man Is Hard to Find" and "The Artificial Nigger."
2. Riding the rails in "The Artificial Nigger," Crane's "The Bride Comes to Yellow Sky," and Nabokov's "First Love."
3. Mr. Head's trip to Atlanta as a journey into the self.
4. Irony, laughter, and the spiritual perspective in O'Connor's stories.

Exercise for Reading

1. As you read, keep a record of all predictions, expectations, and plans announced by the characters. Then note to what degree they are fulfilled. What is the implication of the pattern that emerges?

Related Subject

1. O'Connor claims that the inspiration for this story began with the title phrase alone. Choose a word, a phrase, or an object

that attracts you and explore its potential meaning by writing
a story in which it triggers an important insight in the
central character.

SUGGESTED READINGS

Asals, Frederick. Flannery O'Connor: The Imagination of Extremity.
    Athens: University of Georgia Press, 1982. Pp. 79-92.

Browning, Preston M., Jr. Flannery O'Connor. Crosscurrents/Modern
    Critiques. Carbondale: Southern Illinois University Press,
    1974. Pp. 60-69.

Feeley, Sister Kathleen. Flannery O'Connor: Voice of the Peacock.
    New Brunswick, N. J.: Rutgers University Press, 1972. Pp.
    120-124.

Orvell, Miles. Invisible Parade: The Fiction of Flannery O'Connor.
    Philadelphia: Temple University Press, 1972. Pp. 152-160.

Gabriel García Márquez

"A Very Old Man with Enormous Wings" (page 998)

The word allegories in the headnote presents a challenge to the
reader of this story, and the inevitable failure of any simple
scheme of interpretation to grasp the mystery fully at its heart
reflects García Márquez's central theme exactly. Like the crabs,
which come into the human world from an alien realm, the "flesh-
and-blood angel" constitutes an intrusion of something strange and
unfathomable into the comfortable world of reality-as-we-choose-to-
define-it. Everybody, from the "wise woman" next door to the Pope,
takes a turn at trying to find a slot in which to file the winged
visitor, but no definition seems satisfactory, and even Pelayo and
Elisenda, whom the angel's presence has made wealthy, spend their
money on a house "with iron bars on the windows so that angels
wouldn't get in." When at last the old man flies away, Elisenda
feels relief, "because then he was no longer an annoyance in her
life but an imaginary dot on the horizon of the sea."

In a comment on how he receives artistic inspiration, García
Márquez says, "There's nothing deliberate or predictable in all
this, nor do I know when it's going to happen to me. I'm at the
mercy of my imagination." Without intending to limit the story's
implications, one might associate the angel with this sort of
unpredictable intrusion of the visionary and wonderful into everyday life. As an old man with wings, the angel recalls the mythical
symbol of the artist, Daedalus, except that his wings are "so
natural on that completely human organism" that the doctor couldn't
understand why other men didn't have them too." Bogged down in the
mud, the angel seems less an allusion to Daedalus's son, the

165

overreacher Icarus, than a representation of the difficulty of the artistic imagination in sustaining its flight through the unpleasant circumstances of this "sad" world. True artists are often misunderstood, ill-treated, and rejected in favor of more practical concerns or of the creators of ersatz works that flatter established prejudices. Just so, nobody can understand the angel's "hermetic" language, and when he performs his aggressively unpractical miracles, no one is delighted. Exploited by his keepers, to whom he brings vast wealth, the angel receives as royalties only his quarters in the chicken coop and the flat side of the broom when underfoot. Popular for a time as a sideshow attraction with the multitudes, the angel is soon passed over in favor of the horrible "woman who had been changed into a spider for having disobeyed her parents," a grotesque and slapdash creation of the lowest order of imaginative synthesis, whose "human truth" gratifies both sentimentality and narrowmindedness. But the artistic imagination lives happily on eggplant mush, possesses a supernatural patience, and though functionally blind to the bumping posts of ordinary reality, ever again takes wing. The angel has, perhaps rightly, appeared to his human observers "a cataclysm in repose"; but hear the end, as he sings his sea chanteys under the stars, he definitely comes to resemble "a hero taking his ease," preparing to navigate the high seas beyond the horizon.

QUESTIONS FOR DISCUSSION

1. Why are there crabs in the house? Is it for the same reason the old man with enormous wings has fallen in the courtyard? What other associations does the story make between the old man and the crabs?

2. Pelayo first thinks the old man is a nightmare. What other attempts are made to put this prodigy into a familiar category?

3. How does the old man differ from our usual conceptions of angels? What is the essential difference?

4. Explain Father Gonzaga's approach to the angel. What implications may be derived from his failure to communicate with him effectively -- about the angel and about the church?

5. Comment on the angel's career as a sideshow freak. Who receives the benefit of his success? Why does he fall? Compare what he has to offer with what the spider-woman has. What reasons might people have to prefer the latter?

6. Why do you think the angel tolerates the child patiently?

7. What are the implications of the angel's examination by the doctor?

8. How do we feel as the angel finally flaps away at the end? Does Elisenda's response adequately express the reader's?

TOPICS FOR WRITING

Critical Essays

1. "A Very Old Man with Enormous Wings" and Cheever's "The Enormous Radio" -- the ordinary and the enormous. (Consider the etymological meaning of enormous.)
2. García Márquez's fallen angel -- fairy tale, myth, or allegory?
3. Recharging the sense of wonder: How Garcia Marquez makes the reader believe in his angel.
4. "A Very Old Man with Enormous Wings" and other presentations of the supernatural. (See, for example, Hawthorne, Kipling, and Singer.)

Exercise for Reading

1. Read the story aloud to a selected spectrum of people (at least three) of various ages and educational levels. Tabulate their responses and opinions, perhaps in an interview. Combining this evidence with your own response to the story, try to define the basis of its appeal.

Related Subject

1. Select a supernatural being from a fairy tale or other familiar source (the cartoons involving talking animals that wear clothes and drive cars might be worth considering), and imagine the being as a physical reality in your own ordinary surroundings. Write a sketch about what happens.

SUGGESTED READINGS

McMurray, George R. Gabriel García Márquez. New York: Ungar, 1977. Pp. 116-119.

Morello Frosch, Marta. "The Common Wonders of García Márquez's Recent Fiction." Books Abroad, 47 (Summer 1973), 496-501.

Milan Kundera

"The Hitchhiking Game" (page 1005)

The unnamed young man and woman whose frightening adventure Kundera describes emerge from a vague backdrop as sharply defined personalities, but Kundera reserves his most detailed article for the purpose of making credible the process that calls the reality of those personalities into question. Because he carefully documents each evolving stage of the hitchhiking game as it is experienced by both characters, Kundera is able to convince the reader, not only that this assault of fiction upon real life is motivated, plausible, and even likely, but also that it reveals an important truth applicable to us all.

167

Setting out on a long-awaited vacation from their burdensome
and confining jobs, the lovers are inclined toward experimentation
and play. Each is also inclined, it turns out, to take a vacation
from certain self-imposed and mutually imposed constraints on their
relationship. The girl is cut off from full sensual awareness by
being shy. Her ambition that her relationship with the young man
should be <u>complete</u> ironically limits it. "The more she tried to give
him everything, the more she denied him something: the very thing
that a light and superficial love or a flirtation gives to a person."
The young man likes the jealousy that arises from her worry on this
score just as he likes the girl's shyness. "In the girl sitting
beside him he valued precisely what, until now, he had met with
least in women: purity." But by definition this relationship is
thus limited for him by the lack of what he has found <u>instead</u> of
purity in the women he has known before, and "he worshipped rather
than loved her."

The hitchhiking game offers a way to break free of these
constraints, and its result is to engage the two in a relationship
antithetical to what has gone before. The young man puts the girl
on a pedestal, all right, but in order to humiliate her rather than
to worship her, and the perfect harmony of their bodies as they
enjoy intercourse beyond "the forbidden boundary" comes at the
expense of the unity of body and soul that they have previously
known. Even near the beginning both participants have occasion to
see that the game is getting out of hand, but each is so fascinated
with the sensation of freedom inherent in acting out an alien role
that neither is able to stop its onward progress.

In pretending to be someone other than themselves, the two not
only find the freedom to turn off from the narrow road of their
prescribed destiny, they also lose touch with what they have thought
themselves to be. The young woman <u>vanishes</u> behind a little bush to
emerge as a hitchhiker, and later, after <u>disappearing</u> with a wiggle
behind a screen from the view of the man who propositions her in
French, she seems to the young man to be crossing a "horrifying
boundary" that changes the nature of the self just "as water ceases
to be water beyond the boiling point."

At the end the meaning of their experience becomes clear in the
recognition that the assertion of identity, "I am me," is a
"pitiful tautology." The substitution of any nontautological
content for <u>me</u> plunges one into a frightening indeterminacy that
carries with it a power of decision more burdensome than the
illusory confinement it supplants. As a result of having indulged
in the freedom of playing their game, these lovers must now say, "I
am a man who has demeaned and humiliated his lover," and "I am a
woman who has acted like a whore and enjoyed it."

QUESTIONS FOR DISCUSSION

1. What purposes are served by the opening conversation about running out of gas?
2. Evaluate the young man's attitude toward the girl's shyness and his delight in making her blush.
3. What conflicts about her relationship with the young man trouble the girl?
4. Explain the implications of the paradox that she gets "the greatest enjoyment from the presence of the man she loved" when she is alone.
5. Why do you think the girl starts the hitchhiking game?
6. One of the first results of the game is that the lovers get angry at each other. Why do they keep playing? Does the anger contribute to the continuation of the game?
7. What kinds of freedom does the game bring to each player?
8. At what stage does the game begin to get out of control? Or has it ever been in the control of either participant? Explain.
9. Define the change of atmosphere that takes place at the beginning of section VI.
10. When does the girl fully enter into her role? What does that involve? What purposes does it serve for her? Answer the same questions about the young man.
11. Explain the insight about the girl that the young man reaches in section VII. Does she reach a similar conclusion at any stage?
12. "There's no escape from a game." Is that true? Explain by reference to the story and in general.
13. What is the effect of the young man's forgetting that he is playing a game? Why does he do so?
14. Explain the last sentence of section XI.
15. Why is "I am me" a "pitiful tautology"?
16. How does what takes place in this story differ from organized theatrics? From daily role-playing?
17. Why does the concluding line of the story sound like a sentence to punishment rather than the declaration of a holiday?

TOPICS FOR WRITING

Critical Essays

1. The first paragraph of "The Hitchhiking Game" as a microcosm.
2. Kundera's story as a philosophical parable.
3. What the lovers in "The Hitchhiking Game" gain and what they lose.
4. Kundera's use of stock imagery in "The Hitchhiking Game" (for example, the road, the woods, the dark, dirty, and wandering city).
5. "The Hitchhiking Game" and Flannery O'Connor's "The Artificial Nigger."

Exercise for Reading

1. With a fellow student, act out the scenes of sections III, V,
   VII, and IX. Record your sensations and your awareness of the
   doubly fictitious persona with which you are conversing. How
   would you feel about acting out the rest of the story?

Related Subject

1. Write a sketch in which you portray yourself pretending to be
   someone very different. Perhaps you are habitually polite and
   deferential to waiters in restaurants. Imagine yourself
   behaving in an outrageously assertive manner. Or perhaps you
   are smooth and confident with members of the opposite sex.
   Describe an encounter in which you are tongue-tied and embarrassed. Follow your incident through to a conclusion that
   embodies the insight into your personality that writing it
   suggests.

John Barth

"Lost in the Funhouse" (page 1021)

In a brief comment written for the collection Writer's Choice,
edited by Rust Hills (New York: David McKay, 1974), Barth
describes this story as occupying a medial position in a development
from conventional to less conventional techniques and from youthful
and presumably more personal versions of Ambrose in the earlier
stories in the volume Lost in the Funhouse to later "more mythic
avatars of the narrator." He goes on to repudiate "merely cerebral
inventions, merely formalistic tours de force," and to declare his
hope that the story is "accessible, entertaining, perhaps moving."
Just as Ambrose is portrayed "at that awkward age," so the narrator
who portrays him (a being hard to distinguish from Ambrose on the
one hand and Barth on the other) appears in a transitional stage,
the adolescence of his art. Quoting to himself the supposedly
infallible principles of composition that he seems to have learned
in a creative writing course at school, he struggles forward self-
consciously, complaining that what is supposed to be happening as
he writes does not seem to be taking place. Just as for Ambrose in
the tool shed or at his baptism, observation of the proper forms
does not necessarily bring the expected results. And yet, just as
Ambrose is capable of experiencing unusual transports at inopportune
moments, so the story, as it were in spite of or apart from the
conventions, renders a poignant account of the time and place in
which it is set, of its protagonist's initiation into the mysteries
of life and art, and of the narrator's unexpected triumph over the
difficulties he confronts.

Readers may compare their experience of the story to the difficult progress through a funhouse, with its sudden surprises, its maddening reflections, its obvious contrivances, and the heavy atmosphere of sexuality that pervades it. We enter perhaps violently yawning in the nervous anticipation that shocks are in store, but surely few readers are prepared for the upending of expectation that takes place even in the first paragraph. We stagger forward with the narrator, bumping into the pasteboard screens of his contrivance, glimpsing the pulleys and levers by which the story is operated but nonetheless responding to the images thrust before us. When the narrator complains, "We haven't even reached Ocean City yet: we will never get out of the funhouse," the reader knows he is referring to the story itself as well as to the boardwalk attraction.

Fiction is traditionally supposed to be an imitation of life, made the more credible, as the narrator remarks, by the artifice of illusion. By extension, then, the funhouse can be called an imitation of life, and of that part of life called art (the commentator wanders in these mazes too). While the funhouse may be fun for lovers, for Ambrose and the narrator it begins as "a place of fear and confusion," mastered only by he fantasy of control with which the story concludes. Life, too, which resembles the funhouse in having seduction, coupling, and propagation as its central purpose, appears to the sensitive adolescent a frightening labyrinth that he must enter. The realities of war, death, and suffering -- masked by the diversions of the funhouse or glimpsed behind them -- lie in wait, and perhaps the Operator of the whole show is dozing at the controls. Although Ambrose has theoretical access in Magda to the "fun" life has to offer, he recoils with nausea from his visions of the universal copulation, can bear only the lightest contact with her body, and recalls their precocious experience in the tool shed mainly by reference to the image of a muse-like woman with a lyre printed on a cigar box, her lower parts peeled away. When he loses Magda in the funhouse, Ambrose feels relief, and although he finds his name, with its suggestions of enlightenment (or vision) and divinity, he loses himself in the multiple reflections of the mirrors.

The narrator knows that a conventionally structured story would reach its climax in Ambrose's escape from the funhouse, but what would this story become if its culminating image were the emergence of Ambrose from the funhouse in uneasy companionship with a blind, black Ariadne? Barth's self-regarding experimental narrative technique enables him to beg the question of his protagonist's escape from the literal funhouse and to leave him lost in the figurative one, blocked from enjoying the "fun" but assured of his ability to create through his art even better "funhouses for others."

The discovery of this assurance constitutes a victory for Ambrose over his initial "fear and confusion," and it proclaims the narrator's triumph over the problems of his art with which he has struggled throughout the story. It is a triumph gained in large

measure by means of acknowledging the struggle. Like Joyce's A
Portrait of the Artist as a Young Man, to which Barth alludes more
than once, "Lost in the Funhouse" combines a nostalgic realization
of the circumstances that determine the protagonist's vocation with
the assertion of a provisional theory according to which he intends
to carry it out. Just as Stephen Dedalus's resolution to take wing
is subject to an ironic interpretation that sees it as an expression
of his emotional immaturity, so Ambrose's decision to substitute
the detached manipulation of the funhouse for living his life might
be regarded as an expression of adolescent neuroses that he will
outgrow. Barth makes clear, however, that the combined sensitivity
to and detachment from his experience that make Ambrose an artist
do not simply result from a trauma in the tool shed; rather, as
existing qualities of his personality (perhaps inherited from his
father, whom he resembles as Peter resembles Uncle Karl), they have
conspired to render that occasion a tangible memory for Ambrose
while for Magda it remains, if it lingers at all, an aspect of her
vague but condescending warmth to Peter's little brother. Barth's
handling of the double pas de trois that evolves its intricate
parallels and contrasts in the front and back seats of the La Salle
and along the boardwalk at Ocean City demonstrates that the artist's
way of revealing the hidden realities of life does not have to
follow the repellent naturalism of Ambrose's flashlight view below
the boardwalk or the oversimplifications of his fantasies about the
essential activities of his ancestors and the world at large. No
less than A Portrait, Barth's story is a tour de force whose own
principles of composition criticize the conclusions reached by its
protagonist.

QUESTIONS FOR DISCUSSION

1. How are italics used most frequently in this story?
2. Examine the remarks about nineteenth-century realistic fiction
   in the second paragraph. If Barth's story seeks to convey an
   illusion of reality, what reality does it represent? A
   family's trip to Ocean City or a writer's effort to narrate
   that trip? Or to narrate his effort to narrate that trip?
3. Starting with the fourth sentence in the story, trace all
   references to American history, society, and current events,
   including World War II. How important are these concerns?
   What do you think Barth intends to accomplish by bringing them
   up?
4. Describe the seating arrangements in the car. What parallels
   do you notice between the two rows of people? Later, as they
   walk on the boardwalk similarly disposed, the narrator remarks,
   "Up front the situation was reversed." Explain. The name
   Peter means rock. What objects and qualities are associated
   with Uncle Karl?
5. The narrator worries that "if one imagines a story called 'The
   Funhouse,' or 'Lost in the Funhouse,' the details of the drive
   don't seem especially relevant." What does Barth accomplish on
   this drive with his characters, setting, and theme?

6. What does Barth succeed in communicating about Ambrose by tracing the chain of associations involving cigars, the banana, and Magda?

7. Immediately after chiding himself for having "nothing in the way of a theme," the narrator produces the account of Ambrose's visit to the tool shed with Magda. Explain the thematic implications of that passage. Do they account for Ambrose's moving away his hand as Magda sits down?

8. Why does Uncle Karl warn the young people to "stay out from under the boardwalk"? How are the various elements of this and the next few paragraphs related? Trace the associations in Ambrose's mind; in the narrator's.

9. Who asks, "How long is this going to take?"

10. Why does the narrator remark, "Nobody likes a pedant"? Is his attention to language part of what separates Ambrose from Magda?

11. If diving is a literary symbol, what does it symbolize? Judging from his choice of words, what is Ambrose thinking of as he talks to Magda about Peter's diving?

12. The next two paragraphs leap ahead to the funhouse and back to the tool shed, ending with another grammatical error. What does Barth achieve by thus manipulating chronology, here and elsewhere?

13. Analyze the paragraph that begins, "Let's ride the flying horses!" Whose thoughts are transcribed there? What kinds of alternative plots are envisioned? In the next paragraph, the narrator contemplates still other ways of ending his story. What is the effect of our discovery that one of these endings may be more or less what "actually" happened?

14. Why do Ambrose's initiations -- tool shed, baptism, Boy Scouts -- all leave him cold?

15. Is Ambrose correct in his insight about the point of the funhouse?

16. One effect of Barth's manner of narration is to put off Ambrose's entry into the funhouse until the last possible moment. What does he gain by doing so?

17. Referring to the second diagram, a variant of "Freitag's Triangle," what event or events in the story of Ambrose should be represented by C? By CD? And what events in the story of the narrator's effort to tell the story?

TOPICS FOR WRITING

Critical Essays

1. How "Lost in the Funhouse" resembles Stein's "As a Wife Has a Cow" and O'Faolain's "How to Write a Short Story" -- and how it does not.

2. The realistic narration of "Lost in the Funhouse."

3. The meaning of nausea in Barth's story.

4. The funhouse technique -- obvious imagery, abrupt changes, and surprising drafts from below.

1021-1053 (text pages)

Exercise for Reading

1. "Lost in the Funhouse" resembles an author's journal, or an
    early draft of a traditional story coming into existence on the
    page. Outline that story as it finally emerges, and outline
    the story of the process by which it develops. Do you believe
    that this is an accurate account of how stories are written?

SUGGESTED READINGS

Beinstock, Beverly Gray. "Lingering on the Autognostic Verge: John
    Barth's Lost in the Funhouse." In Critical Essays on John
    Barth. Edited by Joseph J. Waldmeir. Boston: G. K. Hall,
    1980. Pp. 201-209. Especially pp. 206-209. (Originally
    published in Modern Fiction Studies, 19 (1973), 69-78.)

Knapp, Edgar H. "Found in the Barthhouse: Novelist as Savior."
    In Waldmeir, ed., Critical Essays on John Barth. Pp. 183-189.
    (Originally published in Modern Fiction Studies, 14 (1968-1969),
    446-451.

Morrell, David. John Barth: An Introduction. University Park:
    The Pennsylvania State University Press, 1976. Pp. 87-90.

Schulz, Max F. Black Humor Fiction of the Sixties: A Pluralistic
    Definition of Man and His World. Athens: Ohio University
    Press, 1973. Pp. 34-36, 129-130.

Seymour, Thom. "One Small Joke and a Packed Paragraph in John
    Barth's 'Lost in the Funhouse.'" Studies in Short Fiction, 16
    (Summer 1979), 189-194.

John Updike

"Flight" (page 1041)

Allen Dow's problem is to find a way to mount a meaningful
rebellion against a family and a community that expect him to leave,
encourage him to leave, and thereby co-opt his departure. Because
everyone recognizes that his unusual talents exceed the scope
provided by Olinger, his most obnoxiously conceited behavior is
accepted ("the privileges of being extraordinary"), while his
efforts to pursue the normal social activities of adolescence ("the
pleasures of being ordinary") are frowned upon. Allen feels
"simultaneously flattered and rejected."

The ambiguity of his position is focused in his relationship
with his mother, whose desire for him to "fly" springs from her own
disappointment. When her father moved to Olinger from the farm,
she was torn from her childhood home but compensated by the widening
horizons made possible by prosperity. Since the Great Depression,

however, she has found herself imprisoned in a home that is not her own, in a town where she feels unwelcome. By casting Allen in the role of the phoenix, "destined to reverse and redeem" the family misfortunes, she effectively forbids his escape, just as her father forbade her from going to New York. In his peculiar fantasy it is Allen, not his mother, who is represented as the earthworm surrounded and held down by the "huge root."

Youth finds a way, however, and Allen's emergence takes the ironic form of a relationship with Molly Bingaman, the personification of all the comfortable limitations of Olinger that are forbidden him by his special status as outsider, bird of passage, man of destiny. His mother's recognition of the threat his interest in Molly poses to her desires is immediate, but Molly provides Allen with a base for an identity apart from the burden of expectations heaped on him by everyone, a "negative space" into which he can grow. Molly's passivity is her most attractive quality, evident even in her climactic coming out to him, and although Allen never brings himself to tell her so, his love for her is real. When he gives her up as the down payment on his freedom from the "black mass of suffering" that flows from his grandfather to his mother and threatens to overwhelm him, too, his mother both wins him back from Olinger and loses him for herself. The "typical melodrama" of her farewell may be in character, but it admirably expresses the difficulty for both parent and child of letting go.

QUESTIONS FOR DISCUSSION

1. Point out some of the "microscopic accuracies" (see the headnote) that make this story convincing.
2. Comment on Allen Dow's habit of speaking of himself in the third person. Why does he do so? On what occasion does he explicitly not do so? Why?
3. What does the view of Olinger from atop Shale Hill mean to Allen's mother? What is the effect of her remark on Allen? Consider the implications of the town's name.
4. Summarize the history of the Baer family. Is it true that "each generation of parents commits atrocities against their children"? Why?
5. Explain the implications of Allen's examining the snapshot of his mother "on the stained carpet of an ill-lit old house in the evening years of the thirties and in the dark of the warring forties."
6. Discuss Allen's feelings about his grandmother and the asparagus patch.
7. How important is Allen's father to the story? Why do you think Updike stresses his device of committing imaginary suicide with a cap pistol in his classroom?
8. Allen realizes that his mother fights with her father "because she could not bear to leave him alone." Explain the implications of this insight for Allen himself. How does it relate to Allen's mother's ambition for him to be "the phoenix."

9. Comment on Updike's choice of the words <u>mounting</u> and <u>slumping</u> in his account of the debate team's departure.
10. Why does Allen become interested in Molly Bingaman? How important are the circumstances under which they become acquainted? Exactly what is she able to provide for Allen, for example on the train ride home?
11. How is it that Allen's mother can diagnose his relationship with Molly so readily? Analyze her remark, "Don't go with little women, Allen. It puts you too close to the ground."
12. Why does <u>nobody</u> want Allen to go with Molly Bingaman? What benefit accrues as a result?
13. What does his involvement with Molly reveal to Allen about his mother?
14. Why does Updike set the stage for the final scene by discussing the radio? What other music is heard in this scene? What do the two strains mean to Allen and his mother? Compare your response to this passage with Updike's own, as detained in the interview excerpted in Part Two, on page 1200.
15. Why does Allen say he'll give up Molly? Why does his mother say "with typical melodrama, 'Goodbye, Allen'"?

TOPICS FOR WRITING

Critical Essays

1. "Flight" and Olsen's "I Stand Here Ironing."
2. Updike's techniques of characterization in "Flight."
3. Replication of the central conflict as a mode of developing theme in "Flight."

Related Subjects

1. Interview people about their parents' shortcomings. If possible, interview your own parents or other members of your family. Write an essay in which you explore Updike's specula- tion that "each generation of parents commits atrocities against their own children which by God's decree remain invisible to the rest of the world."
2. Does any of the material from your interviews suggest itself as the basis of a story? Try to write one. Follow Updike's example by focusing your theme in a single image such as <u>flight</u>.
3. Study Updike's one-paragraph character sketches. Pick one to imitate, and sketch a character based on a person or people familiar to you.

SUGGESTED READING

Detweiler, Robert. <u>John Updike</u>. Twayne's United States Authors Series, No. 214. New York: Twayne, 1972. Pp. 75-76.

John Updike

"Wife-wooing" (page 1053)

Updike's juxtaposition of the contemporary suburban scene with the elemental concerns of Stone-Age man drawn round the fire at the mouth of the cave or wresting a living from the savage jungle serves at least three purposes. First, it contributes to the story's predominantly comic tone. Second, it serves to satirize the narrator, a poetic fellow and a reader of Joyce, who arrives at such fantasies through his hyperactive verbal imagination and who thereby casts himself in an appropriate, even atavistic role, the fallaciousness of which the denouement reveals. Third, the intrusion of these incongruous images into the story directs attention toward the deepest level of its thematic implications about the structure of relations between the sexes.

Updike defines a spectrum that extends from the total egotism of the baby, "sharing nothing," content as long as his needs are filled, to the complete union the narrator imagines with his wife, symbolized in the "interlocked penumbrae" of "the great rose window" he associates with their honeymoon. A scale of linguistic capacities extends from the wordless baby through the differing competence of the two older children to the "ornate words" of the narrator, once useful in wooing. But to his dismay, his level of communication with his wife has transcended the verbal. His words do not woo her; his gestures betray him; and her words about the dissembler Nixon provide her with a tricky way to escape from his advances. The narrator's poetic fantasies remain as self-contained as the baby's "simple reflections within himself," and his wife's psychological virginity, despite the children that "seem to come out" of her one after another and the blood spilled on the honeymoon, remains as intact as the virginity represented by the rose window of a cathedral.

Thwarted in his desire, the narrator takes refuge in his fantasy of self-sufficient masculine activity: "He arrows off to work" and returns "a steep girder." But his purposeful enterprise degenerates into aimless circles of frustration. When his wife, "girlish" again, comes to him on her own initiative, he discovers that, in love, it is possible to receive unasked what cannot be seized or cajoled. The woman, far more than merely a "wide w," a "receptive o," turns out to have a will of her own, granting grace unpredictably and unbesought, more like the "tall friend of my childhood," who "wills the universe anew every instant," than the object of manipulation addressed by the wooer. In his desire-fueled fantasies, the narrator has forgotten that he is not the only one to sally forth bravely.

QUESTIONS FOR DISCUSSION

1. How does Updike imply the symbolic significance of the family's grouping around the fire?
2. Analyze the wordplay of the narrator's meditations. What purposes does it serve? What does it reveal about him?

3. To what is the narrator's trip for hamburgers compared? What literary genres and eras does the style recall?
4. Why does the narrator begin his seduction of his wife with a reference to their honeymoon? Is it a good choice?
5. What difficulties do the children pose to wife-wooing?
6. Discuss the narrator's thought, "You love the baby more than me."
7. Why is it "tiring" to the narrator that "we sense everything between us" when at the same time he is apparently discontent that his wife retains her virginal integrity, "tall, fair, obscure, remote, and courteous."
8. Explore the implications of the narrator's thought, "We pay dear in blood for our peaceful homes."
9. Why is the narrator relieved that his wife appears ugly in the morning?
10. Explain the terminology of the "momentous moral."

TOPICS FOR WRITING

Critical Essays

1. Poetic techniques in "Wife-wooing" -- figures of sound, allusion, and symbolic imagery.
2. Can this marriage be saved?

Exercise for Reading

1. Read Sonnet 67 from Edmund Spenser's Amoretti (1595) in conjunction with Updike's story. The deer represents the poet's mistress, whom he has been wooing for the previous sixty-six sonnets. This one marks their engagement.

> Lyke as a huntsman after weary chace,
>   Seeing the game from him escapt away,
>   sits down to rest him in some shady place,
>   with panting hounds beguiled of their pray:
> So after long pursuit and vaine assay,
>   when I all weary had the chace forsooke,
>   the gentle deare returned the selfe-same way,
>   thinking to quench her thirst at the next brooke.
> There she beholding me with mylder looke,
>   sought not to fly, but fearelesse still did bide:
>   till I in hand her yet halfe trembling tooke,
>   and with her owne goodwill hir fyrmely tyde.
> Strange thing me seemd to see a beast so wyld,
>   so goodly wonne with her owne will beguyld.

Specify any parallels you see between the two works.

SUGGESTED READING

Detweiler, Robert. John Updike. Twayne's United States Authors Series, No. 214. New York: Twayne, 1972. P. 73.

Philip Roth

"'I Always Wanted You to Admire My Fasting'" (page 1058)

The story's ending points toward an important dimension of Roth's theme: The historical fact that Kafka has become "<u>the</u> Kafka" is more fantastic and improbable than Kafka's own wildest fictions, and certainly moreso than Roth's invention of Dr. Franz Kafka, Hebrew teacher and suitor to Aunt Rhoda in Newark in 1942. Might not Kafka's bizarre narratives have a partial grounding in autobiographical fact, then -- just as Roth's realistic fantasy does? In a headnote to this story that he contributed to Rust Hill's anthology, <u>Writer's Choice</u> (New York: David McKay, 1974), Roth complained that "sometimes serious students of literature tend to read Kafka as though he had written his stories on Mars, or in graduate school, instead of Prague," and that "'I Always Wanted You to Admire My Fasting' came largely out of trying to get my students at the University of Pennsylvania to read Kafka's fiction without becoming Biblical exegists in the process."

Showing how Kafka's writings reflect the troubled consciousness of their author is the burden of section I of the story, in which Roth, drawing not only on the diaries and letters but also on a penetrating insight into Kafka's novels and into stories like "A Hunger Artist" and "The Burrow," defines the personality of the character he imagines to have appeared in the Newark of his childhood. The effect of his concentration on the last phases of Kafka's life is to call into question the absolute philosophical oppositions that Kafka's works seem to invoke. Neither the vision of utter defeat nor the "daydream of salvation" is as true to life as the anxious struggle depicted in "The Burrow" to erect adequate, even beautiful, defenses against an inevitable doom. Roth sees that tale as an expression of Kafka's new life with Dora Dymant. Neither totally cut off from his happiness nor united in a romantic marriage, Kafka huddles with Dora in the last months of his life while the beast chews through his lungs toward the burrow.

But what if death had not come? How would Kafka have lived on? Would escape have meant fame and glory? The daring speculation of section II, bringing Kafka across the Atlantic to Roth's own New Jersey, follows not the improbability of what <u>did</u> happen but the prosaic momentum of what would have seemed most likely. Living on, Kafka has no literary executor to publish his unfinished masterpieces and draw the world's attention to his greatness. He builds a humble career instead on the religious studies to which he was returning in 1923. His affair with Dora dies over a period of years. Marriage, of course, remains impossible for him, though he does not refrain when pressed from attempting to start a relationship with Aunt Rhoda. Philip's father, domineering in such a different way from Kafka's own, attempts to instruct him in "what a family is all about," but Kafka, attempting to follow these fatherly instructions, finds out that he already knows. Aunt Rhoda, locked under the tyranny of her mother and married to a father-substitute institution called "The Big Bear," is as incapable of sustaining a relationship

with Kafka as Kafka was with Milena Jesenká-Pollak. The confrontation of "the Kafka" with the mocking Hebrew school boys and the
condescension of the Jewish middle class, which quite rightly evoke
the reader's laughter, also reveal the intrinsic humanity of the
great genius by casting him as a normal-sized object of sympathy.
Perhaps, further, they suggest that more than one potential artist
and seer has lived and died in obscurity, fated perhaps to suffer
less and produce less for the admiration of posterity.

All great writers are human beings, Roth reminds us; as human as
Roth himself, standing in front of his class at the University of
Pennsylvania or playing cards with his chums behind the synagogue at
age nine. Looking at Kafka, in the meditation that begins the story,
Roth spies not only the ascetic and alarmed face of the burrower, the
artist, but also the familiar features of "half the Jewish boys who
were my friends in high school" and of the millions of Jewish skulls
shoveled from the ovens of the death camps in Europe while Roth was
living his ordinary and protected childhood in New Jersey. Such
stark historical contrasts should shock us as much as any Kafkaesque
horror. Our defense is to hold the contrasting sides apart: Kafka
is Literature; Auschwitz (like the era of the lake dwellers) is
History; real life, for as long as we can sustain the illusion, is
the family album, stroking, and schmaltz. At the end of the narrative we leave Roth, a college student who wants to be a writer,
trying to break down the barriers. His family circumstances are the
opposite of what Kafka experienced, but the burrower-artist has to
keep banging his forehead against them until at last they harden
into material suitable to build "the beautifully vaulted chamber"
of his nonetheless doomed refuge.

QUESTIONS FOR DISCUSSION

1. Why does Roth open the story with the quotation from "A Hunger
   Artist"? What characters in his story resemble the hunger
   artist? How?
2. Roth does not say looking at Kafka is like looking in a mirror.
   Does he, however, imply a feeling of kinship with Kafka? What
   would be the significance of such a kinship in the story?
3. Besides the link of Jewishness, what relevance do the victims
   of Auschwitz have to a story about Kafka and Roth?
4. Why is it thematically appropriate as well as technically
   convenient for Roth to begin his story with an essay?
5. What relationship does Roth see between Kafka and the characters in Kafka's fictions? What does that imply about Roth's
   own fictions? Does this story sustain your conjectures?
6. What happened to Kafka in the last year of his life, as Roth
   discusses them in section I? How does it prepare you for
   section II? What remains unchanged for Kafka, in Berlin and
   in Newark?
7. Contrast the animal in "The Burrow" with the hunger artist.
   Which does Roth prefer as an allegorical representation of the
   artist? How can you tell?

8. Roth interprets "The Burrow" in psychosexual terms. Are similar terms useful in interpreting the story of Dr. Kafka and Aunt Rhoda? Of young Philip, Hebrew school boy, budding Borscht-Belt comic, and would-be author?

9. What factors other than the psychosexual play a role in the stories discussed in question 8? Begin with the real history of the Kafka.

10. How does the insulting nickname "Kishka" help to advance Roth's theme?

11. Comment on the ways the three boys do the alphabet assignment. Relate their responses to the varieties of Jewish experience mentioned in the story -- artistic, ordinary, cataclysmic. Explain the implications of Roth's judgment of Schlossman, "We should all be so lucky."

12. Why is Roth surprised and upset when Dr. Kafka agrees to come to dinner? (Remember that he knows nothing of the Kafka.)

13. Imagine Dr. Kafka's reaction to the Roth family and to Rhoda. "What sort of un-Kafka-like dream had Kafka been dreaming!"?

14. Define Roth's role in his family. How does it differ from Kafka's in his? How are they similar?

15. How is Aunt Rhoda characterized? What does her job at the Big Bear contribute to our understanding of her? To her meaning for Dr. Kafka?

16. Speculate about the contents of Kafka's four "meshugeneh letters" to Aunt Rhoda. Why is the hissed explanation offered by "my brother the Boy Scout" -- "Sex!" -- "no answer and enough answer"?

17. What is the implication of Roth's juxtaposing Dr. Kafka's death with his own rebellion against his father? Is it in the cards for Roth ever to become the Roth?

TOPICS FOR WRITING

Critical Essays

1. Portraits of the artists as young men: "'I Always Wanted You to Admire My Fasting,'" Barth's "Lost in the Funhouse," and Updike's "Flight."

2. How Roth would read "The Metamorphosis."

3. "Looking at Kafka" -- story or essay?

Exercise for Reading

1. Study the story with an eye to terms and motifs that recur in varying degrees of concreteness: verbal, fictive, concrete. To what extent do these recurrences suggest Roth's center of concern?

1058-1079 (text pages)

Related Subject

1. Study the life of one of the writers represented in the
    anthology. Narrate an imaginary event that brings the writer
    as you think of him or her into an environment familiar to you.
    Take into account Roth's insistence on the human stature of
    famous authors.

SUGGESTED READINGS

Malin, Irving. "Looking at Roth's Kafka; Or Some Hints about
    Comedy." Studies in Short Fiction, 14 (1977), 273-275.

McDaniel, John N. The Fiction of Philip Roth. Haddonfield, N. J.:
    Haddonfield House, 1974. Pp. 15-18.

Rodgers, Bernard F., Jr. Philip Roth. Twayne's United States
    Authors Series, No. 318. Boston: G. K. Hall, 1978. Pp. 155-
    156.

Imamu Amiri Baraka

"Uncle Tom's Cabin: Alternate Ending" (page 1075)

The difficulties of this story dissolve when one recognizes
that the narrator, the "I" who imagines himself thrown out the
window by "three elegant Negroes in light grey suits," is close
enough to the author himself to be expressing the kinds of conflicts
Baraka must have gone through in the years preceding the political,
cultural, and artistic transformation detailed in the headnote. The
self-directed irony of the bracketed passage about how "we westerners
love to try to make art out of" our alienation from society is
particularly bitter. The sudden eruptions of literary allusions and
other seemingly extraneous material into the text, along with the
occasional truncated sentences and abrupt shifts of focus, do not
express the specific concern with the act of composition that produces similar results in Barth's "Lost in the Funhouse," but they do
reflect the same predominance of the narrative consciousness over
the story being told.

Recalling an incident in which he himself figured as "Little
McGhee," the narrator openly speculates about its meaning for his
teacher, Miss Orbach, whose first name he cannot quite remember,
although he knows the kind of name it was because he knows the kind
of personality it refers to. This latter-day Puritan is no more
ready to see the blacks she is supposedly helping as human beings
than was Harriet Beecher Stowe, whose novel not only spurred the
abolitionist movement but also fostered the stereotype of black
docility and helplessness now referred to by the name of its title
character. When Little McGhee comes up with the right answer in
arithmetic, and shows in other ways the signs of independence and

182

normalcy that emerge so fully later when the teacher is out of the
room, Miss Orbach becomes uncomfortable.   Her stratagem for getting
him out of her sight is characteristically based on the fantasy that
something is wrong with him, something that requires special help.
The reason Miss Orbach feels uncomfortable, of course, is that
Little McGhee's big eyes are calling out to her desire for contact,
for something she would call "really dirty," a desire she has
repressed underneath "her silent doctrinaire routines." Caught off
guard in the principal's office by the reappearance of those eyes
in Louise McGhee's fact, Miss Orbach immediately falls in love, and
the narrator seems delighted that her love will be both deep and
hopeless, and presumably bring her nothing but remorse.

QUESTIONS FOR DISCUSSION

1. Explain why Miss Orbach is irritated when Little McGhee knows
   the answer.
2. Translate Miss Orbach's rambling thoughts in the second paragraph into coherent prose.
3. The narrator refers to Miss Orbach as an "anchorite." Explain
   how the term sums up her personality.
4. Elaborate on the abbreviated version of American history that
   the narrator gives in the paragraph beginning, "And in this
   class. . . ." How do the concepts of the promised land, the
   apocalypse, and the melting pot fit in? What interpretation of
   Moby Dick does the narrator apparently have in mind?
5. Why would the narrator tell McGhee to get out? Would that be
   a spiritual or a practical injunction?
6. After the "three elegant Negroes" throw the narrator out the
   window, the story becomes a much more straightforward narration,
   easier to read. What makes it so? What limitations in the
   story does the narrator thereby suggest?
7. Why does it trouble Miss Orbach that Little McGhee is looking
   out the window?
8. Explain her reasons for sending him to the nurse.
9. In the fictional economy of the story, what is accomplished by
   the conversation about how to pronounce sandwich?
10. Evaluate Miss Day, and the school she runs.
11. What parallels are there between the last two incidents, which
    Baraka's quick-cutting technique so closely juxtaposes?
12. Why is this story subtitled "Alternate Ending"?

TOPICS FOR WRITING

Critical Essays

1. The intrusive narrators in "Uncle Tom's Cabin: Alternate
   Ending" and Barth's "Lost in the Funhouse."
2. Versions of black experience: Baraka and Ellison.
3. The narrator's conflict in "Uncle Tom's Cabin: Alternate
   Ending."

1075-1094 (text pages)

Exercise for Reading

1. As you study Baraka's story, delete all passages whose connection to the characters and the main line of the plot is not
   immediately clear. Read through your edited version and compare
   it with the original. Compare theme and tone of the two
   versions.

SUGGESTED READING

Brown, Lloyd W. Amiri Baraka. Twayne's United States Authors
     Series, No. 383. Boston: G. K. Hall, 1980. Pp. 84, 87-88.

Joyce Carol Oates

"Where Are You Going, Where Have You Been?" (page 1081)

Pointing to Oates's remark, quoted in the headnote, that she
usually writes "about real people in a real society" should help to
keep discussion away from premature allegorization of mythologizing,
which -- for all its eventual value and interest -- smothers the
story's impact by diverting attention from its realism. Her further
observation that she understands Connie to be "struggling heroically
to define personal identity in face of incredible opposition, even
in the face of death itself," may suggest how to go about answering
the main question that the story poses when considered in naturalistic terms: Why does Connie go out to Arnold Friend?

Connie's life as Oates depicts it takes place in two realms.
Within her home and family Connie feels condemned and rejected, and
she returns the disapproval. Outside these familiar precincts lies
a world defined by movies, the drive-in restaurant, and the ever-
present popular music. It is not the music of Bob Dylan, as Tom
Quirk assures us, but the comparatively mindless, sentimental, and
romantic music against which in the early 1960s Dylan stood out in
such bold contrast. Connie's idea of the world into which, at the
age of fifteen, she is beginning to make her first tentative forays
is shaped by these songs and occupied by boys: boys who can be
snubbed with impunity, boys who merge into one undifferentiated and
safe blur in her mind, boys who offer hamburgers and "the caresses
of love." And that love is "not the way someone like June would
suppose but sweet, gentle, the way it was in the movies and
promised in the songs." To these boys Connie presents herself as
undifferentiated girl, and she is concerned that she look attractive
to them.

The world, however, is occupied not only by frank and tentative
boys but also by determined and deceitful men, by evil as well as
by innocence, by hypocrisy, perversion, and violence -- an exponent
of all of which Connie attracts in Arnold Friend. Although in the
course of their interview Connie sees through his disguise, the

impoverishment of her world provides her no way to resist his
advances. Her home provides no refuge, her father does not come when
she needs him (he has always been essentially absent anyway), and she
is unable to manipulate the telephone because of her panic. Meanwhile, Arnold, who presents himself in the guise of a movie hero,
a teenage "boy," and her lover, offers to take charge of her. He
places his mark upon her and gives her a role to play in a world of
his devising. Because she is cut off from her past and has no idea
of a future, she is at his mercy in determining what to do in the
present. Like her cultural cousin, Nabokov's Lolita, sobbing in
Humbert's arms, she simply has nowhere else to go. Not only does
Arnold show Connie that she is desired, he also provides her a way
to be "good": By going with him she will save her undeserving
family from getting hurt. Connie does not so much decide to go out
to Arnold as she watches an alien being that Arnold has called into
existence in her body respond to his desires. The final ironic
horror, of course, is that she will be raped and murdered and buried
in the desert not as brown-eyed Connie but as the imaginary "sweet
little blue-eyed girl" of Arnold's sick imagination.

Oates acknowledges that her inspiration for the story came in
part from reading about an actual case and Tom Quirk has demonstrated
at length the degree to which the circumstances of "Where Are You
Going, Where Have You Been?" seem to be derived from an article in
Life (March 4, 1955) by Don Moser entitled (in a reference to some
lyrics from a popular song) "The Pied Piper of Tucson." Even some of
the most apparently allegorical details, such as Arnold's trouble
with his boots, which has been attributed to his having cloven hooves
or wolf paws, reflect the facts about Charles Schmid, a wiry gymnast
of twenty-three who stuffed things in his boots, wore make-up, and
drove around Tucson in a gold car playing the hero to a group of
high-school kids until he was arrested for the rape and murder of
three young girls. Quirk's argument that Oates followed the magazine
article's theme in relating this horror in the "golden west" to the
emptiness of "the American dream" points out an important dimension
of the story, and his emphasis keeps the real horror of the incident
in focus.

Gretchen Schulz and R. J. R. Rockwood are aware of the Life
article, but they focus instead on another acknowledged source of
Oates's inspiration, the folk tale. Their discussion of the story's
allusions to and affinities with "The Pied Piper of Hamelin,"
"Cinderella," "Little Red Riding Hood," and other tales suggests why
"Where Are You Going, Where Have You Been?" is such a disturbing
work. Their article offers detailed interpretations of the psychological crises Connie passes through, based on psychoanalytical
interpretations of the meaning and developmental function of the
analogous tales. (They use Bruno Bettelheim as their chief
authority.) But whereas folk tales most often smooth the passage of
their readers through Oedipal conflicts and the reintegration of the
childhood identity into the adult by working through to a happy
ending, "Where Are You Going, Where Have You Been?" taps these
powerful psychic forces in the reader only to pour them out on the
sand.

QUESTIONS FOR DISCUSSION

1. Define Connie's relationships with her mother, sister, and
    father. What is missing from this family? Why does Connie
    wish "her mother was dead and she herself was dead and it was
    all over"?

2. What are Connie's "two sides." In your opinion, is Connie's
    case unusual for a girl her age in our society? In what ways
    is she atypical? What about June?

3. The girls enter the drive-in with "faces pleased and expectant
    as if they were entering a sacred building," and the popular
    music in the background seems "like music at a church service."
    Explore the drive-in religion further. What are its creeds,
    its mysteries? Is it a true religion, a guide to the good
    life? Does Connie believe in anything else?

4. Discuss the similarities between Eddy, who rotates on a
    counter stool and offers "something to eat," and the emblem of
    the drive-in on its bottle-top roof. What else does Eddy
    offer? Compare Eddy with Arnold Friend as we first see him at
    the drive-in.

5. What does Oates accomplish by returning briefly to Connie's
    relationship with her family before narrating what happens "one
    Sunday"?

6. Discuss Connie's daydreams, in which "all the boys fell back
    and dissolved into a single face that was not even a face but
    an idea, a feeling, mixed up with the urgent insistent pounding
    of the music," and in which she associates sunbathing with the
    "sweet, gentle" lovemaking "in movies and promised in song."
    What is the source of the sexual desire reflected in these
    dreams? What is its object?

7. Asbestos was formerly used as a noninflammable insulating
    material. Trace the images of heat and fire associated with it
    in the story.

8. Compare Connie's gentle breathing as she listens to the "XYZ
    Sunday Jamboree" with her breath "jerking back and forth in her
    lungs" when she tries to use the telephone at the climax of the
    story.

9. Why does Connie whisper "Christ. Christ" when she hears a car
    coming up the driveway? Does the effort to see Arnold Friend
    as a Christ figure find further substantiation in the text?
    Does it yield any meaningful insights?

10. Where does Connie stand during the first part of her conver-
    sation with Arnold? Is Oates's blocking of the scene
    realistic? Symbolic?

11. Describe Arnold's car and clothing. What purpose is served by
    his transparent disguise? Why does it take Connie so long to
    penetrate the disguise?

12. Does Arnold have supernatural knowledge about Connie, her
    family, and her friends? Can his apparent clairvoyance about
    the barbecue be explained in naturalistic terms?

13. Account for Connie's idea that Arnold "had driven up the drive-way all right but had come from nowhere before that and had belonged nowhere and that everything about him and even the music that was so familiar to her was only half real." Explain the importance of that idea for understanding what happens to Connie.

14. Why does Connie's kitchen seem "like a place she had never seen before"? How has Arnold succeeded in making Connie feel cut off from her past and unprotected in her home? What is the impli-cation of "the echo of a song from last year" in this context?

15. What is the role of Ellie in Arnold's assault on Connie?

16. Arnold implies that Connie can protect her family from harm by coming with him. How important a factor is this in his winning her over to his will?

17. Examine the passage in which Connie tries to telephone her mother and then collapses in panic and hysteria. Notice its associations with sex and birth. What is taking place in Connie at this moment?

18. Arnold asks rhetorically, "what else is there for a girl like you but to be sweet and pretty and give in?" Explain in what sense this is true.

19. Explain Connie's feeling that she is watching herself go out the door. What has caused this split in her consciousness?

TOPICS FOR WRITING

Critical Essays

1. Arnold Friend's obvious masquerade, and why it succeeds.
2. Popular music and religion in "Where Are You Going, Where Have You Been?"
3. "Where Are You Going, Where Have You Been?" and Shirley Jackson's "The Lottery" -- technique and theme.
4. Arnold Friend and Flannery O'Connor's Misfit.

Exercises for Reading

1. Read the story once while bearing in mind that it is "based on fact" -- something very much like this is known to have actually happened. After finishing the story, write a personal essay giving your reaction. What does this account imply about human nature? About the society reflected in the story.
2. Reread the story with an eye to its allusions to folk tales and fairy tales with which you are familiar. Arnold's "coach" has a pumpkin on it; Connie is nearly asleep when he awakens her; he has big teeth; and so forth. What are the tales alluded to about? Is this story a fairy tale, too?
3. Study the allusions to religion in the story. How would Flannery O'Connor have handled this material?

1081–1109 (text pages)

Related Subject

1. Select an item from the news that grips your imagination, and
   ask yourself why it does. Does it have affinities with folk
   tales or myths? Does it suggest disturbing ideas about human
   nature and society? Write a narrative of the event, perhaps
   from the point of view of one of the participants, that
   incorporates these larger implications.

SUGGESTED READINGS

Gillis, Christina Marsden. "'Where Are You Going, Where Have Your
    Been?': Seduction, Space, and a Fictional Mode." Studies in
    Short Fiction, 18 (Winter 1981), 65–70.

Quirk, Tom. "A Source for 'Where Are You Going, Where Have You
    Been?'" Studies in Short Fiction, 18 (Fall 1981), 413–419.

Schulz, Gretchen, and R. J. R. Rockwood. "In Fairyland, without a
    Map: Connie's Exploration Inward in Joyce Carol Oates's 'Where
    Are You Going, Where Have You Been?'" Literature and Psycho-
    logy, 30 (1980), 155–167.

Urbanski, Marie Mitchell Olesen. "Existential Allegory: Joyce
    Carol Oates's 'Where Are You Going, Where Have You Been?'"
    Studies in Short Fiction, 15 (Spring 1978), 200–203.

Wegs, Joyce M. "'Don't You Know Who I Am?': The Grotesque in
    Oates's 'Where Are You Going, Where Have You Been?'" Journal
    of Narrative Technique, 5 (January 1975), 66–72.

Winslow, Joan D. "The Stranger Within: Two Stories by Oates and
    Hawthorne." Studies in Short Fiction, 17 (Summer 1980), 263–
    268.

Joyce Carol Oates

"The Lady with the Pet Dog" (page 1095)

Starting from a central turning point in the linear narrative
of Chekhov's to which her story refers, Oates spirals out, passing
the center again, cycling past various incidents more than once, and
reaching an account of the beginning of Anna's affair shortly before
the end of the story, where, like Chekhov's lovers, Anna finds herself at a new beginning. This method enables Oates to reflect
Anna's sense that "Everything is repeating itself. Everything is
stuck." At the same time, the recurrent incidents give different
impressions each time they are narrated, demonstrating to the
reader that forward progress is taking place in Anna's idea of
herself, a progress as definite as that of Chekhov's Gurov.

"It was obvious to her that she had, all along, been behaving correctly; out of instinct." With this insight Anna finally achieves the repose within herself that she has previously sought, with inevitably incomplete success, in her husband and her lover alternatively. Oates treats the dissolution of Anna's marriage with imagery of melting and flowing away. When her lover shows up at the theater, she feels filled with congealed mucus, which she identifies both with panic and with love, and she wants it to drain away. As it does, however, she feels her own identity dissolving. Her husband cannot provide it for her; he leads a life of his own within himself. "There was no boundary to her in this house," she feels, and she experiments with suicide. Her lover, by contrast, offers definition. He draws a picture of her; he makes confining, definite gestures with his hands. But allowing him to take her over brings alienation from herself in the form of shame, the bitter consequence of engaging in behavior of which one disapproves.

"What did it mean to enter into a bond with another person?" Anna wonders. "No person could save another," she recognizes. In their last rendezvous of the story, Anna and her lover cling together in a kind of hermaphroditic union that seems absurd to her. When he breaks it off and complains that she is using him to take the blame for her misery, Anna once again contemplates suicide. But with her recognition of his separateness, "that he existed in a dimension quite apart from her, a mysterious being," Anna is saved. When she sees that she loves him not as a part of herself or as a definition of herself but as something other than herself -- and loves him nonetheless -- "she was flooded with a strange certainty, a sense of gratitude, of pure selfless energy." Thus she has not only found her way through the psychological mine field that separates the frontiers of her old life and her new one; she has also redefined herself for herself and learned what it should mean, and what it should not mean, to enter into a bond with another person.

QUESTIONS FOR DISCUSSION

1. How does Oates convey the impact on Anna of her lover's reappearance? What effect does she attain by starting the story with this event?
2. Contrast the way Anna's intercourse with her husband is described at the end of section I, near the middle of section II, and again, briefly, somewhat past the middle of section III. Why does Oates return twice to this event?
3. Anna and her husband feel "shame between them"; riding to Albany with her lover, Anna feels "a declaration of shame between them." Explain the role of shame in this story. What is shame, and what becomes of it here?
4. When Anna and her lover try "to figure out their past" because "there was no future," the lover says, "this is impossible." Explain.
5. At home, why does Anna feel "there was no boundary to her, no edge"?

6. The telephone conversation in section II, in which Anna finally tells her lover not to come over, fades off into a fantasy of a potential future that in turn modulates into a narrative of present events. Why does Oates handle Anna's decision to resume relations with her lover in this oblique manner?

7. Comment on the image of love as fluttering moth's wings. Why is it appropriate at this point in the story? Would it be equally appropriate at the end?

8. Why does Anna want to be free of her lover at the end of section II?

9. What is the effect of reading about the events on Nantucket after some of their consequences have already been narrated? How would our response to this section differ if we came to it first?

10. Is Anna's lover a reader of Chekhov?

11. What is the impact on Anna of her lover drawing her picture? Of his saying to her, "You have defined my soul for me."

12. When Anna comes back from Albany, her luggage is brought to her husband "on a conveyor belt, to be claimed by him." When she goes to her lover in the hotel, he says, "I understand. I'm making no claims upon you." Do these passages reflect what is actually the case in her relations with the two men?

13. Explain why Anna's feelings for her lover keep pushing her toward suicide.

14. Some passages tracing Anna's consciousness consist of nothing but fluttering self-contradictions. How can we be sure her final resolution is not one more of these?

TOPICS FOR WRITING

Critical Essays

1. Oates has said, of this and the other "reimaginings of famous stories" in Marriages and Infidelities, that "these stories are meant to be autonomous stories, yet they are also testaments of my love and extreme devotion to these other writers; I imagine a kind of spiritual 'marriage' between myself and them. . . ." In what ways is Oates's story married to Chekhov's? In what ways is it autonomous? Does that relationship have any connection with Oates's theme?

2. The function of repetition in "The Lady with the Pet Dog."

3. Oates's use of the telephone in "The Lady with the Pet Dog" (and perhaps also in "Where Are You Going, Where Have You Been?").

Exercise for Reading

1. Define the emotional tone and thematic contributions of each incident in Oates's swirling narrative. Does the story in fact make a steady progress toward its conclusion?

Related Subject

1. Select a story from the anthology and follow Oates's example by
    <u>reimagining</u> it as an autonomous story of your own.

Ann Beattie

"Waiting" (page 1111)

Beattie's narration is so oblique that on first reading students
may feel they have missed the point. They will not, however, escape
the mood of numb depression that mutes the narrator's -- and the
reader's -- response to the incidents of the story to such a level
that their connections are obscure and the narrative seems
disjointed. Of course it is not, and discovering its continuities
is a gratification for attentive or repeated reading. The shallow
and abstracted consciousness that dominates the story is that of the
narrator, Sally, who is fixing her attention narrowly on random and
superficial details in order to hide from herself the realization
that her marriage of thirteen years is probably over.   The question
of whether Hugo is asleep or dead releases her emotions, and since
she knows she may have a body on her hands that she cannot bear to
deal with, forces her to become aware of her evasion as well. The
release of Sally's anxiety when the dog reappears also releases her
grief, and the trance that has held her throughout the story
dissolves in tears.

Ray's concluding demand, "Just tell me what you've done,"
expresses his continuing desire to "cheer up" Sally by minimizing
her loss ("Anybody can take a trip. . . . People do what they do")
and by distracting her with pleasantries; but for the reader it
directs attention back to the opening scene and indicates how the
story is unified. What Sally has done is exactly the opposite of
her reupholstering the furniture in a pattern that made John feel
like a prisoner: she has parted with the big antique corner cupboard, eighteenth-century mousehole and all, a trophy from the
earlier era of her marriage, when she and John went to auctions
together. It is "a very large thing to be giving up" and an
unmistakable symbol of the now burdensome past that Sally is
reluctantly letting go.

John has left troubling reminders of himself behind; his letter
from remote, strange Berkeley is just one more of them. In contrast
to what she is losing, represented by the corner cupboard, what
Sally keeps in exchange is as flimsy as the empty beer can she finds
in her driveway: a platoon of solicitous men who phone or stop by --
even the UPS man -- bringing small gifts, small talk, and the
distractions of the city. The best of what is left is good old
Hugo, with whom Sally communicates better than with anybody else --
which is what makes his imminent demise something to dread.

QUESTIONS FOR DISCUSSION

1. What considerations are suggested by the woman who buys the
   corner cupboard? Compare her with Sally; compare her situation
   with Sally's.
2. What is the effect of the association Sally makes with the
   postmark on her husband's letter?
3. Discuss the possible symbolic significance of the coffee tin.
   How do you feel about seeing a jar of instant coffee emerging
   from the quaint antique? What other confrontations of past and
   present are there in the story? What attributes are characteristic of each epoch?
4. What accounts for Sally's sudden feeling that the corner cupboard "seems older and bigger"?
5. Why does Sally stop answering the phone every time it rings?
6. Is thirteen old for a dog? For a marriage?
7. Why does Sally contrast the way they decide whether Hugo is to
   go with John to the way they used to bid for antiques?
8. What does Bobby's call contribute to our understanding of
   Sally's condition?
9. Explain Sally's paralysis in the yard. How many oblique
   suggestions that Hugo -- or something -- has died can you find
   in the section of the story from "No reaction" through the
   departure of the UPS man?
10. Why does Ray visit Sally? Does his visit have the effect he
    intends?
11. Follow the cardinal whose movements Sally keeps track of near
    the end of the story. What does the appearance and disappear-
    ance of the bird contribute to the story's effect?
12. Why does Sally cry when Hugo comes out of the house?
13. What does Ray think Sally has done? What <u>has</u> she done?

TOPICS FOR WRITING

Critical Essays

1. Casual imagery and coherent effect in "Waiting."
2. Compare and contrast Beattie's technique with Woolf's in
   "Moments of Being," Mansfield's in "Bliss," or Babel's in "My
   First Goose."
3. "Waiting" as a comment on our times.

Exercise for Reading

1. Find the order in Beattie's reflection of chaos (see the headnote, page 1110), by noticing the conjunctions and coincidences
   she details. Propound an underlying reason why the narrator
   thinks <u>these</u> thoughts, perceives <u>these</u> images, and makes <u>these</u>
   associations.

Related Subject

1. Write a story from the point of view of a narrator who is
    hiding something from himself or herself. Show how the
    unrecognized truth presents itself indirectly to the narrator's
    awareness.

THEMATIC INDEX

STORY PAIRS

Chekhov, "The Lady with the Dog," 363

Oates, "The Lady with the Pet Dog," 1095

Babel, "My First Goose," 687

Lessing, "Homage for Isaac Babel," 938

Maupassant, "Miss Harriet," 250

Babel, "Guy de Maupassant," 690

Kafka, "The Metamorphosis," 554

Roth, "'I Always Wanted You to Admire My Fasting,'" 1058

ON WRITING

Hawthorne, "The Devil in Manuscript," 32

Poe, "The Oval Portrait," 45

Gogol, "The Overcoat," 50

Melville, "Bartleby the Scrivener," 95

Twain, "A Story without an End," 198

James, "The Real Thing," 215

Stein, "As a Wife Has a Cow," 452

Hemingway, "The Snows of Kilimanjaro," 734

Borges, "Borges and I," 765

O'Faolain, "How to Write a Short Story," 768

Paley, "A Conversation with My Father," 951

García Márquez, "A Very Old Man with Enormous Wings," 998

Barth, "Lost in the Funhouse," 1021

Roth, "'I Always Wanted You to Admire My Fasting,'" 1058

FANTASY AND THE SUPERNATURAL

CHILDHOOD

ADOLESCENCE AND INITIATION

IDENTITY AND RENEWAL

LOVE, MARRIAGE, AND INFIDELITY

PARENTS AND CHILDREN

WAR AND REVOLUTION

LOOKING AT THE WALL

BABYLON REVISITED (F. Scott
  Fitzgerald)
Movie title: "The Last Time I
  Saw Paris"
116 min., color, 1954
Cast: Elizabeth Taylor, Van
      Johnson, Donna Reed, Eva
      Gabor
Directed by Richard Brooks
Distributed by: Films, Inc.

BARTLEBY THE SCRIVENER (Herman
  Melville)
Movie title: "Bartleby"
28 min., color, 1969
Distributed by: Encyclopedia
  Britannica

Movie title: "Bartleby"
29 min., b&w, 1965
Videotape from the American Short
  Stories Classics Series
Distributed by: Michigan Media

THE BRIDE COMES TO YELLOW SKY
  (Stephen Crane)
29 min., b&w, 1965
Videotape from the American Short
  Stories Classics Series
Distributed by: Michigan Media

BYEZHIN PRAIRIE (Ivan Turgenev)
Movie title: "Byezhin Meadow"
30 min., b&w, 1935
Cast: E. Vitka, Boris Zakhava,
      Yelena Teleshova
Directed by Sergei Eisenstein
Distributed by: Audio Brandon

THE CASK OF AMONTILLADO (Edgar
  Allan Poe)
19 min., color, 1979
Directed by Bernard Wilets
Distributed by: BFA Educational
  Media

29 min., b&w, 1965
Videotape from the American Short
  Stories Classics Series
Distributed by: Michigan Media

15 min., b&w, 1955
Cast: Monty Woolley
Distributed by: Audio Brandon

THE DEATH OF IVAN ILYCH (Leo
  Tolstoy)
29 min., color, 1978
Part of the Begin with Goodbye
  Series
Distributed by: Mass Media
  Ministries

THE DOLL'S HOUSE (Katherine
  Mansfield
17 min., b&w, 1967
Videotape
Distributed by: SL Film Produc-
  tions

FIRST LOVE (Vladimir Nabokov)
90 min., color, 1970
Cast: Maximillian Schell,
      Dominique Sanda, John
      Moulder Brown
Directed by Maximillian Schell
Distributed by: Audio Brandon

THE LADY WITH THE DOG (Anton
   Chekhov)
86 min., b&w, 1960
In Russian with English subtitles
Cast: Iya Savvina, Alexei
      Batalov, Alla Chostakova
Directed by Joseph Heifitz
Distributed by: Audio Brandon

THE LOTTERY (Shirley Jackson)
18 min., color, 1969
Distributed by: Encyclopedia
   Britannica

THE MAN WHO WAS ALMOST A MAN
   (Richard Wright)
Movie title, "Almos' a Man"
39 min., color, 1977
Available on film or videotape
Cast: LeVar Burton
Directed by Stan Lathan
Distributed by: Perspective
   Films

THE METAMORPHOSIS (Franz Kafka)
35 min., b&w, 1972
Distributed by John McCarty

OCCURRENCE AT OWL CREEK BRIDGE
   (Ambrose Bierce)
27 min., b&w, 1962
Cast: Roger Jacquet, Anne
      Cornaly, Anker Larsen
Directed by Robert Enrico
Winner at Cannes and American
   Film Festivals
Distributed by: Films, Inc.

30 min., b&w, 1964
Same as 1962 version, with pro-
   logue for its showing as an
   episode of The Twilight Zone
Distributed by: Classic Film
   Museum, Inc.
   Northwest Film Study Center
   Viewfinders, Inc.
   McGraw-Hill Films

PAUL'S CASE (Willa Cather)
55 min., color, 1980
Available on film or videotape
Distributed by: Perspective
   Films

THE ROCKING HORSE WINNER (D. H.
   Lawrence)
30 min., color, 1977
Cast: Kenneth More
Adapted by Julian Bond
Directed by Peter Modak
Distributed by: Learning Corp.
   of America

91 min., b&w, 1950
Cast: John Mills, Valerie Hobson
Directed by Anthony Pelessier
Distributed by: Films, Inc.
               Budget Films

THE SECRET LIFE OF WALTER MITTY
   (James Thurber)
110 min., color, 1947
Cast: Danny Kaye, Virginia Mayo
Directed by Norman Z. MacLeod
Distributed by: Arcus Films
              Jensen's Cinema 16
              ROA Films
              Twyman Films, Inc.
              Westcoast Films
              Audio-Brandon

THE SNOWS OF KILIMANJARO (Ernest
   Hemingway)
117 min., b&w, 1952
Cast: Gregory Peck, Susan
      Hayward, Ava Gardner
Directed by Henry King
Distributed by: Films, Inc.

THE SUMMER (John Cheever)
94 min., color, 1968
Cast: Burt Lancaster, Janet
      Landgard
Directed by Frank Perry

TO BUILD A FIRE (Jack London)
15 min., color, 1975
Also available on videotape
Distributed by: BFA Educational
              Media
              Phoenix

56 min., color, 1969
Narrated by Orson Welles
Cast: Ian Hogg
Distributed by: Audio Brandon
              Kit Parker

THE WHITE HERON (Sarah Orne
    Jewett)
26 min., color, 1978
Distributed by: Learning Corp.
    of America

YOUNG GOODMAN BROWN (Nathaniel
    Hawthorne)
30 min., color, 1973
Directed by Donald Fox
Distributed by: Pyramid Films

DIRECTORY OF FILM DISTRIBUTORS

Arcus Films
1225 Broadway
New York, NY 10001

Audio Brandon
45 MacQuesten P'way S.
Mt. Vernon, NY 10550

BFA Educational Media
2211 Michigan Ave.
Santa Monica, CA 90404

Budget Films
4590 Santa Monica Blvd.
Los Angeles, CA 90029

Classic Film Museum
4 Union Sq.
Dover-Foxcroft, ME 04426

Contemporary/McGraw-Hill
1221 Avenue of the Americas
New York, NY 10020

Encyclopedia Britannica Educa-
    tional Corp.
425 N. Michigan Ave.
Chicago, IL 60611

Films, Inc.
Film and Tape Division
733 Greenbay Rd.
Wilmette, IL 60091

Kit Parker Films
P.O. Box 227
Carmel Valley, CA 93924

Learning Corp. of America
1350 Avenue of the Americas
New York, NY 10019

Mass Media Ministries
2116 N. Charles St.
Baltimore, MD 21218

McGraw-Hill Films
1221 Avenue of the Americas
New York, NY 10020

Michigan Media
University of Michigan
400 Fourth St.
Ann Arbor, MI 48109

Perspective Films
65 East South Water St.
Chicago, IL 60601

Phoenix Films
470 Park Ave. S.
New York, NY 10016

Pyramid Films
P.O. Box 1048
Santa Monica, CA 90406

ROA's Films
1696 N. Astor St.
Milwaukee, WI 53202

SL Film Production, Inc.
P.O. Box 41108
Los Angeles, CA 90041

Twyman Films
329 Salem Ave.
Dayton, OH 45401

Viewfinders, Inc.
2550 Green Bay Rd.
Box 1665
Evanston, IL 60204

Westcoast Films
25 Lusk St.
San Francisco, CA 94107